The Mosaic Decoration of San Marco, *Venice*

Photograph courtesy of the National Gallery of Art, Photographic Archives

Otto Demus

The Mosaic Decoration of
SAN MARCO
Venice

EDITED BY HERBERT L. KESSLER

Published for Dumbarton Oaks, Washington, D.C.

THE UNIVERSITY OF CHICAGO PRESS

CHICAGO AND LONDON

The University of Chicago Press, Chicago 60637
The University of Chicago Press, Ltd., London

97 96 95 94 93 92 91 90 89 88   54321

Library of Congress Cataloging-in-Publication Data

Demus, Otto.
    The mosaic decoration of San Marco, Venice / Otto Demus : edited
by Herbert L. Kessler.
        p.   cm.
    "Published for Dumbarton Oaks, Washington, D.C."
    Includes index.
    ISBN 0-226-14291-4.   ISBN 0-226-14292-2 (pbk.)
    1. Mosaics, Medieval—Italy—Venice.   2. Mosaics—Italy—Venice.
3. Basilica di San Marco (Venice, Italy)   I. Kessler, Herbert L.,
1941–   . II. Title.
NA3788.D45   1988   88-710
726'.527'094531—dc19   CIP

Contents

List of Illustrations

FIGURES

COLOR PLATES

ix

Preface

EVEN BEFORE Otto Demus's four-volume work, *The Mosaics of San Marco in Venice* (© 1984 by Dumbarton Oaks), plans were underway to make available in other forms the materials amassed over a lifetime of study. Because the project to photograph the San Marco mosaics in preparation for the publication had generated far more pictorial material than could be presented in the more than 700 black-and-white and 160 color plates, the University of Chicago Press decided to issue 1,511 photographs in a color microfiche edition. The weighty boxed set with its extensive documentation and technical analysis, on the other hand, seemed richer than many students of San Marco needed and so a single-volume edition was also planned to provide art historians and nonspecialists alike with a compact introduction to the Venetian mosaics that would preserve Demus's history and would offer a generous selection of Ekkehard Ritter's photographs.

Whereas it is reduced in size to approximately one-quarter and omits the scholarly apparatus of notes, bibliography, description of materials, and palaeographic analysis, *The Mosaic Decoration of San Marco, Venice* is not simply an abridgment of *The Mosaics of San Marco in Venice*. Some material has been incorporated from Otto Demus's *The Church of San Marco in Venice: History, Architecture, Sculpture* (Dumbarton Oaks Studies, 6 [Washington, D.C.: Dumbarton Oaks, 1960]); and a few corrections in chapters 9 and 10 on the Miracles of Christ and the Life of the Virgin have been added by Demus. The text has also been restructured so that the synthetic chapters distributed in the original two volumes are now merged. Because of its highly technical nature, and more, because the material has since appeared in a different form in Kurt Weitzmann and Herbert L. Kessler, *The Cotton Genesis* (Princeton: Princeton University Press, 1986), Kurt Weitzmann's chapter "The Genesis Mosaics of San Marco and the Cotton Genesis Miniatures" has been greatly reduced.

Otto Demus read the typescript and proof. Adam S. Cohen assisted in all phases of the preparation of the book. Giles Constable and Robert Thomson, successive directors of Dumbarton Oaks, encouraged the undertaking and supported it in many ways.

HERBERT L. KESSLER

The Mosaic Decoration
of San Marco, *Venice*

History and Critical Survey of the Building and Its Mosaics

1

VENICE STARTED as a Byzantine province in the late sixth century, a *ducatus* under the exarch of Ravenna; but by the year 726, the *dux* (doge), Ursus, was elected by the local tribunes and the national history of Venice had begun. Soon an episcopal see was erected, and increasingly Venice came to play the role of mediator between the Eastern and Western empires. During the ninth and tenth centuries, Venice developed into an independent state, growing into a major maritime power while maintaining a close relationship to Byzantium. Not until the twelfth century did the alliance seriously deteriorate. In 1204, the Fourth Crusade took Constantinople; Venice came to consider the Byzantine capital its own and systematically looted the city.

Venice borrowed, or rather usurped, its patron saint, the evangelist Mark, not from Constantinople but from two nearby cities, Aquileia and Grado. From about the fifth century, the bishops of Aquileia regarded themselves as the successors of Saint Mark, asserting that Mark had founded their church prior to Alexandria's, and in the following century, Grado began to claim its right to the patriarchate, too. The quarrel smoldered until the middle of the thirteenth century, with each city asserting its claims and counterclaims. Long before that, however, Venice had accomplished its own political goals: first, supporting Aquileia's claim to apostolic foundation; second, assisting Grado's claim to be the legitimate successor of Aquileia; third, usurping Grado's claim by acquiring the relics of Saint Mark; and finally, connecting Venice itself with the mythical founder of the patriarchate by the fabrication of the *praedestinatio* legend, Saint Mark's alleged vision that his bones would eventually be laid to rest in the exact location of San Marco. In 829, Venice had already decided not to hand over to Grado the newly acquired relics of Saint Mark but to keep them in Rialto and build a *martyrium* over them, the first step in a long-term policy to keep a firm hold over the patriarch and, perhaps, to force him sooner or later to follow the relics of the patron saint to Rialto. From the second quarter of the ninth century until 1272, all patriarchs of Grado were Venetians, but it was not until the middle of the twelfth century that the patriarch was allowed to take a place in San Marco—on the north side of the presbytery, opposite the doge. The Venetian Church had become a state Church and a national Church.

The transfer of the patriarchate to San Marco in 1807 marked the last stage of a long development and the end of the church as the ducal chapel of Venice. Indeed, the original purpose of San Marco had been to serve as the *cappella ducale*. Even after the church had been rebuilt on a grand scale in the eleventh century, San Marco remained primarily the private chapel of the doge, who was the patron of the church and chief guardian of the relics. It was in San Marco that the doge was presented to the people after his election, that he was invested with the *vexillum Sancti Marci,* and that the *laudes* were sung to him. Solemn events were staged there, and many doges were buried in the church. Probably in imitation of the Byzantine emperor's throne in Hagia Sophia, the doge's throne was placed on the right-hand side of the presbytery.

The rise in importance of the procurators during the thirteenth century marks the church's transition from the doge's private chapel to the state church of Venice. As a state sanctuary, San Marco became the repository for politically important spoils and trophies; every detail of the decorations took on a political aspect, and it became both the symbol and center of the state's power.

The church of San Marco was undoubtedly the most important center of religious and political life in Venice, and the building and its decoration appear to have been shaped, to a great extent, by its function in the Venetian commonwealth, beginning with the erection of San Marco as a palace chapel and ending with its becoming the see of a patriarchate. The history encompasses almost a thousand years, from the translation of the evangelist's relics in 828/29 and the subsequent building of the first shrine, to the final transfer of the patriarchate to San Marco, a measure sanctioning a de facto state of affairs that had existed since the twelfth century.

At the time of its foundation, San Marco was neither a great ecclesiastical center nor was it hallowed by an old tradition, but it was, from the beginning, an apostles' church with all the implications that the possession of apostles' relics held for the Italians of the early Middle Ages. Where the relics came from and which of those that are now in the church or in the treasury were actually acquired in the ninth century cannot be determined with certainty. Those of Peter, John, Matthew, Luke, and Bartholomew in the altar of the Cappella di San Pietro seem to have been present from the time of foundation and must have been acquired expressly for the purpose of surrounding the patron of the church, Saint Mark, with an apostolic cortège and of making his martyrium an apostles' church.

The relics of Saint Mark himself were reputed to have been brought there from Alexandria by two Venetian merchants with the aid of two Greek monks. The narrative of the *Translatio* begins with an ample introduction calculated to prove the divine right of the Venetians to the possession of the apostle's relics. The transfer of the relics must, in fact, have been a rather hazardous undertaking, inspired by the fact that Saint Mark was the disciple of Peter and the author of a gospel that was considered to have been written in Rome for the use of the Italians. Saint Mark was regarded as a specifically Italian apostle; furthermore, he was believed to have been the apostolic missionary of the Northern Adriatic and, as such, the real founder of the partriarchate of Venetia. The Venetians regarded themselves as the first-born sons of Saint Mark and found in this the justification for robbing Alexandria of the saint's relics and transferring them to Venice.

When the relics reached Venice after a miraculous voyage, they were solemnly received and deposited in the ducal palace until a church for them was completed, it is said, in 836. Burned in a rebellion in 976, the first San Marco was replaced by a second church that, in turn, was rebuilt after 1063. According to a thirteenth-century legend, when the new church was about to be consecrated, in 1084/85 or 1093/94, the precious relics—the palladium and glory of

2

Venice—suddenly seemed to have vanished only to reappear miraculously (the *apparitio*). This and other legends reflect a new and proud nationalism of the Venetians and, perhaps, the need to refute the claims of Reichenau to the possession of the relics. Moreover, during the thirteenth century, the motif of the *praedestinatio* was added to the saint's legend, and at about the same time, the ceremony of the Spozalizio del Mar, with which the Venetian state extended its authority over the lagoons and the seas, was introduced.

To the orbit of the patron saint belonged also the relics of his disciples, Anianus, whom Saint Mark had miraculously healed and consecrated bishop of Alexandria, and the Aquileian disciples Hermagoras and Fortunatus. To the original stock seem also to have belonged relics of the Aquileian saints Cornelius, Cyprianus, Hippolytus, and Cyrillus as well as Stephen, Clement, Blaise, Sergius, and Bacchus. Not much was added later.

In spite of the great number of documents and sources dealing with San Marco and its decoration that have been collected, the sum of what is known for certain about the history of the mosaics is not very great. The dates that can be assembled provide only a very general framework.

The present church had two predecessors. The first San Marco was vowed by Doge Justinian Partecipacius in 829, when he instructed his wife in his testament to build a church in honor of the saint whose relics had reached Venice in that year. Nothing is known for certain about the shape and decoration of this church, completed in the 830s by the doge's brother and successor John, and the same is true of the second San Marco, which seems not to have been a new building but a restoration of the first church following a fire in 976.

For the building and decorating of the present church, the third San Marco, sources and material data provide fuller evidence for the date and for the reconstruction of the original shape and subsequent modifications. Most Venetian chroniclers concur in giving credit to Doge Domenico Contarini (1042–71) for having begun the building, to Doge Domenico Selvo (1071–84) for having continued the work, and to Doge Vitale Falier (1086–96) for having completed it. One of the chronicles dates the beginning of the work in the year 1063 and another reports that at the investiture of Doge Selvo in 1071, the church was not yet completed. Several chronicles relate that Selvo began or even completed the mosaic decoration and that he had a mosaic master brought to Venice from Constantinople. Others ascribe the completion of the mosaics to Vitale Falier, who is said to have willed his fortune for the completion of the mosaics. From 1082 on, the church received an annual gift of twenty pounds of gold from the Byzantine emperor.

The consecration of the church is variously reported to have taken place in 1084–85, 1093, or even later, 1102 or 1117. Most likely there was more than one consecration, the first of which would probably have concerned the main altar. If this is true, it may mean that the first decoration of the main apse was completed in 1084. The collocation of the evangelist's relics occurred in 1094, and eleven years later, in 1105, the high altar received the enlarged Pala d'oro that had been commissioned in Constantinople by Doge Ordelafo Falier.

San Marco stood as a cruciform building with five cupolas of somewhat unequal size supported on quadripartite piers and by the corners of solid walls (fig. 1). Each dome is buttressed by lateral barrel vaults, the easternmost vault terminating in the main apse of the church and the western crossarm preceded by an atrium (narthex). The ground plan and its spatial realization were certainly Greek, but the surface relief of the interior walls and facades, with their niches,

3

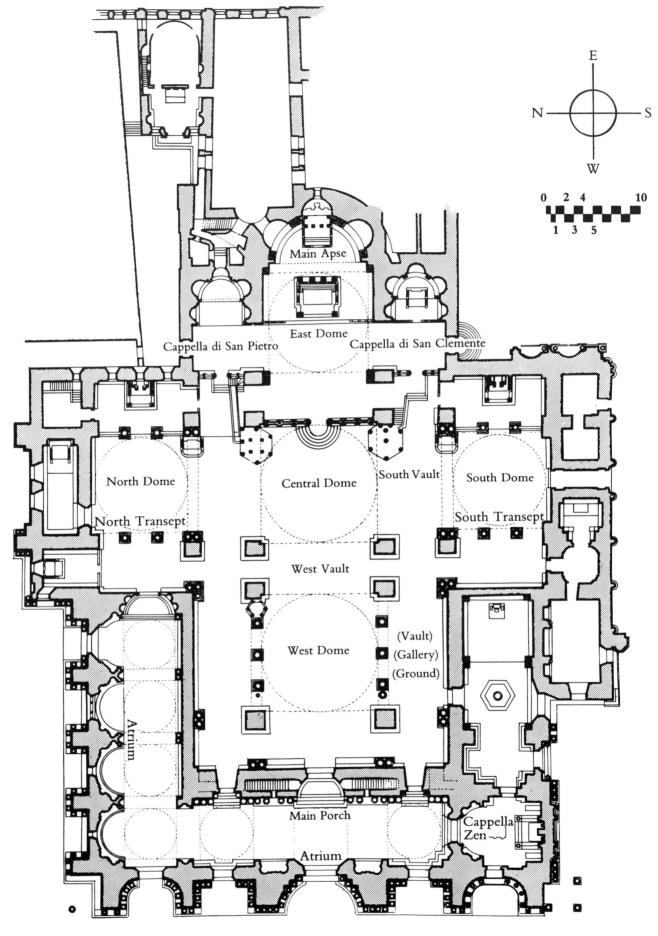

E
N — S
W

0 2 4   10
1 3 5

Main Apse

East Dome

Cappella di San Pietro   Cappella di San Clemente

North Dome   Central Dome   South Vault   South Dome

North Transept   South Transept

West Vault

West Dome   (Vault)
                                                 (Gallery)
                                                 (Ground)

Atrium

Main Porch   Cappella
                                                                   Zen

Atrium

4   Fig. 1. Ground plan *(Opera di San Marco)*

molded arches, and engaged columns of brickwork, was Italian. As early as 1100, the church was compared to the Apostoleion in Constantinople (now destroyed), and there is no doubt that San Marco shared essential features with its sixth-century model: the cruciform shape, five domes, barrel vaults, and four-legged piers. It is equally evident that there are quite important differences. Of these, the most outstanding was the treatment of the eastern arm as the termination of a basilican building with main apse and two side chapels rather than as an equal arm of a truly centralized structure. This is, of course, connected with the different location of the main altar in the two churches. In the Apostoleion, the altar stood in the central square, whereas in San Marco it is in the presbytery. Furthermore, in San Marco the presbytery is raised in order to make room for the crypt. These and other changes transformed San Marco into something of a domed basilica with lateral appendages, but there is no doubt about its fundamental debt to the early Byzantine model.

A very short time after it was completed, in the spring of 1106, a devastating fire broke out at Santi Apostoli, destroying a substantial part of the town, including several churches, and causing great damage to the mosaics of San Marco. Traces of the repairs that the fire made necessary can perhaps still be recognized in the mosaics of the main apse and the main porch. It is difficult to ascertain whether there existed other mosaics in the interior that were destroyed or heavily damaged by this first catastrophe (and restored later). Some remnants of such an early decoration may have survived in the choir chapels; for example, the mosaic of the Sacrifice of Cain and Abel and one or more single figures (Philip) may actually be "survivors" of this sort. It is also tempting to ascribe the archaic character of some other mosaics to the intention of their designers to follow, in some manner, the lead of an earlier decoration.

For the first half of the twelfth century there are very few references to San Marco and its mosaics, and those that survive tell us that work was proceeding in the church during the middle of the century. From the seventies on, there were a number of bequests for the *opera Sancti Marci,* most of which were certainly used for the building of the campanile, though some of the money may have gone into the mosaic decoration. Later chronicles report that under Doge Pietro Ziani (1205–22) a great part of the decoration was completed.

Thus, as regards the twelfth century as a whole—undoubtedly the most important period for the mosaics of the interior of San Marco—the harvest to be gleaned from primary documents as well as from secondary indications is very meager. We hear nothing about the realization of the great program of decoration of the interior, nothing about the reason why essential parts of this decoration were renewed at the end of the century, and nothing about the catastrophe that, in all probability, necessitated these renewals. Consequently, we are thrown back on stylistic arguments if we wish to create some kind of order in the vast body of the church's decoration.

The problem is especially difficult because some of the differentiations of style, technique, and material may be connected with changes in the relations with Byzantium. The chrysobull of 1082, which gave to Venice a virtual trade monopoly in the eastern Mediterranean, and the intimate relationship between emperors and doges at the end of the eleventh century and the beginning of the twelfth must have facilitated the influx of Byzantine artists and mosaic material. Other circumstances may have impeded the development and even hindered the continuation of the work. The crisis that developed soon after the accession of John II Comnenus (1118) and the ensuing war must have had a negative effect

5

on the speed of the mosaic work and—from the Byzantine point of view—the "purity" of its style. A state of tension continued, with several interruptions, through most of the century, culminating in the coup of 1171, when all Venetians living and trading in the Byzantine empire were thrown into prison. Although Venice was less affected than its competitors by the massacre of the Latins in 1182, this desperate measure can hardly have contributed to an entente between the two powers. Even if the chrysobull, the basis of trade relations between Venice and Byzantium, was renewed soon afterward, this did not wholly eliminate the tension between the two states, a tension that finally led to the diversion of the Fourth Crusade to Byzantium.

Whereas it must not be assumed that all relations between Venice and Constantinople ceased during the critical or hostile periods, we can hardly expect to find in twelfth-century Venetian mosaic art, which was so closely linked with Byzantium, an unbroken, undisturbed development.

All this changed greatly at the beginning of the thirteenth century. The taking of Constantinople in 1204 and the establishment of a colonial empire in the eastern Mediterranean certainly provided a new impetus for the decoration of San Marco. There is documentary evidence that in addition to columns, marble plaques, and so on, masses of mosaic material were brought to Venice. The additions to the original program of the interior, the mosaic decoration of the atrium, and the revetment of parts of the interior, of the atrium, and of the facades with precious marble are the result of this windfall. The atrium with the Cappella Zen, the baptistery, and the tesoro are the product of a series of modifications beginning during this period. A special campaign of repairs was carried out in the transept.

That the Venetian school of mosaic flourished in the early thirteenth century and was renowned in other parts of Italy is proved by the fact that Pope Honorius III approached the doge with his request for mosaic masters. A stepped-up pace of mosaic-making after the middle of the thirteenth century can be deduced from a most important document of 1258 in which the procuratori stipulated that none of the San Marco mosaic workers might accept work in any other church or for any other patron before they had completed their task in the basilica; furthermore, they were ordered to take on two apprentices each and teach them their craft.

A precious terminus ante (or ad) quem of about 1270 is provided for the scenes of the Marcian legend on the facade of the church by a passage in the *Chronique des Veniciens* of Martin da Canal, and another of 1277 is furnished by an inscription on the altar baldachin of the Parenzo cathedral, whose mosaics are closely related to certain sections of the San Marco atrium mosaics.

By this time, the decoration of the interior was certainly completed, including the latest additions to the program—the two scenes depicting the miraculous appearance of the patron's relics in the south transept and the Deesis on the west wall, above the main entrance. Work in the atrium continued well into the 1290s. That some mosaic work was still to be done in 1308 can be inferred from an edict of the Great Council which granted special permission for a furnace in Murano to produce a certain kind of enamel even in summer to provide material for the mosaicists of San Marco.

That mosaic is very far from being "painting for eternity" must have been painfully obvious to the Venetians by the middle of the fourteenth century, when the tesserae and mortar bed began to deteriorate through natural decay. Far more extreme were several fires in the course of the fifteenth century; the

6

most devastating, in 1419, destroyed a figure of Christ in the main apse and damaged the mosaics of the west dome and also perhaps those of the south dome. Because the only technician capable of restoring the mosaics had just died, the authorities approached the Signoria of Florence, which sent Paolo Uccello, who seems to have succeeded in reviving the art and technique of mosaic in Venice. When further repairs were needed following a fire in 1439, there was no dearth of mosaicists. Working in close proximity to Florentine artists, an entire school had developed during the work in the Cappella della Madonna dei Mascoli, which was built into the north transept in 1430. Though perhaps not as highly skilled, as sophisticated, or as bold as the Tuscan artists who worked under the direction of Andrea del Castagno in the chapel, the Venetian mosaicists worked in a quieter, flatter style perhaps more specifically suited to mosaic than the plastic quality and hardness characteristic of the painting of the Florentines.

Meanwhile, with the help of appropriations made by the Great Council between 1452 and 1472, the repairs continued slowly. Some of the mosaic work was necessitated by structural alterations such as the rose windows opened in the south transept and in the wall of the south presbytery chapel and the arch inserted between the vault and the south dome. There is something Florentine about the figures on the arch, dated 1458; however, the odd aspect of Saint Paul and Saint Anthony is far removed from the heroic quality of Castagno's apostles in the Mascoli Chapel. It is meant to look medieval—the figures seem to belong to a strange and remote world of the past. The same attitude is found in some works of the south transept: in the figures of Blaise and Nicholas in the south dome and, most striking, in Healing the Man Born Blind. Insofar as he was able, the mosaicist adhered to the original design of the damaged mosaic that he was replacing and was intent on imitating the technical aspects of the old mosaic. A comparison with other mosaics in the same vault makes clear that the scheme of the composition with its rhythmic sequence of figures and groups acting and gesturing toward the right is certainly authentic. The complete absence of any indication of locale and space is also a feature of the original. In fact, the contours of all the figures seem to have been taken from their "predecessors"; the figure of Christ at least may be considered a fair copy of the medieval one. Still, there are a few details that had been severely damaged in the original or that the "restorer" did not choose to copy without "editing" because they were matters of fashion, such as the cut of the hair. There are faces, too, looking somewhat odd—puckered or overmodeled—with knobby noses and staring eyes that are meant to look strange, medieval.

The most monumental and, perhaps, the latest specimen of this "archaeological" current in the restoration activity in San Marco is the Enthroned Christ of the main apse, signed and dated MCCCCVI PETRUS F. There is no doubt that the main features of the figure were copied from its twelfth-century prototype. It is equally certain, however, that it is not a faithful copy; the details of throne and book, the regular, undulating hems of the mantle, and the bulky modeling were assuredly not in the original and reflect the interpretation of the High Renaissance.

The oeuvre of Pietro, in fact, marks the turning point in the "restoration policy" applied to the mosaics of San Marco. Three years after the apse mosaic, the character of the Pietro's work changed completely: the Orant Virgin signed PETRUS 1509 on the arch connecting the Cappella di San Clemente with the main presbytery shows not the slightest trace of having been copied from a medieval

7

model. It is a full-fledged work of the Venetian High Renaissance that faithfully translates into mosaic a Bellinesque cartoon. A similar drapery scheme was also used for the prophet Zechariah, signed PETRUS F, in the east half of the arch between the vault with christological scenes and the south dome. And Pietro's hand can probably also be recognized in the figures of Erasma and Euphemia in two of the pendentives of the south dome and in a number of saints in the arcades.

With the late works of Pietro, and especially with those of his younger contemporary Vincenzo Sebastiani (Bastiani), the intiative passed to painters of renown. Quite often they collaborated for decades with one and the same mosaicist who thus became the faithful executor of their designs. Nevertheless, it also happened that a mosaicist worked on cartoons by different artists, and so the mosaicist became more and more the impersonal tool in the hands of the designers, who do not seem to have given even a passing thought to the problem of how to integrate new figures into old mosaics or even—in some cases—new mosaics into old ensembles.

The greatest onslaught on the mosaics began in the 1520s, led by Titian, Salviati, Veronese, Tintoretto, Palma Giovane, and others, and was carried out by a number of technically very able mosaicists who competed with one another for work in the church. Mosaics were not repaired anymore, or very rarely, but were replaced by new, "modern" creations. And they did not have to be damaged to be replaced, for painters and mosaicists had to make a living. According to tradition, the replacement of all old, "ugly" mosaics by new, "modern" ones was suggested to the procuratoria by Titian. Actually, the worst offender was Tintoretto, with Salviati and Palma Giovane close seconds. None of the Greek painters living in Venice during the sixteenth and seventeenth century were engaged in the work. From the High Renaissance on, San Marco was certainly regarded as a purely Venetian affair.

When the vault of the central bay of the atrium was broken through in order to open up the view into the extended west vault of the church, a new program of decoration was required. The Last Judgment, which originally filled the west vault of the east dome, had to be moved outward to be visible through the rectangular opening, and the west vault of the dome, now freed, was decorated with a cycle of scenes from the Apocalypse, an extraneous insertion into the original program. Practically all of the mosaics of this part are the work of the most famous mosaicists of the period, the Zuccato brothers.

The Tree of Jesse, on the north wall of the north transept, a grandiloquent work on a cartoon by Salviati, with Michelangelesque and Tintorettesque features, was made by the Bianchini brothers in the 1540s. The insertion of this huge mosaic seems to have started quite an avalanche of innovation. The Tree of Jesse, a new subject in the program, displaced the Raising of Lazarus, which was relocated in the atrium together with a new Crucifixion and Death of the Virgin. The most conspicuous part of the decoration of the entrance bay is, of course, the imposing figure of Mark in episcopal garments, which has been variously ascribed to Titian and Lorenzo Lotto.

All these Renaissance and mannerist mosaics are completely independent creations, from the iconographic as well as the formal point of view. This complete freedom was, however, curbed to a certain extent by an edict that forbade "the *proto* [director of San Marco's technical office] and the mosaic masters to have any of the mosaics in any part of the church destroyed unless the notary and *gastaldo* [administrator] had taken note of the particulars of all the figures and inscriptions, so that the old mosaics and the prophecies, which were said to have been arranged by San Gioacchino [Joachim of Fiore], could be remade; . . . before final payment was made, the procuratori [the administrators of San Marco] . . . would examine [the cartoons and decide] whether the work was done according to these models" (Edict of the Procuratoria, 22 December 1566).

In 1610 a new decree was considered necessary, mainly for financial reasons. It was found that the mosaic masters were not using the necessary discretion in destroying existing mosaics, which were often better than those made in their place, and that they simply ordered copies of the parts to be destroyed, without "mature consideration." Three years later and then again in 1684, the injunction against any alteration in the church, especially as regarded the mosaics and the inscriptions, was repeated. It is obvious from the wording of the decrees that economy played a certain part in the decision; however, the great cost does not seem to have been the chief consideration. Most important was the intention of preserving the iconographic program, including the inscriptions, all of which were believed to contain certain prophecies embodied in them by their reputed author, Joachim of Fiore, prophecies important for the welfare of the state. Some of the prescriptions laid down in these decrees aimed also at safeguarding the technical solidity of the work. Stylistic and aesthetic considerations do not appear to have played much of a role; both the artists and the authorities were convinced that the contemporary style was superior to the old.

The fact that the decrees had to be repeated several times does not inspire much confidence in their efficacy. Although one can be reasonably sure that the vetoes and prescriptions were obeyed in the years immediately following the promulgation of these decrees, their effect seems to have diminished quickly enough.

Presumptuous painters and inept mosaicists were not the only enemies of the mosaics. Apart from the fires and earthquakes, which continued to occur, there was danger from the discharge of cannons or mortars and other concussions. In addition, natural decay of the masonry and roofing material made repeated repairs necessary over the years. The history of San Marco from the seventeenth century on is, in effect, one of decay and often of insufficient measures taken against it. The situation was complicated, although perhaps in some respects improved, by the fact that around 1700 the Venetian school of mosaicists was dying out. Early in the eighteenth century, the procurator in charge of repairs had to arrange for Leopoldo Dal Pozzo to come from Rome. A skilled craftsman, he was quite capable of translating the painterly technique and brilliant palette of such contemporary artists as Giambattista Piazzetta (Saint Jerome in the northwest pendentive of the north dome) and Sebastiano Ricci (Venice Venerates the Relics of Saint Mark, on the facade). In the course of many years' work, until his death in 1745, Dal Pozzo also restored and repaired ornamental and figural mosaics with varied results.

Dal Pozzo had apparently failed to train a successor and what came after him was worse. Pietro Monaco, a copper engraver, had neither the skill nor the tact required for the work. His landscape on the south wall of the south organ loft is one of the worst mosaics in the church, both technically and artistically.

The fortune of the mosaics of San Marco reached its nadir in the nineteenth century, especially in the years between 1820 and 1880. It was not so much the creation of new compositions that made inroads on the remaining original parts

9

as the technical restoration of the old mosaics. In most cases, the damaged or endangered parts were removed and replaced by copies made after casts, frequently themselves badly made, often with new material in a slipshod manner and this despite the fact that a new technique had been developed that allowed the mosaics to remain firmly fixed in place while the supporting walls and vaults were renewed from behind or above.

The mosaicists of the first half of the nineteenth century must have done a lot of damage. It was only about the middle of the century that Lorenzo Radi, of Murano, succeeded in producing serviceable gold and silver cubes and some difficult shades of enamel. This technical progress led, in 1859, to the foundation of the Stabilimento Salviati, with which the *fabbricceria* of San Marco made a contract to furnish the necessary mosaic material; in 1867, the firm received the exclusive concession for the restoration. The early renovations were bad enough, but they were vastly superior to those the firm carried out in the 1870s.

Criticism of the poor work of the Società Salviati led to the establishment of the basilica's own *studio dei mosaici*. The accession of Pietro Saccardo to the directorship of the studio in 1883 marks the beginning of a new era. Saccardo brought about a change in principles and technique and his numerous *relazioni,* published partly with F. Berchet, furnish a firm historical basis for our knowledge of the restorations during the last twenty years of the nineteenth century.

Decay continued, in part because of structural deficiencies, in part because of atmospheric conditions that led to the corrosion of the mortar bed and often to a gradual detachment of the mosaic crust from the brick walls and vaults. Sometimes this was remedied by injections of liquid cement; sometimes the masonry had to be renewed, completely or in part. In several instances the technique was applied of fixing the mosaics in situ while the masonry was removed brick by brick from behind or above. With most parts of the decoration, however, the old system of *stacco* was, and still is, resorted to; before the mosaics were detached (in sections of about 1–4 square feet), impressions were made and often painted to obtain faithful copies. In spite of the great care that was, and is, being taken in removing, cleaning, and replacing the sections, the resulting effect was, and is, almost always a partial loss of artistic quality. There is a certain flattening of the mosaic surface. The sutures are often painfully visible, especially on curved areas, and white mortar or cement exudes from the interstices, disrupting the continuity of tone and color. Occasionally, accidents happen. Both the decay and the restorations continue to this very day and will continue as long as the church exists.

As a result of its long and tormented history, the mosaic decoration of San Marco is a complicated medley of original, restored, and renewed mosaics dating from the eleventh to the twentieth century. Most of these mosaics still perpetuate the programs laid down in the eleventh and twelfth centuries and enlarged in the thirteenth. About three-quarters of them have, in addition, preserved their old compositions and, largely, their general stylistic character as well; but only about one-third of the mosaic surface can be regarded as original, and the quality of a good part of this is somewhat impaired by restoration.

Most of the changes in the program took place in the sixteenth century and are not especially hard to spot, and so the medieval plan can be reconstructed with a fair amount of certainty—that is, insofar as the representations of scenes are concerned. The reconstruction of the original series of single figures is, however, a much more difficult, in some cases even impossible, task. The main entrance from the atrium to the interior is surrounded by niches harboring figures of the Virgin, eight apostles, and the four evangelists. In all likelihood, the apselike niche above originally displayed a bust of the Pantocrator and was probably surmounted by a cupola with a central medallion (perhaps Christ Emmanuel) and standing figures (perhaps the prophets or the forefathers of Christ) along its base.

The program of the interior is dominated by the Enthroned Pantocrator in the conch of the main apse (fig. 2); below are four saints, state patrons of Venice. The dome above the altar—the east dome—contains, in the central medallion, a bust of Christ Emmanuel, surrounded by standing figures of the Virgin and thirteen prophets. In the pendentives are the symbols of the four evangelists.

The side chapels of the presbytery, dedicated to Saint Peter and Saint Clement, show in the apses the standing figures of their patrons. In the lower arches and walls are several saints, Christ and the Virgin, the figures of Pope Pelagius and Patriarch Helias of Grado, one Old Testament scene (the Sacrifice of Cain and Abel) and one New Testament scene (or, better, the damaged remains of), the Deposition. In the great vaults and on the walls above (the present organ lofts), we find cycles of the story of Saint Mark and Hermagoras and two scenes from the Life of Saint Peter in the north, with the Translation of Mark's Relics and two scenes from the story of Saint Clement in the south.

The christological cycle begins in the vault between the east and the central domes, with scenes from the Annunciation to the Transfiguration, and it continues in the south vault of the central square, with the Temptation to the Washing of the Feet. The north vault contains the beginning of the Miracle cycle, which branches out into the transept (north, south, and east bays), while the west vault between the central and west domes concludes the christological cycle with scenes from the Passion and Resurrection. Figures of prophets accompany the scenes on contiguous arches and wall spaces.

The central dome is filled with a representation of the Ascension and allegories of virtues between the windows. The evangelists are shown writing their Gospels in the four pendentives, and below them, in the pointed triangular surfaces, are four figures representing the rivers of paradise.

The west dome, containing the Pentecost with representatives of the peoples and tribes between the windows and four angels in the pendentives, is accompanied in the north and south bays by scenes from the lives and martyrdoms of the apostles. A detailed representation of the Last Judgment was depicted on the west vault and, perhaps, originally also on part of the west wall.

The transepts provide space for subsidiary cycles—Christ's Miracles, the Life of the Virgin, and the Infancy of Christ. The dome of the north transept contains scenes from the legend of Saint John the Evangelist, with four church fathers in the pendentives. The dome of the south transept shows four male saints in frontal attitudes and four female saints in the pendentives. A host of standing figures of saints fills the arches of the arcades in both stories.

The extensive decorations of the facade and atrium were executed during the thirteenth century. Other thirteenth-century additions include a number of figures of saints, six large panels on the walls of the western, northern, and southern crossarms, and below them, in the western crossarm, Christ (north) and the Virgin (south), each flanked by four prophets.

A monumental Deesis on the west wall above the main door is the latest thirteenth-century addition to the great decoration. All later mosaics of the interior are substitutions for earlier ones and partly change the program.

Fig. 2. Interior, looking east *(Naya)*

At the turn of the thirteenth century, the decoration of San Marco must have seemed complete. All the vaulted parts of the interior visible from the nave and the transept and the two main entrances—from the piazza and the sea—were decorated with mosaics that represented the history of salvation and the story of the apostles, especially of Saint Mark, the patron of church and state. The mosaic decoration of San Marco even as it appeared about 1200 must have been one of the richest anywhere, with the exception of that in the cathedral of Monreale in Sicily, which possessed a decor that was both larger and more comprehensive from the point of view of iconography. It is certain that this fact was known in Venice, and it is most likely that it was one of the reasons behind a very considerable extension of the mosaic program of San Marco in the thirteenth century.

But jealousy and the spirit of emulation might not have been sufficiently strong incentives for undertaking a new campaign of decoration in San Marco so soon after the completion of the grand decorative scheme and its restoration at the very end of the twelfth century. A new and powerful stimulus was the victory over Byzantium in the Venetian-led Fourth Crusade. The impact of the capture of Constantinople on the political ideology of Venice has been repeatedly described, and its importance can hardly be overrated. The new power called for all the trappings of prestige. In the field of the arts it brought about a movement that can best be described as a kind of proto-Renaissance, as the concomitant of imperialistic archaism, which, having no very old tradition of its own, was forced to create one—if need be by faking and forgery. It found its most impressive early crystallization in San Marco, which, while still the private chapel of the doge, became more and more the church of the state and the people. It was here that the newly acquired power, dignity, and wealth had to be shown to the "nation" and the world.

To aid this endeavor, the interior was enriched with a number of new scenic representations and with a good many single figures, some documenting the continued possession of the relics of Saint Mark, others asserting the recent acquisition of the relics of other saints. The atrium received an entirely new cycle of representations from the Old Testament, surpassing in its richness the Sicilian cycles. In the south vestibule the story of the patron saint was retold with new motifs that linked him ever more firmly with Venice, and on the facade, which was completely rebuilt with ostentatious splendor, the legend of the acquisition of his relics was repeated in great detail. The middle of the fourteenth century saw a recrudescence of this activity, under the doge and historiographer Andrea Dandolo.

But even the ideas and incentives created by the taking of Constantinople and the new status of Venice were not, in themselves, sufficient to initiate and sustain the intense and extended activity that went on in San Marco in the thirteenth century. For the making of mosaics more is needed than ideologies: material, artists, and money are necessary. Some of these were provided by the crusade, for there is documentary evidence that among the booty the Venetians took from Constantinople were not only completely finished works of art but also raw materials for making mosaics. The earliest thirteenth-century mosaic in San Marco, however, that of the Agony in the Garden, certainly shows a new technique and preciousness of material but does not yet exhibit the full development of the new palette that might otherwise be attributed to the booty.

In addition to the possible import of materials, there may also have been an influx of mosaic workers from Byzantium, though there is no documentary

13

proof of this. Moreover, even painters who were not mosaicists could have brought with them model books of various kinds that may have been of importance for Venetian art and thus, ultimately, also for the mosaics of San Marco. We do know, at least, that some of the illuminated books that may have been part of the Constantinople booty played a conspicuous role as models for the mosaics. A further incentive for adding to the existing mosaic decoration of San Marco was the presence of relics of saints taken to Venice from Byzantium: their acquisition suggested the inclusion of the portraits of these saints in the pictorial litany of the mosaics. All the plunder and booty from Byzantium, however, would not have been sufficient to sustain the great campaign of mosaic decoration had it not been for the personal attitudes and wealth of the thirteenth-century doges.

Some of the work in the church may also have been made necessary by catastrophes, as in the twelfth century: there was a devastating earthquake in 1222/23 and a fire in the tesoro in 1231. But the most important and, for the mosaic decoration, crucial work of architectural adaptation does not seem to have been done in response to catastrophes. This work included the removal of the upper galleries in the aisles of the west arm and the transept, the addition of the north wing in the atrium, possibly the construction of some parts of the vaulting system of the west wing, and finally the construction of a richly decorated facade. The removal of the gallery floors may have been connected with changes in the liturgy—the freeing of the ground floor, especially of the side aisles, being done to accommodate the public, including women. It certainly had far-reaching effects on the mosaic decoration, for it permitted the extension of decoration to the perpendicular walls of the aisles, which were now well lighted and visible from below.

Main Porch

THE EARLIEST SURVIVING MOSAICS in San Marco are those in the main porch belonging to the eleventh century. The main porch was the most important of several entrances to the church and contains the most significant decorations. The mosaics have come down to us in a truncated and much-altered form. Today, the entrance is dominated by the sixteenth-century figure of Mark in episcopal robes, which can hardly reflect the original program. Even in Venice, an evangelist would not have been placed above the Virgin and Child. Originally there must have been a bust of Christ Pantocrator, an icon that, accompanied by figures of the Virgin, the apostles, and the evangelists, constituted the normal program in Byzantium as well as in the West. If, originally, there was a dome above the entrance bay, it may have presented the Emmanuel with the prophets and forefathers of Christ, but this is not certain. We can only guess about the mosaics filling the original pendentives and lunettes.

Although differentiated enough in its arrangement—Christ in the conch, the Virgin and eight apostles occupying the niches of the upper register, and the four evangelists in the four large niches of the lower register—the truncated program of the west porch is in itself simple and straightforward. In fact, the combination of Christ and the apostles can be regarded as one of the most normal programs for the decoration of Byzantine narthexes and doorways leading from the vestibule into the naos, although there is no close parallel for the tightly packed arrangement of the decoration of the porch, conditioned as it was by the partly preexisting architectural framework. There is, however, one difference between the San Marco and Byzantine porch programs. The inclusion of the Virgin in not usual in Byzantium, although her portrait appears often enough in the narthex or is in some other way correlated with the main entrance. It is possible that the combination of Pantocrator, apostles, and Virgin was suggested to the Venetians not so much by Byzantine as by Western prototypes and not by doorway but by apse programs.

Mosaics are preserved in only two of the original three or possibly four tiers of arches (fig. 3). Only seven broader niches of the thirteen are at all "inhabitable," the remaining six being too narrow. To use these niches for representations of the Virgin and apostles, two kinds of alterations had to be made to bring the number of spaces to the required thirteen. A figure of an apostle was placed on the flat wall space on either side of the upper row of niches and four additional niches had to be shaped anew in the row below. These were

Fig. 3. Main porch, view looking northeast *(Naya)*

CHAPTER TWO

made somewhat larger to provide suitable frames for the four figures of evangelists, who were thus given pride of place in the porch that leads into the church of the evangelist Mark. The figures are arranged in canonical sequence from left to right: Matthew, Mark, Luke, and John. To underline their privileged position, they are represented in strict frontality, a position that, in the upper row, is reserved for the Virgin alone. The other apostles are turned toward her, that is, toward the center.

In the upper row of figures, symmetry is provided only by the turning of the apostles toward the center and not by facial types or drapery schemes. This is also true of the lower four. Free rhythm rather than symmetry appears to have been the guiding principle of composition.

The strongly emphasized architectural framework of the decoration makes it appear more Romanesque than Byzantine, except that in the West one would expect statuary rather than mosaics to fill the niches. In this, the Byzantine atmosphere of Venice asserts itself.

The iconographic type of the Virgin is the Nikopeia: Mary is represented standing in frontal position holding Christ before her (fig. 4). Her right hand touches Christ's body at the waist and the other approaches his left leg but does not touch it. Although the Child is thus hardly supported at all, he is represented as seated, with his right hand raised in blessing while the left holds a scroll propped up on the left knee. This type of the Virgin, which seems to have evolved from that of a seated figure, is purely Byzantine. The Nikopeia is the presentation of the Emmanuel by the Virgin, and the icon is, therefore, a representation of the Incarnation. The form and proportions of the figure are very much conditioned by the narrowness of its receptacle. To this correspond the straight, vertical contours of the *maphorion* (the long sleeveless tunic with a hood) which at the level of the knees are continued by the equally vertical contours of the garment. The tunic is differentiated from the garment not in color but only by the rich chrysography. In spite of the narrowness and verticality of the figure, the contrapposto in the stance is accentuated enough to impart to the figure a peculiar weightlessness, as if the Virgin were floating above the suppedaneum.

Like the Virgin, the apostles have a slender build and pronounced verticality (pl. 1a). The exceptions to this scheme are the two figures on the flat wall spaces at either end, which are broader and have bolder contrapposto, showing that the character of the others was in large measure dictated by the narrowness of the niches.

The series consists of Peter, Paul, James, Andrew, Simon, Thomas, Philip, and Bartholomew and the four evangelists. The inclusion of the latter and of Paul concurs with Middle Byzantine usage. Generally speaking, the types of the eight apostles also conform to those common in Middle Byzantine iconography, except that Peter is tonsured and holds the keys, features generally found only in Western and Italo-Byzantine monuments. What distinguishes the evangelists in the lower row from the apostles in the upper row is the amount of creative imagination that went into their shaping.

The evangelists (Mark is an exception) and apostles are the work of two different artists who interpreted their models in different ways and even employed different materials and techniques (fig. 5). The style has its closest parallel in Greek mosaics of the first half or mid-eleventh century in the figures of the apostles in the narthex of Hosios Lukas.

Of course, the San Marco mosaics cannot date that early, and, indeed, they

17

Fig. 4. Main porch: Virgin and Child   Fig. 5. Main porch: Luke, head

contain evidence of a later date. They display a softening, in certain respects a weakening and schematization of the Greek style. There must have been some time lag between the latter and San Marco, and we have to assume, then, that the San Marco mosaics mirror a somewhat earlier tradition. The artists seem to have received their training in Byzantium, to have left the capital around the middle of the century, and then to have worked in Venetia for some time before turning to San Marco. Mosaics in the cathedral of Torcello were executed by Greek mosaicists who must have arrived soon after the middle of the century and worked first on the main apse and then on the south apse before executing the main porch mosaics in San Marco. The relationship of these to dated Byzantine mosaics indicates that the San Marco figures date from the last three decades of the eleventh century, perhaps even as early as about 1070. The style of the mosaics is dominated by late Macedonian art and shows none of the

18

characteristics of the Comnenian renaissance. Paleographically, the inscriptions can be divided into two groups. The older one can most likely be dated between 1060 and 1099. The later script is still tied to the eleventh century through older forms, but it already points toward the slightly later group of inscriptions in the main apse.

In the colors used, the more coherent modeling, the overall conception of the figure, and the livelier facial expression, the figure of Saint Mark differs from the others (pl. 1b). The most interesting parallel for this figure is to be found in San Marco itself, namely, in the figure of the same evangelist in the main apse. Although the two figures are not necessarily the work of the same artist, it is quite clear that the author of the porch Mark cut himself loose from the tradition of the older mosaics.

Main Apse and Apse of the Cappella Zen

3

DAMAGED BY FIRE in the fifteenth century, the apse ensemble is not preserved in its original state. Although it seems reasonable to assume that Magister Petrus, the sixteenth-century restorer, copied an earlier mosaic of the Enthroned Pantocrator, we cannot know for sure what figure originally filled the conch. Actually, the image of the Enthroned Christ in the conch of the main apse is not typical of Middle Byzantine monumental iconography; the figure most frequently depicted in Middle Byzantine apses was certainly that of the Virgin, the place of the Pantocrator being the dome. It is possible, however, that the first decoration of San Marco did not yet envisage the inclusion of the cupolas in the program and treated the interior as if it were a basilica for which the representation of Christ in the apse was almost *de rigueur*. In any case, a figure similar to the orthodox Pantocrator of Petrus was most likely already part of the original program.

Distinctly Western is the arrangement of the four patron saints on the semicylindrical apse wall under the Enthroned Christ (pl. 2). To create the space necessary for these figures, four of the seven windows that initially opened into the apse were walled up, apparently immediately after the completion of the building. The four monumental figures, Peter and Mark in the two central spaces, Nicholas and Hermagoras in the lateral ones, are not represented in direct physical connection with Christ. Rather, they share the apse with him, for this is the place of the greatest honor and they are the bearers of Christ's message. Yet the apse program of San Marco remains more closely related to Early Christian, Early Byzantine, and even Romanesque churches—where saints and apostles are arranged below the image of the Enthroned Christ—than to Middle Byzantine ones, which did not, as a rule, display images of patron saints in the main apse.

In San Marco, the four saints of the apse are closely related to the function of the church as ducal sanctuary. All four are state saints; their relics were among the most highly treasured possessions of Venice. Moreover, they embodied ideas that were intimately associated with the official myth of Church, town, and state.

The four figures are linked with one another and welded into an organic whole in a very subtle way—a composition for which the iconographic motifs are only the raw material. The inscription above their heads not only refers to the possession of these saints' relics but praises the saints as patrons and saviors of the state. Of the four, only Nicholas is represented as a single isolated figure, unconnected with the rest. He is shown in full frontality, with the self-contained gesture and wearing the priestly garments of Byzantine hierarchs, blessing with his right and holding the closed book in his covered left hand. Nicholas, distinguished as a patron of the fleet of seafaring Venice, was, in fact, a state saint second only to Mark himself. The other priestly figure, Hermagoras, is treated quite differently. The legendary disciple of Mark and first bishop of Aquileia is placed at the extreme right, turning left to his teacher, with both hands extended toward him in a humble gesture of reverence and submission. He is, thus, introduced not so much for his own sake as a saint to be venerated, but as a companion of Mark, thereby connecting the patriarchate of Aquileia-Grado with the evangelist. His name is inscribed in a manner different from that used for the names of the other three saints, that is, horizontally instead of vertically. This horizontal arrangement gives to the inscription a definite direction, replacing the framing function of the two vertical columns of letters, which makes the other figures appear more self-contained. Moreover, the vertical arrangement is specifically Greek, while the horizontal line corresponds with the Latin custom and is, therefore, most fitting for a purely Latin, even local saint who was not even a historical figure but the product of politically inspired ecclesiastical mythopoeia.

Hermagoras' pose not only connects the saint with Mark, it makes him part of the theme of the apse wall. The three figures, Peter, Mark, and Hermagoras, besides enacting a scene, embody the claim of the Church and thus also of the Venetian state to being an apostolic foundation. The central figure of the triad is, of course, Mark (pl. 3b). He is represented in full frontality, in a balanced attitude, both arms extended laterally; in his covered left hand he holds the closed Gospel book, exhibiting it like a sacred relic. His empty right hand is stretched toward the left, toward Peter, who is turned to the right, toward Mark, and who likewise holds in his uncovered left hand a preciously decorated, closed book, while with his right he makes the gesture indicative of speech (pl. 3a).

In all probability this group is meant to represent the origin of the Gospel of Saint Mark at the behest, in part after the dictate, of Saint Peter, as well as the presentation of the completed and approbated Gospel to the world by the evangelist. In this lies the explanation of the different ways in which the book is carried by the two protagonists; Peter tenders the book with his bare hand, while Mark holds the completed Gospels in his covered hand, as a priest would hold the sacrament or a holy relic. I do not know of any similarly concise and subtle apse program, a program that, with four figures in monumental attitudes, succeeded in realizing a very complex combination of religious and political ideas. The saints appear as the historical guarantors of political and ecclesiastical independence. They are not only remembered and glorified as founding fathers, they actually enact the foundation. As a result, the whole is not so much hieratic representation as dramatic enactment.

The compositional arrangement of the four saints is as subtle and complicated as the program itself. First, the figures are presented as a symmetrical group of four: on the outside two clerics in episcopal garments, with gold, gray, and white dominant, and on the inside two figures in classical garb in white, light ochre, dark blue, and purple-brown. The outer figures are coloristically neutral and recede into the golden ground while the two central

21

figures seem to step out by force of their contrasting colors. The green "meadow" on which they stand bears four magnificent flowering shrubs in gold, red, white, and blue, whereas the two bishops stand on a ground of simple green bands of a wavy design.

The central pair can also be viewed as an almost symmetrical group, the left and right hand, respectively, of the two apostles pointing to the central axis. And, finally, Peter, Mark, and Hermagoras constitute an even more strictly symmetrical group, with Mark's frontal figure in the center, both hands extended so as to appear almost as orant, with Peter and Hermagoras turning toward him. Quite clearly, this compositional arrangement presents Mark as the main figure compared with which those of Peter and Hermagoras seem secondary. Not only is Mark represented in the most conspicuous attitude, he is also distinguished by the strongest contrasts of light and shade. Next to Christ, he dominates the apse.

Fig. 6. Main apse: Nicholas, head

CHAPTER THREE

Stylistically, the present state of the apse mosaics is less dependable than it is iconographically. The figures of Nicholas and Hermagoras have suffered badly. Fortunately, Nicholas's head and hands and the greater part of his drapery are original (fig. 6); of Hermagoras only the head, chest, hands, and a bit of the chasuble are authentic. The two central figures have fared better and can be considered original.

Although the Pantocrator is a replacement, the style and iconography of the sixteenth-century copy indicate that the original did not date from the late eleventh century but from the second half of the twelfth. Thus, either because of a change of program or because of some catastrophe that damaged or destroyed the first mosaic, it was replaced.

The apse mosaics seem to present two phases in the development of a workshop within a generation or less. Nicholas and Peter would begin the sequence: they could have been completed at the time of the consecration of the church for which the main date is given as 1093. To the second phase, soon after the fire of 1106, would belong Mark and Hermagoras. The mosaics of the first phase are still in some way connected with the style of late Macedonian art; the style of the second phase cannot be exactly paralleled in Byzantine monumental painting. In certain respects, both phases are a little behind their times, almost archaic, in spite of certain new traits they contain. The paleography of the inscription indicates a date during the first two decades of the twelfth century.

APSE OF THE CAPPELLA ZEN

The mosaics of the original south vestibule of the church, which during the sixteenth century was adapted to serve as the sepulchral chapel for Cardinal Battista Zen, belong to four different periods. Only the angels of the conch above the doorway leading into the atrium are part of the original decoration of the twelfth century.

The Virgin of the conch is a nineteenth-century creation, although we know from a description that it replaces an original figure of Mary. So much of the original mosaic of the angels was incorporated into the nineteenth-century confection, however, that it can pass as fairly authentic. The inscription of the arch framing the conch is almost completely renewed but the content and literary form are most probably authentic. Their tenor is specifically Venetian with its parallel between Eve and the Virgin, a Western idea. The combination of Western ideas and Byzantine forms found repeatedly in San Marco may be regarded as belonging to the very essence of Venetian mosaic decoration.

The program of the conch is a typical Byzantine apse program (fig. 7). The Virgin flanked by angels was one of the standard programs from Early Byzantine times. In the Middle Byzantine period it was actually the most frequent apse composition, usually with the central figure enthroned, but the standing Virgin with angels is also common enough, especially in the provinces. The angels display a rather rare type of costume, consisting of a white tunic and a colored wrap thrown over shoulders and hips—a kind of reduced toga.

Parallels with other figures in San Marco—the two figures of Mark in the main porch and apse—fix the mosaics securely within the tradition of Venetian mosaic art of the first half of the twelfth century.

23

Fig. 7. Cappella Zen, apse, view looking north *(Alinari)*

CHAPTER THREE

First Phase of the East Dome

4

Though in some respects overshadowed by those of the central dome, the mosaics of the east dome are certainly among the most important parts of the decoration and perhaps the most revealing. They seem to contain the key to the understanding not only of the iconographic program of the church as a whole but also of the stylistic development of the twelfth century on Venetian soil, and this not in spite of, but because of, their problematic state of preservation. Essentially, one can discern work belonging to two different phases, the second representing an extensive twelfth-century restoration, the reason for which may have been some sort of catastrophe, a fire perhaps or an earthquake.

It is readily apparent that the mosaics of the east dome are not homogeneous (pl. 4). The composition as a whole lacks the harmony and coherence of work done in a single, uninterrupted campaign. The general principles of the composition are those of Byzantine Pantocrator domes with a central medallion and radially arranged standing figures. The main axis runs from west to east through the Orant Virgin and the central medallion. Curiously enough, this axis does not divide the dome into two halves equally balanced: to the left of the Virgin, there are seven figures while there are only six figures to the right. Four of the latter—Jeremiah, Daniel, Obadiah, and Habakkuk—with their broader gestures and postures, occupy considerably more space than the others. Furthermore, they are differentiated from the rest in material, color, and style and in the lettering of the inscriptions. They stand apart in every respect, forming a small coherent group (except for the lower part of Daniel, which was replaced during the second phase). Therefore, these three and a half figures are the only remains of the original series, as archaeological, paleographical, and stylistic evidence all indicates.

The half figure of the Emmanuel in the central medallion is a problematic issue from the iconographic point of view. It is essentially a work of the years around 1500, made necessary by the fire in 1419. There is no possibility of reconstructing with certainty the original iconography of the dome. If both the Emmanuel and the Virgin of the preserved program were part of the first phase, this is a unique occurrence, and even if it is assumed that the central medallion originally contained an image of the Pantocrator, the inclusion of the Virgin in his cortège would still be unusual. Moreover, it is not possible to reconstruct the original list of prophets on the strength of the four that are preserved. All we can say is that in all likelihood there was one figure fewer.

The types of the four prophets of the first phase are those current in Middle

Byzantine painting, but a few realistic traits are worth noticing: the forceful modeling of the hands, with tendons, muscles, and fingernails clearly indicated; the little skin folds at the elbow of Jeremiah. an almost unique detail; the attempt at three-dimensional representation of the rolled-up ends of the scrolls; and the spatial projection of Obadiah's scroll with the letters diminishing in size from top to bottom.

The proportions of the composition differ profoundly from those of most Byzantine cupolas, where the central medallion is relatively much larger, dominating the aspect of the dome, while the prophets appear as secondary elements, mostly placed between windows. In San Marco it is really the prophets who seem to have the most important role and whose figures fill the greater part of the surface. This is as much a formal as an iconographic feature: it emphasizes the importance of the special message embodied in the prophets, and at the same time it is in keeping with a general tendency toward spreading the figures evenly across the gold surface and thus toning down the great contrasts in size characteristic of purely Byzantine decorations.

A close analysis of the style suggests that the four figures of the first phase of the dome can be regarded as products of a workshop that continued the style of the main apse mosaics after a certain interval. During this interval, the concept of the draped figure had changed from a fairly integrated statuesque organism to an overdifferentiated, somewhat manneristic relief. This development can be followed even in the sequence of the three figures themselves (Daniel must be excluded). Jeremiah marks the beginning of the series (pl. 5a). The figure stands somewhat apart, and we are inclined to see in it the creation of a master of marked personality who, in view of the high quality of this mosaic, would have to be regarded as the leader of the workshop. The somewhat different character of this figure may also be due in part to its having been the first to be executed after a certain lapse of time, not only in the east dome itself, but in the whole of San Marco. Some experimental traits might be explained by this assumption. The figures of Obadiah and Habakkuk seem to have followed, with an ever increasing tendency toward agitated mannerism (fig. 8). The broken zigzag style is most strongly developed in the last figure, Habbakuk, which is weighed down by a multitude of splintery shapes.

From the point of view of style, the main overall characteristics of the four figures of the first phase of the east dome are their classicism, with its preference for noble and beautiful forms and features (fig. 9); the tendency toward an ever stronger differentiation of the relief of the body with its concomitant loss of plastic totality; a growing linearism, the elements of which are straight, angular, and broken lines containing little or no suggestion of three-dimensional development; and a shading that is achieved by the juxtaposition of contrasting shades and by hatching rather than by continuous modeling.

The search for parallels and possible sources of the style of this phase of the east dome leads first to the apse mosaics of San Marco itself and to other mosaics of the Adriatic area. Beyond that, they are connected to the neo-Hellenistic, classicist current in Byzantine monumental painting. Comparisons with these make it quite clear that the first phase of the east dome in San Marco must date from the first quarter of the twelfth century, and this date is borne out by comparisons with manuscript illumination and enamels and is confirmed by the paleography.

26

Fig. 8. East dome: Daniel, Obadiah, and Habakkuk

Fig. 9. East dome: Daniel, head

Choir Chapels

5

THE MOSAIC DECORATION of the two choir chapels of San Pietro and San Clemente constitutes an iconographically and formally homogeneous unit. The arrangement of the various parts is, by and large, symmetrical with the exception of the two outer walls of the chapels at the floor level: the north wall of San Pietro is decorated only with medallions of Saint Theodore and Saint Pantaleon set within scrolls, while the corresponding south wall of San Clemente depicts Cain and Abel presenting their offerings. Except for that of the outer walls, the program is conditioned by the differentiation of function according to which San Pietro was the domain of the Church and San Clemente that of the doge. In accord with this differentiation, the mosaics of San Pietro evoke the "prehistory" of the Venetian Church, with the foundation of the patriarchates of Aquileia and Alexandria, which Venice claimed to have "inherited," and the statement of those claims against Aquileia with the representation of Patriarch Helias of Grado petitioning and Pope Pelagius granting them. In San Clemente, the ducal motif is represented by the *translatio* of the relics of Saint Mark, the palladium of Venice, and parallel to Pelagius and Helias, the figures of Christ and the Virgin in close proximity to the ducal throne.

All the figures are balanced in symmetrical pairs. In the apses stand the two patrons of the chapels, Peter and Clement. Saint Peter, clad in apostolic garments, blue tunic, and light brown toga as is usual in Byzantium and Venice, is standing in slight contrapposto: he blesses with his right hand and holds both cross-staff and keys in his left (fig. 10). Clement wears episcopal costume of Western type, with alb, dalmatic, chasuble, stole, pallium, maniple, and miter (fig. 11). The low, conical, rounded form of the miter was current in the early and middle twelfth century. The difference in attitudes of Peter and Clement is to be explained by the difference in their rank: the orant gesture and the inscription define Clement as intercessor.

The choice and placement of the church fathers on the east and west walls of the two galleries are somewhat peculiar: Ambrose and Augustine above Saint Peter, John Chrysostom and Gregory Nazianzenus above Saint Clement—two Western and two Greek fathers, distinguished from one another by their Latin and Greek name inscription and costumes. No apparent reason can be found for placing the Latin fathers with Peter and the Greek ones with Clement. Similarly, the division of the four apostles among the two chapels, Matthew and Andrew in San Pietro, Philip and James in San Clemente, cannot be explained by their

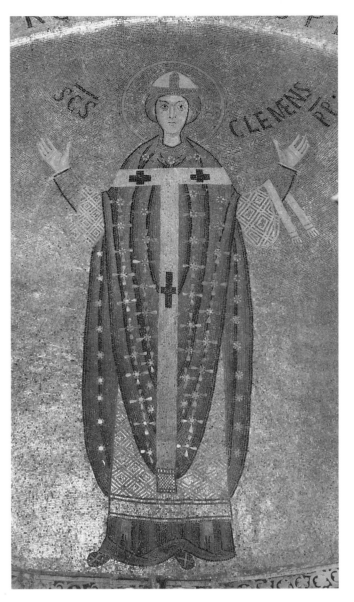

Fig. 10. Cappella di San Pietro: Peter *(Böhm)*

Fig. 11. Cappella di San Clemente: Clement

relics' having their resting place in the two altars, respectively, since the San Clemente altar did not contain any apostle's relics. Moses and Elijah in San Pietro and Sergius and Bacchus in San Clemente are in the arches preceding the apostles.

Most interesting are the figures in the arches between the choir chapels and the presbytery, figures that express clearly the respective functions of the two chapels. In all likelihood, there was only the figure of Helias of Grado in the west half originally—personifying the claim of Venice to be the legitimate successor of Aquileia in the patriarchate, against the claim of Aquileia itself. The figure opposite Helias in the east half of the north arch, Pope Pelagius, presents the answer to Helias's prayer in two long inscriptions. The claim of primacy over Istria existed as early as the middle of the eleventh century. The Dalmatian claim was eagerly pursued by Venice throughout the first half of the twelfth century and was realized in 1155. In 1180, Grado renounced its claim to the metropolitan rights over the Istrian bishoprics. The most likely date of the monumental

29

formulation of the claims of Grado is, therefore, the first half of the twelfth century.

The arch opposite shows the Orant Virgin and the Enthroned Christ, the two figures connected with one of the customary places (or thrones) of the doge. The figure of the Virgin dates from the sixteenth century, but the medieval prototype can still be felt in the Renaissance mosaic, and there is no reason to doubt the iconographic authenticity of the figure. The iconographic type of the Enthroned Christ is also authentic, and a few parts of the figure are original.

The most important parts of the decoration of the choir chapels are, of course, not the single figures but the two intimately connected narrative cycles of the vaults and the upper wall spaces of the galleries, namely, the Life of Saint Mark and the Translation of Mark's Relics. The former, filling the vault and the north wall of the gallery of San Pietro, have come down to us in a badly restored state. Some insertions were made in the fourteenth century, but it was in the 1870s that most of the damage was done. Beginning in the upper left of the vault, the sequence proceeds:

1. Saint Peter Consecrating Saint Mark
2. Mark Healing the Leper (Athaulf)
3. Mark Baptizing Athaulf
4. Saint Peter Consecrating Hermagoras Bishop
5. Hermagoras Baptizing
6. Mark Preaching
7. Mark Baptizing
8. Mark Sailing to Alexandria
9. Mark Healing Anianus
10. Martyrdom of Mark
11. Burial of Mark

The designer, or his theological advisor, was able to draw from a large body of literary sources that had received its accepted form in the eleventh century. From the texts, he selected those scenes and motifs that were in some way related to Venice. The scenario had thus to contain Mark's consecration as *protepiscopus Italiae* and first patriarch of Aquileia, the authorization by Saint Peter of Hermagoras as Mark's successor, Mark's mission to Alexandria, the founding of the church of Alexandria by the installation of Anianus as Mark's successor, the martyrdom of the evangelist, and, finally, the miraculous preservation of his relics, attested by their solemn burial. These motifs are related to the foundation of the Venetian Church in connection with Aquileia and Alexandria and to the cult and final acquisition of the relics, the latter motif being spun out in the mosaics of the Cappella di San Clemente.

Mark's consecration by Peter as bishop of Aquileia (or the *provincia Italiae*) is not contained in any of the texts of the Life—where Mark is ordained bishop of Alexandria, not of Aquileia—or in any of the cycles, not even that of Aquileia itself. This suggests that the scene was expressly invented or adapted for this cycle. The first scene of the cycle is thus the opening statement of the pictorial claim of Venice for the apostolic origin of the patriarchate connected directly with Saint Peter (fig. 12). Mark Healing the Leper, though heavily restored, is iconographically reliable. The fact that Mark is wearing apostolic costume stresses, by contrast, the ceremonious nature of the preceding scene, where Mark is dressed in episcopal regalia. Of Mark Baptizing Athaulf, all but the figure of Mark is the pure invention of the nineteenth-century restorers.

30

Fig. 12. Cappella di San Pietro, vault, west half, upper register

The lower tier of the west half of the vault is dedicated to Hermagoras, the disciple of Mark and first bishop of Aquileia (pl. 5b). The presentation underlines the apostolic origin of the Aquileian patriarchate; for example, in the scene of the saint baptizing, Hermagoras is clad not in episcopal costume but in classical garments usually reserved for apostles (fig. 13). In fact, he is introduced as a "near apostle," the legitimate successor of Mark. The state of preservation of the scenes in the upper tier of the east half of the vault, representing in all probability Mark's Mission in the Pentapolis, is very complicated, but the distribution and positions of the figures can be taken to render, more or less correctly, the original composition. The lower tier of the east half of the vault is better preserved (fig. 14). The most interesting detail is the ship in the scene of Mark's Voyage to Alexandria. It is a merchant ship of the *navis* type, with all its parts clearly recognizable and drawn with a specialized knowledge not merely rare, but unique in this period. It is not depicted in a conventional and conceptual manner as figures, landscapes, and architectural elements are, but is "copied" after an actual working model of contemporary design.

The continuation of the story on the north wall is comparatively well preserved. The martyrdom is abbreviated and the burial follows immediately (pl. 6a and fig. 15), and together the two scenes constitute the basis for the story of the relics in the vault above the Cappella di San Clemente.

The state of preservation of the relics cycle is neither better nor worse than that of the preceding ones. There are traces of Gothic renewals and additions, Renaissance changes, and nineteenth-century restorations. The cycle comprises the following scenes:

1. Saint Mark's Body Being Removed from the Tomb
2. The Relics Being Carried Away
3. The Ship with the Relics Being Examined by Muslims
4. The Vessel Departing from Alexandria

31

Fig. 13. Cappella di San Pietro:
Hermagoras Baptizing

Fig. 14. Cappella di San Pietro,
vault, east half, lower register

Fig. 15. Cappella di San Pietro: Martyrdom of Mark

5. The Vessel Being Saved from Shipwreck
6. The Ship Arriving in Venice
7. Reception of the Relics

The mosaics illustrate the salient points of a story that originated in and for Venice; the tradition was unknown or unaccepted outside the region. The textual narrative, though certainly based on earlier sources, was edited during the eleventh century. The *Translatio,* which formed an essential part of the national myth of Venice, begins with an ample introduction calculated to prove the divine right of the Venetians to the possession of the saint's relics.

The mosaics of the Cappella di San Clemente represent the oldest full cycle of the *Translatio* that has come down to us. The upper tier is almost entirely original. It begins with a kind of preface, a definition of locale in the shape of an arcade inscribed ALEXANDRIA, and it continues with the removal of the body, a naive representation, characterized as the lifting of the body out of the sarcophagus (fig. 16). The four figures holding the body are not bending over the coffin—which seems to float in midair—but are standing upright. The next episode in the upper tier of the east half of the vault shows Tribunus and Rusticus, the Venetian merchants who acquired and transported Mark's body,

33

Fig. 16. Cappella di San Clemente: Removal of Mark's Body

Fig. 17. Cappella di San Clemente: Transportation of Mark's Relics

carrying the relics in a basket on their shoulders very much like the spies of Moses bringing back the cluster of grapes from the land of Canaan (fig. 17). In front of them, on the south wall, stands a single Saracen designated by the inscription KANZIR KANZIR as one of the customs officers deceived by the merchants' ruse of covering the relics with pork. The lower tier contains only the examination of the Venetian ship by the Muslim harbor guards, hardly any part of which is original though the composition as a whole seems trustworthy. The following scene, the Vessel Departing from Alexandria, consists only of the Venetian ship on the waters.

The narrative then continues in the upper tier on the west half of the vault with the Vessel Being Saved from Shipwreck (pl. 7). The scene is followed by the ship's arrival in Venice and the reception of the relics. The representation of the arrival is only a bad copy of the original; no action is portrayed, only the ship coming to rest. Utmost caution is needed in evaluating the iconographic authenticity of the reception scene (fig. 18). It is possible that the relics were not shown at all originally, that their actual presence under the main altar, opposite the mosaic of the reception, made their representation superfluous. Such a

CHAPTER FIVE

connection between the two spheres, that of the image and that of reality, is far from uncommon in the twelfth century. In contrast to other depictions of the subject, including that of the facade of San Marco, the scene includes neither a casket nor the church of San Marco, nor—and this is the most important difference—any action or narrative. What then was the reason for the choice and the development of this odd pictorial scheme? The answer must be sought in the influence of, or desire to imitate, the most famous and most authoritative "processional" image in the region, the sixth-century dedicatory image of Justinian in San Vitale at Ravenna, which also combines the bringing of gifts with a representation of the highest authorities of Church and state. It is no mere chance that this earliest depiction in San Marco of the representatives of the supreme powers of Church and state occurs in connection with the relics of the patron saint.

Fig. 18. Cappella di San Clemente: Reception of the Relics in Venice, left part

Although the cycles of the life of Saint Mark and the *Translatio* belong so intimately together as to form a unit, there are certain structural differences. In the first cycle, we are taken twice to Rome and Aquileia, then to the Pentapolis and Alexandria, following the mission of Mark in a number of scenes meant to illustrate the foundation of the churches of Aquileia and Alexandria. Finally, we are witness to his martyrdom and burial, which means the depositing of his relics. Most scenes are set pieces, familiar from other hagiographical cycles: consecrations, sermons, baptisms, healings. Except for the rendering of the ship in Mark's Voyage to Alexandria, there is nothing specific about them, and the effort that went into their pictorial redaction is minimal. For the *Translatio* there are no set pieces and no compositional models, except for the Justinianic dedication mosaic. Everything else had to be invented ad hoc. The intention of the author of the program was to give the beholder the opportunity of accompanying the relics from their first resting place to their final destination and thus to remove any doubts about the reality and completeness of the *Translatio*, doubts that might have arisen in view of Alexandria's claim to have retained the head of the saint or Reichenau's claim to have abducted the relics from Venice. It was this need for a convincing statement that led to the adoption of a certain objective realism in the rendering of naval matters, the material for which Venice could provide better than any other place. The story of the *Translatio* was for Venice more than a legend: it was an integral part of the ideological foundation of the Venetian Church and state.

Two scenes from the Life of Saint Peter are represented on the north wall of the gallery of the Cappella di San Pietro, Herod Interrogating Peter (pl. 6b) and Saint Peter Being Liberated from Prison (based on Acts 12:3–11). These specifically Petrine scenes may have been chosen because, immediately thereafter, "Peter went to the house of Mary, the mother of John, whose surname was Mark." (Acts 12:12). As a whole, the mosaic is a curiously awkward production, based on a local cycle of Acts illustrations. Furthermore, since the mosaic is practically hidden behind the organ, only nominal restoration has occurred leaving the mosaic the most badly damaged in San Marco.

The choice of two scenes from the Life of Saint Clement on the opposite wall of the appropriate gallery—The Mass of Saint Clement and Sisinnius' Attempt to Have Clement Arrested—is no less arbitrary and unusual. Possibly, the latter was chosen to parallel the Petrine scene opposite: each represents a foiled attempt at imprisonment.

The program of the choir chapels is by and large homogeneous; is this true also of the style? With the exception of the mosaic of Cain and Abel and the apostles Philip and James, it is. Cain and Abel may be a remnant of the earliest decoration preceding the fire of 1106 and is a more or less isolated piece of work (figs. 19 and 20). Philip and James are similar cases, perhaps the first attempts at a restoration after one of the catastrophes of the twelfth century.

The homogeneity of the rest of the chapels is revealed in the overall composition, the decorative arrangement of the constituent parts, and the relation to the architecture. More than elsewhere, the gold ground dominates the system; scenes and figures stand out more as isolated motifs than as coherent compositions. In spite of the looseness, however, the single parts were arranged according to an overall decorative concept with complicated interrelations between them. Walls and vaults are treated as units with strict symmetry governing their decoration. It is very likely that formal considerations even influenced the selection of scenes and motifs to be represented. The symmetry

36

Fig. 19. Cappella di San Clemente: Abel

Fig. 20. Cappella di San Clemente: Cain

is also apparent in the palette and distribution of coloristic accents.

Except for the relics cycle, the scenes are isolated and pictured singly, and there is no attempt to achieve any kind of continuity. The very laconic narrative style has its best parallels in Western cycles.

The work was, of course, divided among several mosaicists and may have taken a considerable time. San Pietro is certainly more archaic than San Clemente, even as regards the compositional design. Within the two complexes, work must have proceeded from top down. A certain progress can be noted: the attempt to extend a scene from one wall across an angle to the next wall, and the creation of a "seascape" in San Clemente could be regarded as being the result of this progress. The executors seem to have had the same technical training and to have drawn from the same repertoire of types. All the architectural forms are derived from Western, pre-Romanesque prototypes. They are abstract and conceptual, with little functional differentiation; and none stands in a landscape or on any kind of terrain. Flat, conceptual forms are also found in the few pieces of "furniture." The costumes are odd mixtures of Byzantine and Western elements; some features were copied from Byzantine models, while others were

37

drawn from actual garb. To the intentional realism of certain costumes, the garb of the Saracens and heathens—half-naked savages—forms a curious contrast. This is certainly a piece of propaganda, as is the rendering of the two henchmen in the martyrdom as Moors.

Movement is, on the whole, restrained, even stiff, and has nothing of the speed and urgency characteristic of the dynamic style of late Comnenian art. Most of the attitudes are definitely archaic; the figures seem pressed to the picture plane in a fashion found more often in the West than in Byzantium but there not later than the eleventh century. The drapery patterns are also as flat, stiff, and frozen as is compatible with a minimum of movement. The design of the draperies is clearly influenced by Byzantine models but there is little effect of continuous, convincing relief; the lines are more like incisions in a flat surface than concentrations of shadows along plastic folds. The facial types are also simplified and generalized versions of Byzantine models, but they show little of that quality that makes Byzantine figures almost character portraits. The generalizing and toning down of special accents and specific forms are characteristic of the style of the workshop. With the exceptions of Anianus' face in the healing scene and the faces of the executioners in the martyrdom scene, the expression of emotions has as little place within the possibilities of this style as the rendering of individual features.

In the linear treatment of hair and beard, the San Pietro apostles stand between the figures of the main apse and those of the second phase of the east dome. The modeling techniques indicate that the mosaicists had some Byzantine training—probably through Byzantine craftsmen in Venice. Despite this and other technical connections with Byzantine mosaic art, it is unlikely that even the technicians, not to mention the chief designer of the mosaics of the choir chapels, were actually Greeks. The non-Greek characteristics, which may even be called Venetian, are too prominent. One such characteristic is the predilection for specially cut marble or enamel pieces, round, tear-shaped, or square—shapes that are rare in Byzantine art. There is also a somewhat barbaric love of showiness, of material splendor in its almost indiscriminate use of decorative wealth.

As far as extant works are concerned, the style of the choir chapels as a whole has no antecedents in Venice or the Adriatic. This does not mean that this style was imported unaltered from outside, from Byzantium or the Romanesque West. On the contrary, the recourse in certain instances to Ravennate models indicates that there was a strong local factor active in its genesis. The Byzantine elements are mostly typological and technical. The stylistic character might be accurately defined as a typically Venetian mixture of Byzantine and Romanesque elements. In all likelihood, the material, stone and enamel, that went into the making of these mosaics was also Venetian.

Unfortunately, there are no dependable objective data for establishing the actual date of the mosaics. A date in the first half of the twelfth century is likely, probably even in the first quarter. The paleography indicates that the choir chapel inscriptions were set about the second or third decade of the century.

38

North Dome

THE MAIN THEME of the north dome is the Life of Saint John the Evangelist. In the center is a cross-shaped motif with inscriptions and between the windows are the symbols of the four evangelists and further inscriptions. Four standing figures of church fathers occupy the pendentives (pl. 8). The main subject is so arranged that a figure of Saint John, in the frontal attitude of an orant, stands isolated on the east axis, while five scenes from his life are placed around the circumference. The frontal figure and much of the narrative are very heavily restored and two church fathers (besides Ambrose) are baroque replacements. With the exception of the evangelists' symbols and columnar bases, the whole can be regarded as iconographically authentic.

The Saint John cycle is intimately connected with the dedication of the altar in the east aisle (or chapel) underneath. Before the thirteenth century, when a stone relief was placed on the east wall, the frontal figure of the orant saint on the east axis of the dome may even have had the function of an altar panel. Cycles consisting of the frontal figure of a saint surrounded with scenes from his or her life are quite frequent in the twelfth and thirteenth century, and the scheme goes back at least to the eighth century. John is represented as an old man with a long white beard and scanty, somewhat curly hair—a Byzantine type (fig. 21). The orant pose is in keeping with the function of the image as the center of the cycle and, at the same time, as the altar icon of the east chapel of the north transept. Though such a figure is quite normal in an apse, the San Marco John is unique in a cupola. Even more exceptional, is Saint John's costume, which is not a dark tunic and light toga, but a dark blue tunic and a deep, brilliant green toga, both decorated with numerous gold stripes outlined in red, which by the complicated folding and knotting of the garments appear to be cut up into a multitude of gold rectangles.

The cycle of the life comprises five scenes:
1. John Raising Drusiana
2. John Raising Stacteus
3. John Destroying the Temple of Diana
4. John Drinking Poison
5. The Resuscitation of the Two Poisoned Men and the Conversion of Aristodemus and the Ephesians

The fact that this cycle of the Life of Saint John in San Marco is the earliest to have survived makes it difficult to establish the character of its source. The

Fig. 21. North Dome: John

scenes all belong to the Ephesian narrative, from which the mosaicist selected and composed a typical *virtus* cycle, which opens with a resuscitation and ends, fittingly, with the triumph of the saint, the conversion of the people of Ephesus.

In spite of numerous patchings, John Raising Drusiana is largely original (pl. 9a); the tripartite scheme is repeated in all other scenes of the dome. The next scene is nearly identical to this one; except for the praying mother and the shroud, all distinguishing details of the story have been suppressed. The next three episodes form a closed subcycle representing the conversion of Aristodemus, the high priest of Ephesus.

From whatever source, possibly a templon beam, the theological advisors of the designer of the San Marco cycle might have drawn their inspiration, it is quite clear that the narrative was given a thoroughly new redaction in accordance with the principles of cupola decoration. The number of scenes was limited to the five that could be accommodated in the available space. All secondary features of the selected scenes were eliminated to make the episodes easily readable, and all unnecessary architectural and landscape accessories were removed.

The figures are stereotyped to a degree rare even in medieval art. Saint John, for instance, is repeated four times with hardly any variation and the witnesses are practically uniform. The only thing really evident to the uninformed beholder is that the scenes depict miracles, but the specific content and the course of events are not made clear at all. Each scene is uniform, comprising the performer, the object, and the witnesses, and each is absolutely self-sufficient. In this, the San Marco cycle resembles certain Byzantine saint cycles, although the latter usually contain a wealth of accessory details.

Placing legendary scenes in a cupola was in itself something that ran counter to the principles of Byzantine iconography and decoration and also had no precedent in the West. It must be conceded, then, that the designer of the north dome made an astonishingly good job of his difficult task. First, he designed an axial cross by the cross-shaped inscription of the central medallion and stressed the main axis by inserting in the east the frontal figure of Saint John, which marks the beginning and end of the cycle. The orant figure is flanked by two more figures of the saint in mirrorlike symmetry (made possible by the inversion of the last composition), and the most symmetrical middle motif, the collapsing altar of Ephesus, is placed opposite, on the west axis (fig. 22). The

Fig. 22. North Dome: John Destroys the Temple of Diana

transverse axis is marked by two "pillars"—one the figure of Saint John, on the right, and the other a narrow group of bystanders, on the left.

In addition to the axial regularity, there is the principle of concentric rings to establish a firm compositional order. It begins with the small ring of letters in the central medallion, which, in its turn, is surrounded by the closely knit ring of the main inscription. The next ring is formed by the figural compositions and the last by the windows with inscriptions in the wall spaces between them. The extremely well-ordered and firm pictorial architecture is equaled in San Marco by the west dome with the Pentecost, which is, in fact, closely related.

The mosaics are stylistically homogeneous except for the church fathers which, as indicated by the figure of Ambrose, are by a different hand, though closely linked to the main part. The figures in the dome are short, even stocky and squat, for no attempt was made to counteract perspective foreshortening. The number of types is as restricted as the number of attitudes and movements; this is equally true of faces, draperies, and other elements. Even the modeling is schematized to the highest degree.

The mosaics of the cupola are much less Byzantine than those of the porch and the main apse, being more closely related to the choir chapels, of which they are, in most respects, a continuation. A date slightly later than the choir chapels—perhaps still in the first quarter of the twelfth century—is confirmed by the shape of the inscriptions and the appearance of new paleographic forms.

South Vault

7

THE SOUTH VAULT of the central dome contains four scenes from the Life of Christ: the Temptation and the Entry into Jerusalem in the east half, the Last Supper and the Washing of the Feet in the west half (pl. 9b). Although the decoration of the vault underwent extensive restoration in the nineteenth century, the iconography is reliable.

Inscriptions surrounding the openings of the tribune below and on the northern face of the arch separating vault and south dome refer to the scenes, and further references are found on the scrolls of the prophets next to the tribune openings and on the narrow south arch. This is the most completely preserved combination of scenes, prophets, and related inscriptions to be found in San Marco. David, Jeremiah (fig. 23), and (in part) Daniel are stylistically authentic; Zechariah, Moses, and the second David are works of the sixteenth century.

The cycle begins with the Temptation of Christ, which shows numerous traces of reassembling and repair but is, as a whole, authentic. The scene is represented in three phases. The well-shaped, winged Satan of the Temptation in the Desert corresponds more to Byzantine notions than to Western grotesques. The second phase shows Christ standing on the roof of the temple, which is figured as a frail ciborium rising from a crenellated wall. In front of his tall, slender figure is Satan urging him to throw himself down. Both figures are repeated in every trait in the third episode, in which Satan shows Christ the riches of the world (pl. 10a). The general iconographic character of the sequence points to a Middle Byzantine prototype of the eleventh or early twelfth century (pl. 10b). The mosaic contains no specifically Western traits nor any that would have to be dated later than about 1100.

The Entry into Jerusalem is the best preserved of the representations in the vault. Although all the elements of the composition are to be found in Middle Byzantine works, the shape of these details and especially of the composition as a whole is specific—the latter belonging to that type in which the several motifs are strung from left to right with as little overlapping as possible.

Despite patchings and restorations, the Last Supper can be regarded as iconographically authentic. Christ and Peter sit opposite one another on upright cushioned benches; all the apostles have their left hands placed on the table while they gesticulate with their right hands; John rests his head on Christ's shoulder (fig. 24). The apostles respond to Christ's announcement of Judas' treachery, and at the same time, Christ institutes the Eucharist, holding the bread in one hand and blessing with the other. The merger of the two themes appears to be

Fig. 23. South vault: Jeremiah

Fig. 24. South vault: Last Supper, Christ and John

the fusion of a Byzantine model with Western iconographic ideas.

The Washing of the Feet has suffered from restoration. Most of the details conform to Middle Byzantine usage, but some peculiarities indicate that the mosaicists assembled details from various models and interpreted and arranged them in an uninspired and monotonous way.

For the scenes, the mosaicist must have looked to book illumination, probably of the later eleventh century and not in the current style. Although he exchanged some motifs for others that were more familiar to Italian minds and eyes, he made few corrections. More important was his compositional editing. All representations show the same sober and impersonal interpretation, the same monotonous and additive rhythm. The stereotyped and regularized qualities are so strong that they represent positive aesthetic values and must be regarded as the result of a conscious restraint, a specific will to form. This almost impersonal

44

art—though somewhat different from that of the choir chapels—does not obtrude itself in any way. The compositions are completely subordinated to the demands of iconographic clarity and decorative orderliness, filling the allotted space in the most economical manner. The gold ground is the most important element, not even broken by inscriptions. It is an ascetic "antipictorial" style in which spatial effects and overlapping are eliminated, the result being midway between the Byzantine ideal of the picture and the Romanesque principle of interrelated patterns. In these mosaics, the only force of cohesion is rhythm sustained by forms and color.

The style of these mosaics has parallels in the mosaics of the Cappella di San Pietro, but there are also significant differences, most notably a strengthening of the plastic sense of the figures. The latter must result from a direct study of Byzantine models, as must the smoother, more rhythmical flow of the lines, the more "correctly" Byzantine types of figures, and other features. This corroborates the conclusions drawn from the iconographical data that the designer of the christological scenes of the south vault had recourse, among other models, to a Byzantine manuscript of the second half of the eleventh or the beginning of the twelfth century and that the chief executing mosaicist—whether he was the designer or not—had also had an opportunity to study modeling techniques in Byzantine mosaics. This only provides a terminus post quem, of course, and it should be noted that the copying of earlier works during the twelfth century can be traced—not only in the provinces, but also in Constantinople itself. Technically, the mosaics of the south vault are related to those in the San Pietro chapel and should be dated to the first half, even to the first quarter, of the twelfth century.

45

South Dome and Single Figures of Saints

8

Fig. 25. South dome: Leonard

THE SOUTH DOME is the most astonishing and most disappointing part of the decoration of San Marco (pl. 11). It contains nothing but a central medallion with a cross and four standing male saints and female saints in the four pendentives. Surely this is the most unusual cupola decoration in mosaic, for whereas a few parallels exist on a small scale in Byzantine churches, nowhere is found such a large dome with saints that do not fill it. The male figures are the Venetian state saints, Nicholas, Clement, Leonard, and Blaise. The first three, also represented elsewhere in San Marco, may have been repeated in the south dome because of their importance as protectors of the government and the people and of the army and navy of Venice. Leonard, the main figure on the east axis, is also an altar icon, as is John in the north transept. The iconography does not, however, account for the problem of form, or rather of lack of form; for that the only possible explanation is artistic bankruptcy, the breakdown of artistic leadership in this part of the church's decoration.

The filling of the pendentives with the so-called Grado martyrs Dorothea, Erasma, Euphemia, and Thecla is equally well founded from the point of view of the program—they, too, are state saints of a kind—and equally unsatisfactory in composition. Single figures are inadequate fillings for pendentives and rarely occupy that space in Byzantine buildings.

Leonard is depicted as a normal Byzantine martyr, with a little cross in his right hand and his left raised in front of his breast, palm outward (fig. 25). Clement, however, cannot be regarded as more than a bad copy of the original. How much of the artistic degradation can be blamed on the restorer is difficult to say, but some of the weakness of the figure was certainly inherent in the original. The iconographic scheme of Nicholas and Blaise is copied with little change from that of Nicholas in the main apse—further proof of the complete lack of inventive force here.

The master who was responsible for the four female saints in the pendentives had more imagination and, it seems, greater technical skill. Unfortunately, only Dorothea is preserved in original form (fig. 26). Erasma and Euphemia are works of the fifteenth century and Thecla was done in 1512. Dorothea is represented in the costume of Byzantine royalty, except for the embroidered cap. Even the manner of presenting the delicate wreath recalls an empress holding an orb. Stylistically, the entire complex seems to be the work of a local workshop.

Insofar as they have retained their original form, the numerous single figures of saints in the arches of the ground floor and tribunes in the cupola piers that open toward the main body of the church belong to the family of the south dome. Whether figures of this group also filled all the arches of the upper register in the tribunes of the cupola piers is difficult to determine, as practically all of them are baroque. A few figures in the tribune of the southeast pier of the central dome suggest that from the start the intent was to fill the arches of the upper story with figures of the same workmanship and that a beginning was actually made.

The south arch of the southeast tribune of the central square has retained its original program. It contains two pairs of figures; the eastern pair represents the archangels Michael and Gabriel holding a shell-shaped medallion of the Emmanuel (fig. 27). The other pair portrays Saint George and Saint Theodore—in style very close to the mosaics in the Cappella di San Clemente. George and Theodore are represented elsewhere in San Marco; their placement here may be due to the fact that this was the ducal area. The two figures seem to have become models of practically all other representations of saints in the arcades of the church, of which most have been disfigured by far-reaching restorations.

The models of the main types were quite clearly early Byzantine works, specifically mosaics. Saint Sophia in Kiev offers close parallels datable to the 1040s—which, though not outstanding, are better than the belated and provincial imitations produced by mediocre craftsman on the fringe of the local workshop in San Marco.

Fig. 26. South dome: Dorothea

Fig. 27. Central dome, southeast pier: Michael and Gabriel with medallion of Christ Emmanuel

47

Miracles of Christ

9

ALTHOUGH THE MIRACLE CYCLE has suffered from restoration more than any other part of the decoration has, there is good reason to assume that the scenes largely correspond to the original program, except for the lacunae that resulted from the opening of the rose window and the introduction of the huge Tree of Jesse.

No linear sequence is followed in the cycle, but the beginning must be sought in the central square and the series seems to follow in a clockwise direction. (Parentheses indicate that the mosaics are later work, but subjects are probably original.)

North Vault of Central Square
1. (Healing the Syro-Phoenician Woman's Daughter combined with the Raising of the Widow's Son)
2. (Supper in the House of Simon)
3. (Healing the Leper)
4. (Miracle at Cana)

North Bay of the North Transept
5. Healing the Paralytic at Capernaum
6. Stilling the Tempest
7. Healing the Dropsical Man
8. Miraculous Draught of Fishes

East Bay of the North Transept
9. (Healing Ten Lepers)
10. (The Woman Taken in Adultery)
11. (Healing the Centurion's Servant)
12. (Healing the Woman with an Issue of Blood)
13. (Cleansing the Temple)

East Bay of the South Transept
14. Feeding the Five Thousand
15. The Samaritan Woman at the Well
16. Healing the Man Born Blind
17. Christ Calling to Zacchaeus
18. (Christ Walking on the Water)
19. (Healing the Paralytic at the Pool of Bethesda)

South Bay of the South Transept
20. (Healing Two Demoniacs at Gadara)
21. (Feeding the Four Thousand)
22. (Healing Peter's Mother-in-Law)
23. (Healing the Woman with a Spirit of Infirmity)

Together with the scenes that are now missing, the Raising of Lazarus and Raising of the Daughter of Jairus among others, San Marco would have had twenty-nine scenes. The scenes are not in any kind of chronological sequence according to one or another of the Gospels, nor do they follow an artificially created harmony. Instead, the scenes are arranged formalistically. The first vault, for instance, combines two feasts and two healings; the north bay of the north transept contains two healings opposite one another and two miracles set on water. The east bay of the north transept pairs two healing miracles; the common theme of another is impurity. The east bay of the south transept represents two healings effected through life-giving water. Feeding the Five Thousand is perhaps connected with Christ Walking on the Water because both are set on the seashore, a rather loose connection characteristic also of the other scenes at the end of the cycle. Among the more subtle juxtapositions are those that match events involving men with similar ones concerning women: Daughter of the Syro-Phoenician Woman/Leper; Samaritan Woman/Zacchaeus; Centurion/Woman with an Issue of Blood.

The principle of arranging the somewhat amorphous mass of miracles with the help of common motifs of content or form can also be found in Byzantine cycles, but more commonly the organization followed liturgical practice—of which nothing is found in San Marco. Certain of the scenes were accompanied by prophets though none has survived; this, too, was rare but not unprecedented.

Because all the mosaics of the north vault of the central square are works of the third quarter of the sixteenth century, not even the program can be taken for granted. The iconography of the mosaics in the north bay of the north transept, on the other hand, is certainly authentic. The basic iconographic scheme of Healing the Paralytic (pl. 12a) conforms in all details to the eleventh-century Byzantine type, as does Stilling the Tempest, which, however, was interpreted by a less than mediocre draftsman who had little understanding of the niceties of Byzantine iconography. Though the preservation of Healing the Dropsical Man is among the worst in San Marco, the iconography conforms generally to Byzantine examples; so does that of the Miraculous Draught of Fishes, which surely was based on an illustrated Byzantine Gospel book.

The mosaics of the east bay of the north transept are rich baroque compositions and are very different from the laconic schemes of the old mosaics; only a very few motifs may go back to their medieval predecessors. The four scenes on the vault of the east bay of the south transept, by contrast, retain their original compositions, although the entire scene of Healing the Man Born Blind and several of the other figures are very much restored. Feeding the Five Thousand seems to follow a conservative Byzantine prototype in which the archaic symmetrical group of the Blessing of the Loaves was combined with a narrative development of the entire scene from left to right. The inscription does not contain any suggestion that the representation may have had a Eucharistic meaning; the equation of the physical feeding with spiritual nourishment is already inherent in Scripture. For the Samaritan Woman at the Well, the

49

designer used a Byzantine narrative redaction in which the various phases of the episode appeared side by side. Healing the Man Born Blind is an interesting example of fifteenth-century restoration activity; iconographically, it belongs to the mainstream of Byzantine illumination, as does the badly preserved Christ Calling to Zacchaeus.

The scenes on the east wall of the bay and the vault of the south bay are exuberant baroque compositions that have preserved hardly any elements of their medieval predecessors.

So homogenous is the character of the entire cycle, in general, and of the preserved medieval scenes, that a single prototype can be assumed for the mosaics—surely a rather archaic eleventh-century Byzantine Gospel book. The compositions of the north bay of the north transept seem somewhat clumsier and more awkward than those of the east bay of the south transept, which are more monumental, more mature than the former. It is apparent that the author of the latter profited from the experimental groping of the former, which would mean that work, like the iconography, progressed in a clockwise direction. The scenes of the north and south transepts seem to be the work of two different but closely related workshops. Their closest stylistic parallels are to be found in the mosaics of the San Pietro and San Clemente chapels; in fact, the north transept seems to continue the style of the San Pietro mosaics and the south, those in San Clemente. This would suggest the possibility that the workshop of the north group continued the tradition of the north chapel and that of the south group, the practices of the south chapel. This also means, of course, that the Miracle cycle is somewhat later than the mosaics of the choir chapels. It is difficult to say more about the style, however, because after the thirteenth century, the mosaics were much damaged and restored. Some details retain an eleventh-century character, others that of the thirteenth; most are shapeless products of still later interference.

CHAPTER NINE

Life of the Virgin and Infancy of Christ

THE LIFE OF THE VIRGIN is represented in two parts in the west bays of both the north and south transepts and is accompanied by a few single figures of prophets and saints. The south part was completely transformed at the end of the seventeenth century. The north part has retained its medieval compositions but has also suffered from later restorations. It is very likely that most of the present mosaic surface is a product of the thirteenth century.

The first scene, the Rejection of Joachim's Offerings in the Temple, though a baroque fabrication, includes elements that reflect the Byzantine tradition. Judging from the inscription, the next scene originally contained three episodes but the baroque artist severely curtailed these to gain room for the Return from the Temple. Even though the Search of the Records is very rare in monumental art, it may have been part of the original program, as were the Annunciation to Anne and the Withdrawal of Joachim to the Wilderness. It is almost certain that the original mosaic depicted the Lament of Joachim, Annunciation Witnessed by the Shepherds, and Joachim and Anne Meeting at the Golden Gate, the first two combined in one scene as in most Byzantine depictions. The Birth of the Virgin and Anne Nursing the Child Mary were most likely represented as separate episodes. In keeping with its high position in the hierarchy of Marian subjects, the Presentation of the Virgin in the Temple is represented in one grand composition on the west wall of the bay, probably with a sort of annex showing the Virgin Nourished by an Angel.

In establishing the sequence and analyzing the iconography of the second part of the Marian cycle, we are on firmer ground, but the cycle representing the transition from the Life of the Virgin to the story of Christ—which was to a large extent remade in the thirteenth century—still raises many questions. The first scene, the Calling of the Suitors, is followed by the Handing-over of the Virgin to Joseph, which is somewhat better preserved than the former and is certainly authentic from the iconographical point of view (fig. 28). The next two scenes represent the Annunciation at the Well and the Handing-over of the Purple to the Virgin (pl. 12b), the latter modeled on a depiction of the Trial by Water. Both of the next two scenes, the Visitation and the Scolding of Mary by Joseph, have suffered greatly through restoration but can be regarded as iconographically authentic. Next are shown the First Dream of Joseph and the Journey to Bethlehem (fig. 29), both of which are better preserved than the preceding scenes. The cycle is then continued on the west wall of the bay with three scenes from the Infancy of Christ: the Third Dream of Joseph, the Return

Fig. 28. North transept: Calling of the Suitors and Mary Handed Over to Joseph

Fig. 29. North transept: First Dream of Joseph and Journey to Bethlehem

CHAPTER TEN

from Egypt, and the Twelve-year-old Christ in the Temple. The mosaic was so extensively renewed that it must be considered a bad copy of the lost original.

The San Marco mosaics constitute one of the most detailed monumental cycles of the Life of the Virgin and Infancy of Christ, but it is not unique in its time. Several parallel cycles in Russia and Georgia suggest a common, Constantinopolitan source, probably a late eleventh-century Protevangelion of James illustrated in Constantinople—with a Gospel source for the terminal scenes.

Unfortunately, the state of preservation of the mosaics is such that their style can be analyzed and judged only to a very limited extent—and then, only those of the north transept. It seems that at least two masters and one assistant divided the work among themselves, but the differences remain within the compass of the style and technique of one workshop, as is indicated by the monotonous uniformity of the style, technique, and color of the material. The homogeneity is also proved by the unity of design, the "vertical symmetry," which consists in the mirroring of shapes in the two registers. The dependence on the model, however, was so strong that little or no attempt was made to establish symmetrical correlations across the width of the vault.

The prophets in the apex have been heavily reset. All that can be said is that there is a complete linearization of their draperies and faces, the expression on their faces is sober, and they are comparatively simply and logically designed. Saints Julian and Hermagoras are characteristic. Both have connections to the mosaics belonging to the orbit of the "local workshop"; they must be dated a good deal later than other figures from the shop. All the stylistic evidence points to a more advanced date in the twelfth century or even the beginning of the thirteenth. There can be no doubt that the narratives are of the same date, even though their style was so heavily conditioned by the model that the contribution of the Venetian mosaicists is difficult to assess.

There are, however, features that must be taken as embodying the stylistic interpretation of the model by the Venetian masters. Among these are the accentuation of the knees and hips in some figures, the heaping of repetitive forms of the drapery, and the hard modeling of drapery. Generally speaking, the style seems to have grown out of the local tradition, the earliest preserved works of which are the mosaics of the choir chapels. It has little or nothing to do with the style of the north dome, although this, too, is a product of the local school, albeit a very specialized one. As a matter of fact, there are no other mosaics in San Marco that are closely related to the style of the Life of the Virgin. There is, however, one that may be regarded as an earlier parallel, namely, the Incredulity of Thomas. The germane features are the reduction of modeling to hard contrasts of light and dark in a graphic "black and white" technique, and the geometrical treatment of forms, many of which are repetitive, especially in the figures of Thomas himself and Peter.

The aesthetic quality of these mosaics is not very high. The designer seems to have done little to translate his model into the language of monumental art: the mosaics are hardly more than mechanically enlarged copies of book illuminations, presented in a rather rough, simple technique that completely lacks the refinement of the central dome or the west vault, a technique that suits very well the dull emptiness of the scenic representations. These late and, as it were, tired products of the local workshop also lack the archaic dignity of the earlier works of the school: they are *retardataire* and provincial and may have been executed as late as 1200 or at the very beginning of the thirteenth century.

West Dome

11

THE WEST DOME, with its representation of the Pentecost, is one of the most impressive and intriguing parts of the decoration of San Marco (pl. 13). It is impressive not so much with regard to the artistic quality of details as with regard to the composition of the whole; it is intriguing because of its stylistic complexity and the bad state of preservation. The west dome, like the east, raises the question of whether the mosaics were all made at the same time or in two distinguishable phases.

Fires caused severe damage to the western parts of the church in the fifteenth century; among the restored parts in the west dome are the Libyans and certain details. Later restorations—down to the 1950s—can be recognized in other parts of the dome as well. As a result, the mosaics reveal varying degrees of authenticity and originality, but there is hardly a part that has not been tampered with at one time or another, and yet, iconographically they can still be regarded as authentic.

No absolutely convincing proof can be found of any restoration or alteration prior to the fifteenth century, but it is very likely that repairs and mendings were made in the late twelfth century. Although the original was certainly the work of different hands, everything speaks for the assumption that the cupola and pendentives were decorated under the leadership of one master. Technically and stylistically, the entire group is fairly homogeneous, even to a sharing of types between the apostles and the nations.

The composition of the Pentecost dome is a perfect wheel, the axial symmetry of which is observed not only in line and mass but also in color. At the hub of the wheel is the golden throne with purple chlamys, book, and dove, in a circular glory whose concentric rings are colored dark blue, medium blue, silver, and white. From the geometrical center of the circle, behind the throne, radiate twelve silver rays in such perfect symmetry that each ray is the exact continuation of the ray on the opposite side: they are perfect diameters. The rays descend on the heads of the apostles, striking their haloes at the highest point, where they are met by red conic shapes, the flames of the Holy Spirit. The apostles are seated on golden thrones (fig. 30), the evangelists being distinguished by golden folds, full frontality, and the golden books they hold in their left hands (pl. 14a and fig. 31). Between the sixteen windows beneath are pairs of nations according to Acts 2:9–11. Four angels occupy the pendentives and accentuate the Saint Andrew's cross formed by the frontal evangelists.

As in all monumental representations of the Pentecost, this is not the

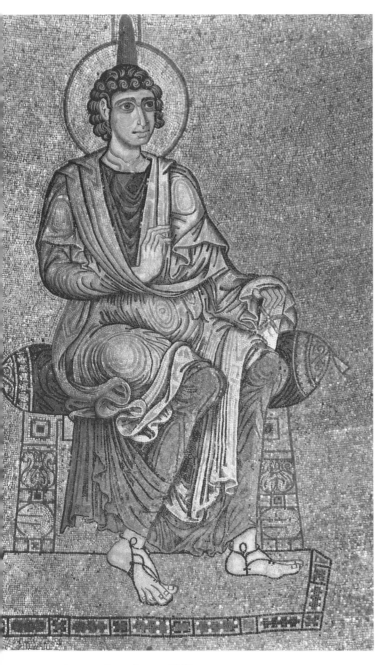

Fig. 30. West dome: Philip

Fig. 31. West dome: Luke

pictorial record of an event, but the symbolic representation of the institution of the Church and its infusion by the Holy Spirit that is depicted. The apostles are not shown at the moment of their receiving the Holy Spirit but in their role as the founders and inspired teachers of the Church.

Whereas the San Marco scheme shares most features with other Middle Byzantine representations of the Pentecost, it also contains such unique elements as the placement of the nations between the windows (rather than in the pendentives), which freed the pendentives for angels, often connected with the *Hetoimasia,* that is, the empty throne. The *Hetoimasia* had clear Trinitarian associations, with the Gospel standing for the Son and the dove for the third person of the Trinity. It will be remembered that Pentecost and the Feast of the Trinity were celebrated on the same day in the Orthodox church.

The fully differentiated apostles conform to the normal liturgical list of

55

Byzantine iconography, with Paul and all four evangelists. The nations between the windows are among the most interesting representations of foreign peoples in art. Each pair of figures consists of bearded men and beardless youths who seem to be disputing with each other (fig. 32). The designer of the mosaic gave each pair distinct costumes without repetition and without having recourse to nondescript garments. Although in the beardless youths, the mosaicists repeated facial types, in the bearded faces, all possible shapes and colors of beards are to be found, some of them highly individualized. The Arabs are rendered as half-naked savages and the Egyptians as Moors (fig. 33). These two examples alone show that there was no ethnographic basis for the choice of types and costumes. But the gusto with which the pseudo-realism of the nations was developed distinguished the iconography from its Byzantine sources and betrays the spirit of Venice, and this spirit may also be seen at work in the geometrical schematization of the composition.

Because of the unsatisfactory state of preservation of the mosaics, it is difficult, if not impossible, to define the shares of individual mosaicists who, under the leadership of a head master, must have worked on the vast surface of the dome. Within the series of apostles, however, there are different levels of

Fig. 32. West dome: Cappadocia

Fig. 33. West dome: Egiptum

quality attributable to differences in training and ability. By far the figure with the best arrangement and modeling of the drapery as well as design and execution of the face is that of Luke. The delicate coloring and modeling found in all parts of the figure suggest that one single mosaicist set the whole, and the fine harmony of shades, together with the sureness of drawing, makes it almost certain that we are dealing here with a work of the leading master.

The twelve figures seem, generally, to consist of two groups—one favoring simple, straight-lined patterns, the other complicated and undulating ones. The straight-lined group includes James, Simon, Luke, Bartholomew, Andrew, and John; the undulating ones are Paul, Peter, Mark, Thomas(?), Philip(?), and Matthew. If the mannerist component of the style is rather subdued in Luke and one or two other figures, it certainly comes to the fore in the greater part of the cupola's mosaics. It is, however, not the only striking element: another is the figures' archaism. The figures are characterized by extremely large wide-open eyes, large ears, and long, fleshy noses with the tips drawn downward (pl. 14b). In the three-quarter views the noses are strongly curved. The beards are designed in a manner less detailed than in the later figures of the second phase of the east dome: there are fewer spiral involutions, and those that do occur are much less plastically modeled. Moreover, the design is more abstract and geometrical, as is the hair, which is arranged in ornamental patterns, mostly symmetrical, even in figures represented in three-quarter projection. The heads have little expression, and most of them display a kind of bovine heaviness. Generally, the draperies are odd combinations of severe and playful forms, and the design is rather flat, with very few elements indicating three-dimensional extension.

Though less schematized, somewhat less provincial, and nearer to Byzantine standards, the mosaics must be the products of a branch of the local school. The tradition of the workshop was sufficiently strong and the training of its members sufficiently comprehensive to enable the mosaicists to apply the formulas to different tasks. But the humble character of the workshop could not provide models for the enthroned apostles. Generally speaking, the workshop lacked altogether the practice to cope with monumental figures. For this task, the leading master had to look toward Byzantium, where executing seated monumental figures was among the most frequent tasks.

The heavy, complicated design of the drapery, with its open folds and loose undulating ribbons, has its parallels—not in Constantinople—but rather in Macedonia. The actual models must have been fairly recent, but all elements of the so-called dynamic style of the later twelfth century are lacking. Of course, some of the abstract geometricity of the design, especially that of the grand composition of the cupola as a whole, must be ascribed to the specifically Venetian interpretation of the Byzantine models.

The heavily restored state of the Pentecost makes it difficult to pin down the date. The only certainty is that the mosaics are a good deal earlier than those of the second phase of the east dome. Although they represent the beginnings of an animated style, a forerunner of the dynamic style, they should still be dated in the first half of the twelfth century and not too late within this period. The paleography indicates that the inscriptions should be dated after the choir chapels, that is, after the second or third decade of the century, but a more precise date is not possible. Thus, the mosaics of the Pentecost dome are survivors, together with all other products of the local school, of the period before the catastrophe(?) that made large-scale restorations and even full renewals necessary.

57

Second Phase of the East Dome

12

WITH THE PROPHETS of the second phase of the decoration of the east dome there begins an entirely new chapter in the history of Venetian art. We do not know when the east dome was so heavily damaged that the replacement of about two-thirds of the mosaic surface became necessary, nor do we know whether this extensive repair was made immediately after the damage or after the lapse of a considerable period. We do know that the figures of the Virgin and nine prophets were made in the course of this repair work, and it is possible that the half-figure of the Emmanuel was also made at the same time, either as a renewal of an original figure of the same iconographic type or, improbably, as a replacement of an original Pantocrator bust.

The theological concept and the representational type of Christ Emmanuel, the incarnate Logos, are based on the most important messianic prophecy, that of Isaiah 7:14 (taken up by Matthew 1:23), where this name is given to the son to be born of the Virgin. The representation of the childlike Emmanuel is restricted to Byzantium and its sphere of influence, where it crystallized rather late, only from about the eleventh century. The stars stress the divine character of the Logos before its Incarnation, and the rainbow frame is the same as that of Byzantine Pantocrator images.

The figure of the Virgin in the east axis of the dome stresses the Incarnation motif (fig. 34). She is the door through which the Logos entered humanity. The tallest and largest figure in the dome, she is iconographically identical with the Orant Virgins of Byzantine apses. The motif of the Incarnation is also underlined by the greater part of the prophecies written on the scrolls of the prophets, whose figures belong to the second phase of the cupola decoration: Isaiah, David, Solomon, Malachi, Zechariah, Haggai, Zephaniah, Jonah, and Hosea. Six of the prophecies are messianic, as are the four of the first-phase prophets incorporated in the new program (pl. 5a). They foretell the Incarnation of the Logos and are thus in harmony with the main theme of the dome. Hosea, on the other hand, points toward the Resurrection; Zephaniah and Jonah refer to the Last Judgment. Some of the prophecies offered by the figures of the east dome are very common in Byzantine and Italo-Byzantine monumental programs, but there is no doubt that the author of the program was a trained theologian and that he selected his texts with great care.

The costumes and the facial types of the nine prophets of the second phase are on the whole those current in Byzantine art during the twelfth century (pl. 15). The two prophet kings, of course, stand apart; the other seven figures can

Fig. 34. East dome: Virgin

be divided into main groups on the strength of their different interpretations of the contrapposto. The first type, including Haggai, Isaiah, Zephaniah, Jonah, and Hosea, shows a rhythmical contrapposto, with the most striking motifs of the drapery appearing on the free leg and thigh. Although the modeling differs profoundly from that of classical figures, the arrangement still preserves the memory of such schemes. This is not the case with the second type, comprising Zechariah and Malachi. Although here the basis of the figure scheme is also a sort of contrapposto, the two legs are treated in almost the same way.

These groups do not quite correspond to the respective shares of the mosaicists. The master of Isaiah, for instance, could also have designed the three contiguous figures—the Virgin, David, and Solomon. A second was responsible for the next two figures, Malachi and Zechariah. A last group, following the first type, is not as homogeneous as the others. Jonah is completely renewed, and Zephaniah is somewhat isolated by an extremely hard technique of modeling and by differences in material. Thus, one can refer to an Isaiah master, a Malachi master, and a Haggai master, the latter perhaps a composite personality.

59

The Isaiah master was undoubtedly the strongest personality and thus, in all likelihood, the leading mosaicist of the workshop (pl. 16a). His vigorous, energetic style, with its plastic protuberances and form-designing, wrinkly folds, and strong contrasts of light and shade in rather neutral colors, is profoundly different from the style of the first phase. The figure of the Virgin shares many features with that of Isaiah, but as a whole is rather stiff. It seems that the master followed an earlier model, perhaps the predecessor of the present figure, which would account for the archaizing character. The most telling feature is, of course, the chrysography of the *maphorion,* the gold has ceased to be used as a light or highlight and has become strictly a very tight, linear pattern.

Even with its somewhat subdued colors, the figure of David is truly regal, partly because of its costume, which is rendered in the hieratic mode, the folds drawn in a simple, forceful, and abstract manner with no continuous modeling

Fig. 35. East dome: Haggai

at all in the red mantle and very little in the light tunic. The face lacks the finesse of Isaiah's, suggesting that it is the work of an assistant (pl. 16b). Solomon is by the same master, and, like David, that figure is a very able interpretation of contemporary Byzantine models by a mosaicist trained in Byzantine technique.

Malachi and Zechariah are the work of the same, not overly gifted, master. The modeling is very forceful as far as details are concerned, but there is no resulting conception of the body as a whole. In the faces, especially, technical tricks take the place of free modeling.

Haggai belongs to the last group; his attitude and drapery are more elegant, more Hellenistic than those of the two preceding figures (fig. 35). The contrapposto is well balanced and, at the same time, dynamic. Moreover, the figure is the only one that shows the classical motif of the sling of the toga. The technique of modeling differs from that employed in the preceding group: vigorous dark lines cut deep into the surface and provide the pattern, while fine gradations produce a light relief. Though the scheme of the face is derived from that of Isaiah, the expression is emptier, devoid of the concentrated energy and self-assurance. Zephaniah shows similar weaknesses, and although Jonah has suffered more than the others, what survives is reminiscent of Zephaniah. Hosea forms a pair with Jonah.

The figural style of the second phase can be characterized generally as a special form of the so-called dynamic style of Byzantine painting, which has been described in terms of the agitated draperies, violent contrasts of light and dark, and overall unity through intricate surface patterning. The San Marco version of this style is not very extreme; there are no agitated movements or exaggerated attitudes, no flying or floating folds. The proportions of the figures are normal, even a little stocky, and the expressions, though somewhat savage, show little excitement. The dynamic style still seems to be in a nascent stage. The question of the exact date of the second phase of the east dome is beset with difficulties, in part because the new dynamism has not taken hold of the entire figure but only of the surface relief, and even this lacks the *brio,* the streamlined speed of the lineaments of the true dynamic style. The most probable date would be 1170–80, the time of Sebastiano Ziani (1172–78), to whom popular tradition ascribed the entire mosaic decoration of the church. The paleography indicates a beginning date for the inscriptions in the third quarter of the twelfth century.

It seems likely that evangelist symbols were already represented in the pendentives in the first phase, but the only one that has survived in an authentic state—Luke's ox—belongs to the second phase. In it, the mannerist heaping of wrinkles and humps is developed to an almost absurd degree. Most likely it was Rome—not contemporary Byzantium—that provided the models for these symbols.

SECOND PHASE OF THE EAST DOME

Central Dome

13

THE MOSAICS OF THE CENTRAL DOME and its pendentives date from the great renewal of the twelfth century following the catastrophe whose traces are visible in the east dome. In fact, their style bears the imprint of a dominant personality who can be labeled the Master of the Ascension. The state of preservation of the dome is on the whole satisfactory. Only the figure of the Virgin is completely new, having been replaced in the nineteenth century. The two beardless apostles were also restored earlier.

The Ascension mosaic is probably the most impressive and best-preserved cupola composition of the theme that has survived (pl. 17). In the zenith of the dome, Christ, clad in gold and silver, is seated on an arc of light with his right hand raised in a gesture of blessing and his feet resting on a second, smaller arc (pl. 18). His figure is outlined against a circular, star-studded glory of concentric rings—their blue color deepening toward the center—which is carried aloft by four angels. The winged glory is surrounded by the standing figures of the Virgin, two angels, and twelve apostles. Between the windows stand sixteen allegorical figures of virtues and beatitudes. The strongly concentric pattern of figures is continued in the pendentives, where the architectural motifs accompanying the evangelists are drawn sideways to establish visual contact with the apex motifs of the four central vaults. The gaps in the inscription and in the row of trees create an empty space around the Orant Virgin, a golden void that enhances the sanctity of the figure, the only one presented in full frontality. Together with the two flanking angels (fig. 36), the figure of the Virgin constitutes the center of the main view of the dome as it presents itself to the beholder looking east, toward the altar.

The differentiation in the attitudes of the figures, Virgin, angels, and apostles is the one specifically scenic element preserved in cupola representations of the Ascension. The figures are connected with each other and with the central iconographic motifs of the ascending Christ solely by their various attitudes and the fluent rhythm of their turnings. Otherwise they are presented in almost statuesque isolation, taken out of the context of a scenic, historical representation so that they seem lifted into the sphere of timelessness and ideal space. The rhythm that leads the eye of the beholder from one figure to the other appears at first glance to be very free, almost incoherent. On closer inspection, however, a definite regularity manifests itself, a subtle scansion that brings life and order to the row of posing and turning figures. The eastern group centers on the Virgin; Peter and Paul and the angels turn toward her (pl. 19a). All the other

Fig. 36. Central dome: Angel to right of Virgin

apostles are arranged in groups of two, corresponding quasi-symmetrically with one another on either side of the east-west axis. The row of virtues and beatitudes is more freely arranged, but here, too, an articulation of the series in pairs is more or less consistently carried out. By its rhythmical, one might almost say musical quality, the Ascension dome in San Marco outranks almost every other cupola decoration of the Middle Byzantine period.

The allegorical figures between the windows may have been inspired by the personifications of the tribes in the Pentecost dome. They are the only specifically Western element in the iconography of the dome, which otherwise is purely Byzantine. The interpretation of the Byzantine scheme, the harmonious composition with its equilibrium of geometrical regularity and rhythmic freedom are, however, Venetian, as is probably also the choice of certain types.

The iconography of the single figures and the analysis of their types corroborates the conclusions drawn from the study of the iconography of the theme

63

in general, namely, that the leading master, while adhering to time-honored metropolitan schemes, kept an open mind with regard to modern trends, which he interpreted in a specifically Venetian manner. The central motif of the ascending Christ is a case in point. Most features are usual in earlier Byzantine examples, but the blessing gesture is halfway between the "orthodox" Byzantine and the so-called Western type, and the sideways turning of the legs is a modern feature that seems to be connected with the rise of the dynamic style. The rather bad-tempered, even a bit aggressive, expression of the face also belongs to that phase. All this points to an origin of the type well within the second half of the twelfth century.

In selecting the apostles, the Master of the Ascension or his theological advisor deviated from the normal Byzantine list, including Paul and Mark and eliminating James the Less (and Luke from the liturgical series). This is probably due to the Western tendency to follow as closely as possible the historical lists, while in Byzantium all four evangelists were often portrayed. The types of the apostles, on the other hand, conform by and large to current Middle Byzantine types.

The execution of the figures in the Ascension dome is quite homogeneous. There are, however, certain real differences—above all, differences in artistic quality. The half-series beginning with Saint Paul is more imaginative in design and more perfect in execution than the one beginning with Saint Peter in the north half of the dome. The faces of James and John (pl. 19b) and the expressive attitudes they share with their neighbors Paul, Matthew, and Bartholomew would be difficult to match in the other half. The homogeneity at a high level of differentiation of forms and perfection of technique is surely due to the commanding personality and surpassing artistic genius of the leading master, who laid out the composition, selected models for the single figures, drew their outlines, established vocabulary and grammar of the stylistic microcosm, set the tone and standard for the technical execution, and generally supervised the work so closely that his assistants became his extended hands.

What was the background of the chief master? It is certain that he was connected in some way with the mosaics of the second phase of the east dome, the figure of Isaiah being closest to his work. In any case, the difference in date between the two domes cannot be great. In the hothouse atmosphere of a great undertaking in the later part of the twelfth century, a comparatively short time would be sufficient to account for changes from the style of the prophets to that of the apostles, especially if one credits the possibility that these changes were the outcome of a development that took place during the interval that seems to have separated the work in the east dome from that of the central cupola. It is certain that the leading master was receptive to stimuli from the most recent phases of contemporary Byzantine development. These stimuli must have affected him on two different levels: on the large-scale level of composition and figure types and on the more minute level of details. Both may have been transmitted in part by notebooks or model books, giving the Master of the Ascension access to a late variant of the so-called dynamic phase of late Comnenian painting. The decisive qualities of this style are the consistent separation of plastically modeled "islands" and streamlined bundles of folds, accompanied by a nascent feeling first for the relief, later on for the plastic wholeness of the limbs, and finally of the entire figure: the arrangement of the linear design in concentric shapes or radial forms issuing from common centers; the appending of secondary shapes (flying ends, hanging folds) to the primary

Fig. 37. Central dome: Andrew

shapes of the bodies; the heightening of expression in movements, gestures, and features; and the strengthening of contrasts in light and shade (fig. 37). The apostles have something of the smooth, elegant, and "oily" movements of the later variant of this style and show something of the characteristic unification of the figure with the emphasis on its general shape and outline at the expense of internal modeling, as well as something of the fragile beauty of the faces and the silky sheen of the garments. They still lack the artificiality of the final phase of the style and other traits such as soft folds that look as if they had been squeezed out of a tube. From the point of view of the Byzantine development, a date in the 1180s would be quite possible for the Ascension dome, but a somewhat later date cannot be excluded. The source of the specific current of Byzantine art that was the chief constituent of the Ascension style must be sought in Constantinople itself.

In addition to the local Venetian and the Byzantine elements of the Ascension style, there also appear Western, that is, Romanesque, elements. This is suggested by the special springy quality of the lineament and the taut elasticity of the configurations that shape the draperies of Paul and John, to name only two of the most outstanding cases. The reduction of plastic modeling to linear elements goes beyond the Byzantine norm and approaches Western usage.

Because the normal series of allegories of the virtues was insufficient to fill the spaces between the windows, the nine beatitudes were added. The series comprises: Charity, Hope, Faith, Justice, Strength, Temperance, Prudence, Humility, Kindness, Compunction, Abstinence, Mercy, Patience, Chastity, Modesty, and Constancy. The most important figure, Charity—the beginning of the series—is not beneath the figure of the Virgin but in the north axis because there is a window in the axis position. The figures of Fortitude (fig. 38) and Temperance are placed beneath the figure of the Virgin, forming a triangular group with it.

The combination of virtues and beatitudes in San Marco is strictly religious rather than humanistic and is specifically Western. Just as the central position of the Ascension itself—as a representation of the highest Venetian state festival, the Sensa—is very likely to have had political overtones, so, too, the combination of the virtues with the Judgment aspect of the Ascension must be seen in this context. The inscription around the ascending Christ refers to the Judgment, and the virtues stand for the ethical norms and ideals according to

Fig. 38. Central dome: Fortitudo (Fortitude)

Fig. 39. Central dome: Compunctio (Compunction)

which judgment will be given. The iconographic types and ideas behind the allegories point to the West as the area of origin and to the twelfth century as the period. Venice seems to have used specifically modern sources.

As is the case with the apostles of the Ascension, the series of allegories is not just the sum of independent single figures but constitutes a skillfully composed and articulated whole. The figures confront each other in pairs, approaching or moving apart from each other. They are represented in movement, in a kind of dance that is even livelier than that of the apostles above (fig. 39). One feels their movement as a quality of style rather than as depicting action. Flying ends of the garments continue the movement of the figures themselves as flourishes continue the movement of letters and words in a line of handwriting. The scarves, particularly, conceived as independent parts of the costume, are among the most characteristic features of the dynamic style. As is the case with the attitudes and movements of the apostles, those of the virtues have a stately dignity (pl. 20a). Despite certain internal variations, the group gives an overall impression of homogeneity. This impression extends even further, to embrace the entire cupola. The figures of the virtues are so closely akin to those of the apostles that their design at least must be ascribed to one artist, the leading master of the workshop. Of course, it is only logical to assume that more than one mosaicist was employed in the actual setting of the tesserae.

Technically, the virtues display refinements that are unique in San Marco, and what is entirely new about these figures is their expressive power (pl. 20b). The sources of these technical refinements and modeling practices are, in the last resort, certainly to be sought in Constantinople, but the iconographic models of the figures were Western: French and Italian allegories and representations of the wise and foolish virgins. The assimilation and development of Byzantine techniques and recipes, their marriage in a synthesis with Western prototypes, and their quickening by a truly Venetian spirit must all be regarded as the achievement of a Venetian master. With these figures, and the mosaics of the central dome in general, Venetian mosaic art came of age. Without disavowing its Byzantine origin, it ceased to be dependent on the direct importation of artists, models, and forms. It ceased to be colonial art.

The evangelists in the pendentives of the central dome have suffered badly from restorations. What can be made out of the original style suggests that the figures reflect a particularly late variety of the dynamic style, which had been transformed into something lifeless and at the same time overcomplicated.

The pointed triangles below the evangelists contain the four rivers of paradise represented as standing half-nude men, each holding a large amphora from which pours a stream of water that collects in a puddle (pl. 21). The bottom parts of the pendentives are each filled with a tree. They are connected with the evangelists because of their numerical aspect—the number four—and the idea of life-giving water that connects them with the Gospels. Most of the monuments in which the connection between the rivers and the evangelists was intentionally realized are from the eleventh and twelfth centuries and especially from the second half of the twelfth. In these the rivers are often further combined with the four cardinal virtues, a combination that, on a much larger scale, has also been realized in San Marco. All known combinations of rivers, evangelists, and virtues are Western. It therefore must be assumed a priori that the general iconographic prototypes of the four Venetian figures were Western, not Byzantine. The somewhat grotesque figures are less reminiscent of ancient river gods—in spite of the huge amphorae they carry—than of Western

67

medieval demons, personifications of the forces of nature, more heathen than classical, crowned rulers of unredeemed regions. There are some elements, however, that make it certain that the designer also profited from Byzantine works. The anatomy of the bodies, especially of the chest and abdomen of Tigris, is typically Byzantine. All these elements, Western and Byzantine, are completely integrated into the Veneto-Byzantine style of the Ascension workshop.

West Vault

14

THE PASSION AND RESURRECTION CYCLE is placed in the west vault of the central dome and includes the Betrayal of Judas, the *Ecce homo* (with the Mocking of Christ and the Carrying of the Cross), and the Crucifixion in the south half, and the Holy Women at the Sepulcher (in the apex), the Anastasis (Harrowing of Hell), Christ Appearing to the Women *(Noli me tangere),* and the Incredulity of Thomas (pl. 22a) in the north half. The Descent from the Cross is added as an isolated picture in the presbytery. The west vault was restored repeatedly.

The Betrayal of Judas represents Christ standing in an almost frontal attitude, his impassive face slightly averted from that of the red-haired Judas, who has approached Christ from the left and is embracing him with both hands (pl. 22b). In his left hand, Christ holds a closed scroll; his right appears from behind Judas's back with a blessing gesture directed toward Malchus. It is grasped at the wrist by one of the henchmen who are crowding in from the left, while a number of Pharisees form a closed group at the right, one of them seizing Christ at the shoulder. The last figure at the right is turning away from the scene: his gesture and an open scroll in his left hand with the word *crucifigatur* connect him with the following phase of the narrative, the *Ecce homo.* At the extreme left Peter is represented on a somewhat reduced scale, kneeling on the collapsing body of Malchus, whose ear he is cutting off with a knife (pl. 23a). Malchus turns around toward Christ and lifts his right hand in an imploring gesture. Judas is the only figure isolated from the compact mass.

The rendering of the Judas scene is characterized by a number of traits that connect it with the Byzantine development but, at the same time, distinguish it from the dominant currents. Christ and Judas form a slender pillar rather than, as customary in Byzantium, a triangle, and Judas approaches from the left rather than the right. The Peter and Malchus episode is also found on the left side, whereas in Byzantine and Western examples it is usually on the right. Christ's gaze, averted from Malchus, thus has a somewhat absent expression. The clear separation of armed henchmen on one side and Pharisees on the other occurs more often in Italo-Byzantine works than in those of the central Byzantine regions, where the two groups are usually mixed together. The most conspicuous and unique feature of the San Marco Betrayal is the Pharisee at the extreme right with pointing finger and holding in his left hand an open scroll. He is the connecting link to the *Ecce homo* that makes the representation of the Betrayal definitely part of a narrative context, and this fact dominates the composition.

Iconographically and formally, the Betrayal cannot be a faithful copy of any Byzantine or Western prototype: it was designed for the place it occupies and for the context of which it is a part. Practically all the single motifs, however, follow well-established models. What were these models? What were the designer's sources? Which currents did he follow? There is not a single element that is not Byzantine, and most features point to the twelfth century. But the designer of the composition approached his task in an eclectic manner, taking his material from more than one current of Byzantine iconography and interpreting as well as arranging it in a very personal, and at the same time very Venetian, manner. He toned down the agitated dynamism, reinterpreted the central triangle of his Byzantine models, separated warriors from Pharisees and thus made two groups out of the undifferentiated mass of figures, and, most important, he placed the Malchus episode on the same side with Judas, thus imparting to the whole group a definite movement toward the right in the direction of continuous narrative.

The *Ecce homo* has a similar structure, though it also combines elements of the Mocking of Christ, the Crowning of Thorns, and the Carrying of the Cross (pl. 22b). It is closely connected to the preceding scene by the Pharisee holding the scroll reading "CRUCIFIGATUR," which answers the question on the scroll of Pilate, "REGEM VESTRUM CRUCIFIGAM?" What is represented in the main scene is, as in practically all medieval representations, the mocking by Pilate's Roman soldiers and not the earlier mocking in the house of the high priest. Christ is represented standing in full frontality, clad in a blue tunic and vermilion mantle with gold and purple tablion (the stitched insignium of office), a truly regal garment. The green, compact crown of thorns also resembles a royal diadem. Christ's face is sad and impassive (pl. 23b). He is surrounded by the mocking soldiers, of whom two stand and three kneel. The latter figures gesture in mock adoration; the man on the left seizes Christ by the shoulder and is shouting or spitting. The one on the right lifts his right hand as if to strike Christ. All five soldiers are beardless, showing grotesque profiles, and three of them have red hair, which characterizes them as low and wicked.

Although it accords with contemporary Byzantine and Italo-Byzantine examples, the representation in San Marco is distinguished by two features, the breaking of the strict symmetry by the differentiation of the tormentors and the addition of one more figure at the bottom left. The differentiation serves to enhance the expressiveness of the action.

The Mocking is transformed into the *Ecce homo* by the addition of the figure of Pilate with his scroll. Pilate wears a richly ornamented, princely garment consisting of a long green tunic and blue mantle, both embroidered and studded with pearls and precious stones. Between Pilate and Christ the figure of Simon of Cyrene with the cross on his shoulders is wedged in. The inclusion of Simon was the reason for the addition of the fifth tormentor on the lower left, which provided the broader base needed for the figure of Simon. Simon's expression is sad and full of sympathy.

Except for the scrolls, all the individual motifs were taken from current Byzantine models. What is exceptional is the interweaving of these motifs to form a compound picture combining all three themes in such an economical and ingenious way. What is more, the use of inscribed scrolls seems to be entirely foreign to central Byzantine art, except for prophecies. They are used very frequently in Western art, on the other hand, for clarifying and dramatizing a picture by recording the spoken word of the participants of an action. The use of inscribed scrolls for the production of "dialogic" pictorial narrative offers a genuine parallel to the *sermon dialogué* in liturgical drama. If the inscribed scrolls in the Passion scenes of San Marco are a Western element, their specific shape is, however, thoroughly Byzantine. They are shaped exactly like the stiff rectangles in the hands of Byzantine prophets. Western thought has once again been cast in Byzantine form.

The Crucifixion is on the whole well preserved and, from the iconographic point of view, completely authentic (fig. 40). On the left is the Virgin, accompanied by four holy women in attitudes of sorrow. Behind John, on the right, there appear the centurion and three male figures, one of them characterized by his hood as a Pharisee (pl. 24a). To the right and left of the cross are the lance- and sponge-bearers in their characteristic attitudes. At the foot of the cross, on either side of the cave with the skull of Adam, are seated two soldiers holding Christ's garment between them, and above the cross are eight

Fig. 40. West vault: Crucifixion

half-figures of grieving angels. Christ himself is represented more as standing on the square suppedaneum than hanging on the broad cross. His body and arms are slightly curved, the hands spread out with the thumb upward. He is represented as dead, with empty eyes and with blood and water flowing from the wound in his chest.

Compared to Middle Byzantine examples, the mosaics contain several rare or exceptional traits: four holy women represented in emotional attitudes and with expressive features, three figures accompanying the centurion; the soldiers throwing dice or playing morra; and eight—instead of four—angels. All the other motifs—the gestures of the Virgin (pl. 24b) and Saint John, the lunge of the centurion, the lance- and sponge-bearers—are characteristic of Middle Byzantine iconography.

The movement of the centurion is somewhat exaggerated, and this, together with the intensely sorrowful attitudes of the holy women, may be taken as typical of the expressive tendencies of the late twelfth century (fig. 41). The other distinctive features are more closely associated with nonmonumental art forms than with Middle Byzantine mosaic art. One wonders whether San Marco was not influenced by an earlier famous representation, and in this connection one cannot help suspecting that this earlier source was the mosaic of the Apostoleion in Constantinople. It seems likely that the designer studied the composition of the Apostoleion and embodied in his design not only general features but perhaps also some details, while preserving the freedom of his eclectic attitude. In designing the details he must have used contemporary Byzantine and possibly also Italo-Byzantine models that furnished him with the formulas of the poignant attitudes of the holy women and possibly also the gestures of the chief figures. This eclectic melding of motifs in a paratactic composition is as characteristic of the iconographic attitude of Venice as it is of the Venetian principles of form.

Although the scene of the Holy Women at the Sepulcher was completely renewed in the later fifteenth century, the copy was intentionally faithful to the original. The general iconographic type of the scene is familiar from many Byzantine representations. The women approach the tomb from the left; one of them is turning away, as if frightened by the angel who sits on a square stone and points to the opening in the rock tomb in which the empty linen is visible. Below is a group of sleeping soldiers. The appearance of three instead of two women and the position of the angel's wings (hanging down) distinguish the San Marco composition from Byzantine examples.

The Anastasis contains most of the features of the Byzantine type of composition (pl. 25): carrying the cross in his left hand and seizing Adam's wrist with his right, the dominating figure of Christ strides over the prostrate figure of Hades, who grips Adam's foot; with Eve behind, the figure of Adam kneels on the edge of the sarcophagus; David, Solomon, Saint John the Baptist, the patriarchs, the crossed doors of Hades with keys, locks, hinges, and pins are strewn around in the dark cavern framed by the contour of the hill. A number of traits distinguish the composition from most other representations of the theme and make it sui generis. One is the strongly asymmetrical arrangement of the dramatis personae, which is to be explained by the tendency toward expression: the figures to the left of Christ with their imploringly raised hands are a massed personification of entreaty, of the prayer for salvation, while the static figures on the right represent the testimony of the prophets and John the Baptist (pl. 26a). This is also the reason why the hands of Eve are bare rather

72

Fig. 41. West vault: Crucifixion, holy women, heads

than veiled and hidden in her red garment. Eve's hands are an indispensable link in the chain of imploring hands that descends from the upper left to Adam's hands, in a grandiose repetition of identical forms. Although the turning and the inclination of the head of Christ are paralleled in most Byzantine representations, the intensity of feeling in his face rarely occurs there. The emotionalism also expresses itself in the dynamic stride. There are few parallels to the figure of Hades and none as impressive (fig. 42); its size alone is exceedingly rare.

None of the representations of the Anastasis that have come down to us is really related, as a whole, in iconographic material or in interpretation to the San Marco mosaic. The mosaicist seems to have conceived his work using Middle Byzantine iconographic material and to have cast these details and composed them into a new whole filled with the emotional spirit of the great San Marco workshop, without in any way offending Middle Byzantine canons and concepts. Even where he deviated from practically all Byzantine Anastasis representations, he adhered faithfully to Byzantine types. The mosaic is a grand example of a very personal creation by a master who was thoroughly conversant

73

Fig. 42. West vault: Anastasis, Satan, half-figure

with contemporary Byzantine art but interpreted the raw material in a way that must be called Venetian.

Christ Appearing to the Women is perhaps the most unfortunate of all the mosaics of the West vault (fig. 43). It has been severely damaged and twice restored. It is difficult even to determine whether it represented the *Chairete* (Matthew 28:9–10) originally or the *Noli me tangere* (John 21:14–17), the first being favored in Byzantium, the second in the West. In fact, San Marco seems to have fused the two scenes. Generally speaking, the iconographic character of the scene is as unspecific as possible; the interpretation of the subject is as unimaginative and as trite as the artistic quality of the execution is poor.

In the arrangement of figures, the Incredulity of Thomas is nearly symmetrical—five apostles stand on either side of Christ (pl. 26b and fig. 43). On the left, in front, is the figure of Thomas, who bends down so that his forehead is beneath Christ's elbow. With the index finger of his right hand, he almost touches Christ's wound. The series of apostles is not the historical one because Paul is represented leading the left group as counterpart to Peter on the right.

The mosaicist's aim was not the expression of emotion but the shaping of a ritualistic image of the apparition of Christ, the solemn representation of a theophany with the apostles as unmoved witnesses with stereotyped gestures. This is also expressed in the sacred niche of the door and in the open scroll of Thomas with his testimony. This latter is, of course, a non-Byzantine feature grafted onto an otherwise strictly Byzantine iconographic scheme.

Of the Deposition, only two fragments are preserved. However, in the environs of Venice there is a representation of the scene that is in all probability a faithful copy of the destroyed mosaic, namely, a fresco in the crypt of Aquileia that can substitute for the lost mosaic, at least from the iconographic point of

74

view. The fresco and the mosaic display the iconographic type in which the Virgin takes an active part by assisting Joseph in holding the horizontally projecting upper body of Christ and by pressing her cheek to the face of her son. The specific intention is, however, not so much action for its own sake as arrested action for the sake of presenting the body of Christ for veneration. It is a kind of *ostentatio* similar to that of the *Ecce homo*. This type must be placed toward the end of the evolution of Byzantine Deposition iconography, and so, it is unlikely that the model for the Venetian and Aquileian works was older than the second half of the twelfth century. In other words, the author of the lost mosaic of San Marco and his copyist in Aquileia followed a more or less contemporary prototype.

The iconographic material contained in the Passion and Resurrection cycle is, on the whole, taken from contemporary Middle Byzantine art. No specific source or prototype for it can be found, although it is not impossible that the mosaic decoration of the Apostoleion exerted a limited influence on it. It is likely that the compositional schemes used in these mosaics came from a model-book type of collection that was drawn eclectically from various sources, monumental and even miniature, with a preference for dignified movements and actions: there is nothing in these mosaics of the exaggerated speed that characterizes the iconography of so many contemporary Byzantine works. Thus, it is likely that most of the figure schemes were derived from Constantinopolitan sources. In some cases, however, models seem to have been chosen to show iconographic

Fig. 43. West vault: Appearance to Marys and Incredulity of Thomas

types or single motifs preferred in the Italo-Byzantine area, though none of these is foreign to Byzantine art. The inscribed scrolls, however, are distinctly un-Byzantine: the entire principle underlying this use of the spoken word of the characters is almost exclusively Western. Western influence also seems to have been active in the telescoping of several scenes into a single composition and in the use of pivot figures. Compared with the iconography of the scenes from the Temptation to the Washing of the Feet and of the Miracle cycle, that of the Passion scenes is much more modern and shows a more personal redaction. On the emotional and sympathetic level there is a new and very individual spirit at work in the recombination and reinterpretation of the iconographical material.

The vault is treated as a compositional unit, with the golden ground providing the canvas on which the single scenes are projected as colored silhouettes held together by continuous bases. The compositions of the lower registers, two on either side, are somewhat heavier and more compact and consist of rectangular blocks of closely packed figures. The compositions of the upper tiers form a large, loose composition on each side, and the golden ground invades the pattern of figures to a greater extent. However, even these compositions, though they are not as crowded as the lower ones, are comparatively full and coherent.

The greater density of the lower-tier compositions gives to the whole a certain stability, an architectural solidity that counterbalances the greater height of the upper tiers and the larger patterns of the two scenes with their taller figures. The chief point is the opposition of the two main icons, the Crucifixion and the Anastasis; the scenes below appear as secondary illustrative material. The general structure of the compositions was conditioned by the desire to fill the whole width of the vault and by the fact that there are no frames to serve as points of reference and to hold the pattern of the figures together. Consequently, the compositions are not centered but are paratactic with a tendency toward establishing flanking pillars of figures, or groups of figures, at the sides. The chief means of holding together the compositions are rhythm, the repetition of similar forms, and the placing of special coloristic accents.

It is clear that the general layout of the mosaics of the west vault was established by a leading master who also supervised the execution in a loose way. The actual work was done by a number of mosaicists, with the Master of the Thomas scene and his assistants deviating so strongly from the general line that they seem to belong to a different workshop with a different training. Actually, the Master of the Thomas also collaborated in other parts as well. In addition, the three most important heads in the Crucifixion, those of Christ, the Virgin, and John, are the work of the technically most competent and refined mosaicist in the whole of San Marco (pl. 24b and fig. 44). The superb structure of these heads is built up of minute particles, mere slivers of stone and enamel; the average size of these particles is about a quarter of those employed in the hands and about one-eighth of those that make up the garments. Indeed these heads may be proclaimed the most technically refined pieces of wall mosaic in existence. Very close in style and quality to the latter, which must be by the chief master, are the Judas and *Ecce homo*. The strongly rhythmic design of the figures and faces of these mosaics, as well as the bravura of the compositions, are closely akin to the general stylistic habitus of the central dome, especially of the virtues. The palette of this master is more colorful, his draperies are livelier and more organic than those of the Crucifixion, in which we sense a stiffening process.

The style that best deserves the epithet "dynamic" is not that of the Judas

76

Fig. 44. West vault: Crucifixion, Christ, head

and Pilate mosaics but that of the Anastasis. The expressive deformation of the faces is strongest, the relief of the drapery more plastically differentiated, the lens-shaped joints more convincingly rounded than in any other part of the vault. The baroque mannerism of the Anastasis is more conspicuous since the mosaics directly below, the *Noli me tangere* and Thomas scenes, form such a strong contrast. In these two mosaics, the figures are as frozen and stiff as the entire compositions and as flat. The two styles, the expressive and dynamic mannerism of the Anastasis and the dry, abstract schematism of the Thomas scene, must have existed side by side since the Master of the Thomas collaborated in the Crucifixion, which in turn is closely related to the Judas and Pilate scenes by the three main heads, as well as to the Anastasis. This multiplicity of styles, the existence side by side of such divergent, even contrasting, possibilities is a specifically Venetian trait. The conglomeration was made possible only by the special circumstances of the later twelfth century, when the development of style, up to then consistent and logical, was replaced by a rapid change of styles during which evolution was turned into revolution. Small wonder that in the hothouse atmosphere of San Marco otherwise successive phases appeared simultaneously.

77

Most of the stylistic material that went into the shaping of the lower Passion scenes comes from the repertory of the central dome mosaics, whose chief master may also have supervised the decoration of the west vault. There are hardly any elements that could be identified as new Byzantine influences, with the sole exception of the intensified local color. The Anastasis shows a different facet of the dynamic style, which is connected not so much with the apostles of the dome, as with the evangelists of the pendentives. It is very likely that the Master of the Anastasis knew and was influenced by recent Byzantine works. The mannerist and expressive tendencies are strengthened, the faces are wilder, more haggard, and more charged with emotion, and the types more Oriental, almost grotesque.

The style reaches its peak in the Crucifixion. The deeply melancholic faces of the Virgin and the holy women have an almost concave shape; they are so haggard that with the exception of the cranium and forehead, they seem to have hardly any mass. The same is true of the bodies. These stylistic qualities and the passive, introspective expression of the figures correspond to the rising of an antidynamic style in which all temperamental qualities were rapidly lost and agitated curves were replaced by rigid, straight, mostly perpendicular lines and strictly vertical contours. The breaking up of the composition that is fore-shadowed in the mosaic of the Crucifixion is also a characteristic of the last part of the century. Thus, there can be no doubt that the Crucifixion shows the impact of the most recent tendencies of the evolution of Byzantine painting; the same is true of the Thomas scene. The Master of the Thomas must have been conversant with the abstract-decorative current in Byzantine art, one of the most recent in Byzantine painting. This helps date the mosaics of the west vault to the later 1180s and perhaps the early 1190s.

Some Western influence can also be detected in these mosaics. The most conspicuous is the shaping and functional role of the terrain in the Judas and Pilate scenes. This consists of a row of triangular hills with rocky outcrops, partly overlapping each other, in several layers differentiated in color, so that the general aspect is of a faraway chain of mountains.

Western elements of a different kind appear in the remaking of the Life of the Virgin in the north transept, the author of which seems to have continued the practices of the Master of the Thomas.

Lives of the Apostles

15

ICONOGRAPHICALLY AND TOPOGRAPHICALLY, the scenes illustrating the lives of the apostles belong to the orbit of the Pentecost dome—the lateral vaults of which they fill—but stylistically, they are a continuation of the mosaics of the Passion cycle, although they contain some different elements. Unfortunately, only the half of the cycle in the vault supporting the dome on the south side has been more or less preserved in its medieval version. The cycle in the northern half is a seventeenth-century replacement that seems to preserve the scenario of its medieval predecessor. The twelve lives are so arranged that two each are placed on the perpendicular walls on either side of the west arm, and four each on either of the two vaults, with two scenes in each half, one above the other.

The series of apostles whose lives and martyrdoms make up the cycle does not correspond to any of the lists represented elsewhere in San Marco. It is identical, however, with that of most collections of *passiones* and seems, in fact, to have been modeled on one of the earliest series. There exists nearly complete conformity between the San Marco sequence and Western sacramentaries, whereas the Greek lists follow a different sequence.

The baroque series comprises the following episodes:
1. Peter and Paul: dispute with Simon Magus before Nero; the fall of Simon; Peter's crucifixion
2. Paul: beheaded
3. John: boiled in oil; enters grave alive
4. James the Greater: dispute with high priests; beheaded
5. Andrew: crucified
6. Thomas: before King Gundaphorus; transfixed with lance

The original south series includes:
7. James the Less: pushed from roof of temple; killed with fuller's club; burial
8. Philip: has idol of Mars destroyed; raises men poisoned by breath of dragon; the apostle venerated; burial
9. Bartholomew: preaching; flayed
10. Matthew: baptizes the king of Ethiopia and his family; killed with sword while celebrating mass
11. Simon: overthrows idol of sun; a figure with drawn sword alludes to the killing of the apostle
12. Jude (Thaddeus): mirror image of preceding mosaic

Each of these twelve mosaics is thus a succinct cycle illustrating the missionary activity, death, and in three cases the burial of the apostle. Cyclic illustrations of this kind are preserved in Middle Byzantine manuscripts and also existed in monumental painting. The model was not an Acts source but must have illustrated a menologion or synaxarion (Eastern liturgical books containing saints' lives) based on apocryphal sources, or else illustrations of a specific collection of apostles' legends.

Although the Disputation with Simon and his Fall also appear in Byzantine representations, placing the scene in Rome and including Nero make it likely that the prototype was an Italian or Italo-Byzantine representation. Whereas John's self-burial is common to Eastern and Western recensions of the legend, his being boiled in oil in Rome at Domitian's behest belongs exclusively to the Latin tradition. The martyrdom of James the Greater is based on Acts, but its pictorial source cannot be determined. The Martyrdom of Andrew was re-arranged by the baroque master, whereas the original mosaic of the Martyrdom of Thomas, on the other hand, may have contained most of the elements found in the baroque composition.

The original series of the lives on the south side of the west arm begins with James the Less and Philip (pl. 27). The two apostles are often grouped together because their feasts are on the same day and their relics are preserved together in Santi Apostoli in Rome. San Marco gives all the essential details of James's martyrdom (fig. 45); the saint's tonsure is an allusion to the tradition that he was the first bishop of Jerusalem. Clearly, the architecture is an ideal representation of the Dome of the Rock. Although the imagery conforms well to Western parallels, the burial is probably connected with the possession of the apostle's relics.

In Western versions of the *Passio Philippi,* the apostle Philip preaches the Gospel in Scythia. When he is forcibly led to the idol of Mars to sacrifice there, a dragon appears from the base of the statue, kills the son of the priest and two tribunes with its poisonous breath, and makes others ill. The apostle promises to heal them if the idol is pulled down and the cross of Christ erected in its stead. As soon as this is done, the dragon disappears, the sick are healed, and the dead resurrected. The people become believing Christians and venerate Philip, who stays another year, after which he returns to his home in Asia Minor, where he dies peacefully and is buried in Hierapolis. That is exactly what is represented in San Marco.

The close proximity of the lives of Bartholomew (fig. 46) and Matthew corresponds to an early tradition of sending forth the apostles in pairs (Mark 6:7 and Luke 10:1) and to the intimate connection of the two legends. Bartholomew's missionary activity in India corresponds to an important branch of the tradition: the typical figure of the teaching apostle who holds a scroll in his covered hand is quite frequent in Byzantine art, the scroll meaning here the Gospel that the saint is preaching (pl. 28a). The most interesting feature of the mosaic is the flaying of Bartholomew, a means of execution found exclusively in Western representations though not before the twelfth century. The two figures in the tympanum of the arcade under the scene should probably be interpreted as idols.

Like that of Bartholomew, the mosaic of Saint Matthew consists of two scenes, one depicting his missionary activity and the other his martyrdom. The narrative follows an abridged version of the Latin *passio,* according to which Matthew, after many miracles, converts King Egippus of Ethiopia and baptizes

80

Fig. 45. South aisle: Martyrdom of James

Fig. 46. South aisle: Bartholomew Preaching and Martyrdom of Bartholomew

81

him along with his entire family and household (pl. 28b). Egippus builds a church in which Matthew preaches for twenty-three years. After the death of Egippus, his brother and successor Hyrtacus desires Egippus's daughter for his wife, but she, having taken the veil, refuses him at Matthew's instigation. The incensed king orders Matthew to be killed with a sword at the altar of his church. The motif of the martyrdom during mass seems to be characteristic of Western representations.

The martyrdoms of Simon and Jude concludes the series of apostles' lives. They are symmetrically arranged on the south wall to the left and right of the group of windows, one scene mirroring the other. The two scenes are abbreviations of the Latin *Passio Simonis et Judae,* a long and miraculous contest of the two apostles with magicians in Persia, in the course of which the saints are led to the temple of the sun and the moon, respectively, Simon to sacrifice to the idol of the sun god, who is riding in a golden horse-drawn chariot, and Jude to the idol of the moon, who rides in a silver chariot drawn by oxen (fig. 47). Instead of sacrificing, the saints exorcise the demons dwelling in the idols, who appear as black "Ethiopians" and flee with a loud clamor, whereupon the incensed priests and the multitude set upon the apostles and kill them. The mosaic depicts the two idols exactly as they are described in the *passio,* but adds a new feature: the two demons (here green instead of black), not fleeing but attempting to hold up the falling idols.

Clearly, the textual basis of the lives was a Western, Latin martyrology or passional. This source did not furnish the compositional models, however. What we have in the way of pictorial cycles in the West is entirely different. Much nearer to the form of the narrative governing the mosaics are illustrations in Greek manuscripts where we find similar strip-compositions that combine several phases of the narrative. Most of the abridged Byzantine cycles have one peculiarity in common: they represent as the opening phase of the martyrdom story the confession and condemnation of the saint by a seated ruler or judge in front of whom the accused stands. Now, this seated figure of a ruler or judge occurs in all the cycles of the north aisle of San Marco but nowhere in the south half. This can hardly be connected with the baroque renewal of the northern part, nor can it be mere chance. It seems that the originals of the north half of the cycle were designed by a master who adhered more closely to the Byzantine type of scenario than his colleague in the south part. On the basis of this discrepancy it is, perhaps, not unreasonable to assume that the baroque half-cycle in the north vault is a substitution, not of mosaics contemporary with those extant in the south aisle, but of an earlier series that here had survived until the seventeenth century—while it had been replaced on the south side by new compositions soon after the damage. It is, in any case, certain that the designer of the cycles in the southern part, while following the general structure of Byzantine narrative sequences, steered clear of the prevailing monotonous pattern of Byzantine martyrdom cycles. As a corollary of this apparent freedom, we find in this part of the San Marco cycle a less logical linking of scenes, a false continuity that suppresses important links of the narrative and willfully introduces new artificial ones.

We have to assume that the designer of the lives in the south aisle used a Western textual source and perhaps a Greek compositional pattern. He did not, however, adhere too closely to the text, and he held even less closely to the illustrative scheme. He did not copy but arranged and even invented more or less freely within the given textual and compositional framework.

Fig. 47. South aisle: Martyrdom of Jude

The principles that govern this great art of monumental composition on
curved and flat walls in a three-dimensional ambient were, of course, developed
and elaborated in Byzantium in the second half of the twelfth century. The types
of the apostles in the south aisle are, by and large, those current in Byzantine
representations. The most interesting component of these figures is their
clothing. While the apostles are clad *all'antica,* the Jews, Pharisees, and priests are
attired exactly as in the Passion scenes, with long tunics, mantles, and head
scarves. Others wear Arab headgear. The male Ethiopians expecting baptism
are wrapped in sheets and wear turbans, with white cloths wound around
pointed caps. The garments of the princesses in the same scene are Byzantine,
richly embroidered and studded with pearls, similar to the costumes of the
virtues in the central dome. The crowns of Egippus and Hyrtacus imitate
Byzantine forms, and the *loros* of Hyrtacus is a reproduction of the imperial

83

Byzantine costume. The clerics who assist at the burial of Philip are clad in albs and wear stoles and are tonsured like James. An unusual feature is the mail collar and hood of Hyrtacus's sword-bearer.

The exotic attire and weapons of the Indians, Scythians, and Persians—the first and last with long pigtails—can all be found in Byzantine illumination. Thus, there can be no doubt that the designers of these mosaics were fully conversant with the Byzantine way of representing exotic peoples. This must be especially emphasized in view of the fact that the textual basis of the representations was in most cases Western. As regards these costumes, there is in the entire cycle only one feature that may be of Western origin: the embroidered pattern in the shape of a rinceau on the thigh of the headman of the Indians.

Except for the Dome of the Rock, which stands for the Temple in Jerusalem, all the architectural motifs are purely conceptual. Here, too, the materials, that is, the single motifs, are in principle derived from Byzantine art, whereas the special configurations under which these motifs appear in the mosaics are more characteristic of Western than of Byzantine usage. This applies especially to the regular, symmetrical, and decorative way in which turrets, cupolas, and houses are arranged on top of the arcades, as against the freer, irregular agglomerations in Byzantium. It appears that the arcades with their architectural crowning motifs have in San Marco a very definite meaning as topographical indications. Thus, it is likely that the motif next to Mark in one of the pendentives of the central dome signifies Alexandria; in other instances, the place name is affixed or at least mentioned in nearby inscriptions. These named architectural motifs are all formed as arcades with complicated superstructures. Simple arcades without superstructures designate single specific buildings. This distinction between cities and countries on the one hand and specific buildings on the other exists in Byzantine art.

The slight but perceptible differences that appear in the narrative structure and rhythmic composition of the two halves of the south vault are accompanied by other dissimilarities. The James and Philip half seems to be weaker and perhaps a little more conservative than the Bartholomew and Matthew half. The figures in the latter half are more elegant, smoother in their movements, and modeled more convincingly as three-dimensional bodies: Bartholomew, for instance, has clearly marked light and shaded sides. And there are differences in other figures as well. It would be rash to conclude from this that the two halves of the vault are the work of two different hands and that a third master was responsible for the Simon and Jude scenes. More likely there existed a division of labor, with specialists working on the faces and costumes of the exotic figures and others on the architectural motifs. All in all, it must have been a smoothly functioning workshop under the guidance of a very able master whose art is quite clearly based on the style and palette of the Betrayal of Judas on the contiguous vault of the main dome. At the same time, it is clear that the style of the apostles' martyrdoms is a somewhat more recent development, later by a very few years but pointing in the direction of thirteenth-century smoothness.

All in all, the palette is a miniaturist's rather than a monumentalist's, just as the compositions are miniature compositions adapted to and arranged for monumental purposes. In spite of the dominant Byzantine elements, there is so much that is specifically Venetian in the iconography, composition, typology, and style of the San Marco mosaics that any comparison with works outside Venice can touch only the surface or upon general principles, while the essential and specific qualities remain unrelated.

84

The stage of general development to which these mosaics belong is characterized by a preference for diminutive prettiness, which in Byzantium finds its purest expression in the so-called rococo movement and in the West in the classicist strains of early Gothic. Some figures, especially that of Saint Matthew, show in addition the characteristics of the early monumental style, if only in a diminutive form: a certain broadening, so that the figure reaches normal proportions, as against the extreme slenderness in the dome and Passion mosaics, quiet movements, and, above all, a logically designed drapery of almost classical simplicity. The date of the actual setting of the cycle cannot have been far from the turn of the century and took place possibly at the beginning of the thirteenth.

Program and Decorative System

16

THE PROGRAMS OF SAN MARCO are highly complex because of the multiplicity of ideas that had to find expression in the pictorial decoration of a church that was at once the private chapel of the doge, the shrine of the relics of the evangelist Mark, one of the most popular places of worship, and, in practice if not in theory, the state church of Venice. San Marco was the place of the coronation and the solemn *promissio* of the doge and the scene of most great festivals, including Ascension Day, on which, later on, the marriage of Venice and the sea was performed. The decoration itself was not carried out in one campaign but in several, and, therefore, the programs were neither planned nor executed as a unity but grew from small beginnings. Some of it may have been realized first in wall painting and only later translated in mosaic step by step. Even sculpture played its part in the program—combined with mosaics on the facade from the beginning, elsewhere merely adding finishing touches to the existing mosaic programs, as with the angels of the Last Judgment. In the thirteenth century these were placed high up on the pillars of the central dome, an interesting *post festum* stressing of the eschatological aspect of the dome's Ascension as a Second Coming.

Two great catastrophes, a fire in 1106 and possibly an earthquake sometime after 1150, made renewals necessary. During these repairs new conceptions and ideas that had developed in the meantime were incorporated in the mosaics.

The program of the main apse certainly had the greatest importance for the shaping of the successive amplifications of the decoration: it seems to have conditioned the program of the east dome, and it also set the tenor for the grand program of the whole interior.

A record almost contemporary with the rebuilding of San Marco states explicitly that the church was built after the model of the Apostoleion in Constantinople, and later sources repeat this statement. There is no reason to doubt that San Marco was an intentional imitation of the apostles' church built as a sepulchral edifice by Constantine, rebuilt by Justinian I, and destroyed in 1459. San Marco, too, was an apostle's church, and, given the close relations between Venice and Byzantium in the eleventh century, it was almost inevitable that the Venetians should have modeled their church after the great Constantinopolitan shrine.

The model chosen for the new San Marco was not a standard product of contemporary Byzantine architecture but a highly experimental and complicated work of a period long past, a work that was generally far removed from the mainstream of Byzantine architectural development. Of course, an ecclesiastical building of the sixth century could not be copied *tale quale* in the eleventh. Among the most important of the changes concerned the eastern part of the church, where a tripartite sanctuary was added. By this addition, the original, truly centralized ground plan of the Apostoleion was given a definite orientation, the central bay now being not the center of spatial radiation but only an accentuated step in the west-east movement from entrance to apse. The altar was moved to the presbytery, and the floor level there was raised to make room for the crypt. The longitudinal tendency was also stressed by using smaller domes in the transepts and reducing the arcades. Structurally as well as optically, San Marco is not truly an equilateral cross but rather a domed basilica with lateral appendages. Another important difference, and one that has a great deal to do with the optical effect, is in the fenestration. Whereas in the Apostoleion only the central cupola had windows, all the domes in San Marco are fenestrated, and all are smooth—rather than ribbed—half-globes.

Despite all these differences, San Marco can still be regarded as a copy of the Apostoleion in the medieval sense of the term. It is not, however, a mechanical copy but a very sensitive adaptation of a great model and a work of art in its own right. It was sufficiently close to the Apostoleion—perhaps even in its measurements—for the model to be recognized and was at the same time thoroughly adapted to the new and specific requirements of the cult, for which more than one altar was required and for which the main altar had to be above the principal relics, contrary to Byzantine usage, according to which the location of the altar was independent of that of the relics. This shift of the main altar eastward and the addition of one central and two lateral apses were the most important single factors by which the strictly centralized plan of the model was altered and the longitudinal character of the entire interior established.

Factors of style also militated against the mechanical copying of the Constantinopolitan model. San Marco is, after all, a work of the eleventh century and its architects must have been alert to contemporary fashions and trends. It reflects the strong tendency of Middle Byzantine architecture toward the spatial unity of the interior. Apart from the crypt, Western features are due mainly to the collaboration of Western technicians and workmen in the articulation of the blind windows, the rows of arches, and the walls with niches.

It is logical to assume that the Venetians, having chosen the Apostoleion as a model of architectural form, should also have studied its mosaics with a view toward using, if not copying, their decorative and iconographic system. The evidence suggests that the mosaic decoration of the Apostoleion was a conglomeration of parts that belonged to more than one period. The church was certainly redecorated as soon as possible following the end of Iconoclasm (A.D. 843), most probably under Basil I, and so what the Venetians saw was essentially ninth-century work.

Using the medieval descriptions as the basis of a reconstruction of the Apostoleion mosaic program shows clearly that there was a certain general analogy in the distribution of the program in the two churches, for in each the cycle was divided into three categories: domes, primary vaults, and secondary vaults together with wall spaces. More specific is the placement of scenes across the zenith of the primary vaults. But of the representations contained in the domes only one is in the same place in the two churches, namely, the Pentecost in the west dome. The Pantocrator, who in the Apostoleion occupied the central

87

dome, changed aspect (as Emmanuel) in the east dome of San Marco, a displacement undoubtedly connected with the moving of the main altar from the center to its present place in front of the apse. The Ascension, in the south dome of the Apostoleion, occupies the central cupola in San Marco. The system of San Marco could be interpreted as a logical adaptation of that of the Apostoleion, the moving of the altar entailing the displacement of the Pantocrator, with the Ascension being moved in to close the gap.

No connection between the two churches can be made in the main vaults supporting the central dome nor in the subsidiary cycles of the secondary vaults. In the secondary vaults of the western cross arms, however, there is a much more palpable relationship between the two churches in the presence of episodes of the missionary activities of the apostles. What seems certain, nonetheless, is that the martyrdoms and burials of the apostles cannot possibly have been represented in the Apostoleion, and it is just these aspects of the lives of the apostles that were given prominence in San Marco. Thus, it cannot be claimed under any circumstances that San Marco followed slavishly the model of the Apostoleion as regards the illustration of the lives. What can be said is that the Constantinopolitan program exerted a generic influence on the mosaic decoration of the west arm of San Marco: the common theme in both churches was the Pentecost and the subsequent missionary activity of the apostles. The combination in the two churches of the Pentecost in the west dome and representations of the missionary activities of the apostles in the contiguous vaults is—among the extant monuments—unique. That the influence of the Apostoleion was most strongly felt in the western part of San Marco is surely not a matter of chance: the Venetians wanted their church to be an apostles' church, and it was only logical for them to follow the Constantinopolitan model most closely in those parts of the program that were specifically dedicated to the apostles.

In judging the program of San Marco in terms of contemporary Byzantine decoration, we must take into account the fact that the architectural frame of the Venetian church is entirely different from the normal type of post-Iconoclastic church architecture. The authors of the San Marco program could hardly have adapted the current Middle Byzantine type of program because it was from its very origin intimately connected with entirely different types of ecclesiastical buildings. As in these, the most important parts of the program of San Marco are, of course, to be found in the domes and the apse. This statement, however, requires immediate qualification. Only three of the five domes of San Marco contain subject-matter that can be called important in relation to Byzantine iconographical thinking; the transept cupolas, with scenes from the Life of Saint John the Evangelist in the north and four figures of saints in the south, have nothing to do with Byzantine cupola decoration. From all the preserved monuments as well as from descriptions, the conclusion follows that Middle Byzantine art knew only three "workable" compositions for domes: the Ascension, the Pentecost, and most important of all, the Pantocrator. San Marco made use of all these cupola schemes, lining them up along the main axis of the church. For the two remaining cupolas, those of the transepts, there were no prototypes in contemporary Byzantine art: they were consequently filled in a manner that has little to do with the principles of Middle Byzantine monumental decoration.

As regards the pendentives of the San Marco domes, two sets are in keeping with Middle Byzantine usage. The seated evangelists of the central dome are usually connected with the Pantocrator scheme, but they also occur in

88

connection with the Ascension. Angels in full figure (not often found in the pendentives of Middle Byzantine churches) fill the pendentives of the Pentecost dome in place of the tribes and nations that were the customary motif in Byzantium. The pendentives of the third dome contain the four evangelist symbols, an arrangement that hardly occurs in Middle Byzantine churches, where seraphim are preferred. This choice was connected with the theological ideas embodied in the program.

The program of the apse and perhaps also of part of the east dome precede that of the grand mosaic program. What the authors of the latter had to do was to integrate these existing programs into the new plan, possibly by some adaptations and certainly by the addition of a few figures, not in the apse itself, where there was no room, but in the presbytery. The figures of the four hierarchs, which in Byzantium usually appear in the bottom register of the apse, were added to the presbytery walls, and although two western as well as two eastern fathers are portrayed, this scheme is certainly a Middle Byzantine feature.

Middle Byzantine principles can also be seen to underlie the structure and arrangement of the narrative cycles. There is, first, the subdivision of the christological cycle into distinct primary and secondary parts. The primary cycle is placed in the main vaults that support the central dome. Although it is not a "pure" feast cycle in the strict Middle Byzantine sense, it contains most of the traditional scenes of this cycle. The comparatively detailed representation of the Passion goes beyond the canon of Middle Byzantine art, which is restricted to the Betrayal and the Crucifixion. The other scenes can, however, be found in detailed narrative cycles. The way in which the Crucifixion and the Anastasis are accentuated by being placed in the upper part of the vault so that they face each other across the entire width of the nave, is a specific trait of centralized programs of the Middle Byzantine period. It is also in accordance with contemporary Byzantine principles of arrangement that the Christ of the Anastasis walks toward the altar and not away from it. Between the Crucifixion and Anastasis, the authors of the program inserted the scene of the Holy Women at the Sepulcher, which, if it does not belong to the feast cycle itself, is very frequent in early and Middle Byzantine christological cycles. Its placement in the apex of the vault, in the main axis, shows that great importance was attached to the scene. It is presented as a parallel to the Transfiguration in the apex of the eastern vault. Thus, two axes cross each other. The cycle progresses with the Apparition of Christ to the Two Marys and the Doubting of Thomas, both scenes belonging to the enlarged Middle Byzantine cycle. Another christological theme, the Descent from the Cross, which was not part of the classical feast cycle but was frequently included in the enlarged sequence of Passion scenes, sometimes even replacing the Crucifixion, was represented in San Marco in an odd place, as if by an afterthought, namely, on the south side of the presbytery, on the western face of the quadripartite pillar between the central and eastern domes.

The Miracle cycle of San Marco is one of the richest to have come down to us from the Middle Byzantine period. Apparently no important scene was left out and none cannot be found in contemporary Byzantine programs. It is, however, a special feature of the program in San Marco that the Miracle cycle should have been treated as a separate entity but at the same time interwoven with the main christological cycle. Here the principles of centralized and narrative programs seem to be in conflict, with the result that San Marco follows neither of them consistently. Otherwise, the San Marco cycle shows hardly any specific traits.

89

Another secondary cycle, consisting of two parts, the Life of the Virgin and the Infancy of Christ, is arranged in the western bays of the transept, contrary to what would be expected in a purely narrative cycle, in which these scenes would, in part, precede the christological cycle proper and, in part, be interpolated into it. But as the scenario of San Marco does not follow the rules of chronologically consistent narrative, the Marian cycle is treated as a separate entity, a treatment frequently found in Middle and late Byzantine decorations. As a matter of fact, the Life of the Virgin was treated not so much as a subject in its own right but as the "prehistory" of the Life of Christ, whose infancy is depicted in conjunction with and as a direct continuation of the Marian cycle.

The manner in which the Gospel cycle is accompanied by prophets in full figure displaying texts related to individual scenes is also connected with Middle Byzantine models. And the plan to decorate the side chapels of the choir with representations related to the cult of the patron saints and their relics is, generally speaking, quite in conformity with Middle Byzantine practice. It is perhaps not mere chance that the Life of Saint Peter was illustrated in the north chapel as it was one of the most frequent themes represented in the *prothesis* of Middle Byzantine counterparts. The representation of the titular and patron saints as in the south chapel of San Marco is not uncommon in Middle Byzantine churches. Taken as a whole, the complex of the choir chapels is the real *martyrion* of the evangelist, and the program of its decoration is, as in most Byzantine examples, dominated by those principles that governed the programs of Early Byzantine *martyria*. In these programs, the legends of the saint's relics had as much a place as his life and martyrdom.

Several other features in the mosaics of the choir chapels of San Marco might have some relation to Middle Byzantine programs. One of these is the Sacrifice of Cain and Abel on the south wall of the Cappella di San Clemente. The isolated Old Testament theme could be explained in two different ways: either as a reminiscence of Ravennate presbytery programs, which is the likeliest explanation, or as an echo of Middle Byzantine decorations of side chapels. In both cases, the Eucharistic connotations are obvious.

Another motif, possibly connected with or derived from Byzantine bema programs, is that of the archangels Michael and Gabriel holding and presenting an *imago clipeata* with a portrait of Christ, here in the type of the beardless Emmanuel. It occurs mostly in the presbytery but also in the *diaconicon,* the deacon's room, or the narthex.

One last part of the program possibly connected with Middle Byzantine programs consists of the representation of saints, those in the side apses as the patrons of the chapels and those of the arches and walls. Both kinds are almost *de rigueur* in Byzantine side chapels that were dedicated to particular saints. Byzantine choir chapels did not harbor exclusively representations of those saints whose relics were guarded in these chapels, but the possession of relics did play an important part in their decor. This is the case in San Marco.

Generally speaking, the parallels between the program of the choir chapels of San Marco and Middle Byzantine decorations do not seem to amount to much, but they do show that the authors of the program possessed a certain knowledge of decorations of this sort and were conversant with the principles that governed their arrangement. This also holds true for the general distribution of images of saints in the main body of the church, with apostles, priests, and healers in the eastern part, and ascetics and hermits in the western part.

The western part of the church, that is the westernmost vault and probably also the original west wall, bore a representation of the Last Judgment. This was, ideally, also the arrangement in Middle Byzantine church buildings, where, however, it appeared more often in the narthex than in the naos, especially in domed churches. Here again, the Venetians seem to have followed the lead of contemporary Byzantine programs.

The influence of Middle Byzantine principles of arrangement was still felt in the thirteenth century, when the decoration of San Marco was supplemented by a number of scenes in large panels that filled the previously empty lower spaces of the outer walls of the transept and the west arm, wall spaces that became visible from the main body of the church only after the removal of the gallery floors. The newly created panels in the west arm are related to the Passion cycle by the Agony in the Garden and to the Last Judgment by a representation of paradise. In the east bay of the north transept, the Emmaus scenes and the Communion of the Apostles were placed as near as possible to the sanctuary, the normal Middle Byzantine place for the Divine Liturgy. The corresponding bay in the south transept can be interpreted as a side chapel dedicated to Saint Leonard; consequently, the panel on the east wall represented the life of the saint, as was customary in Byzantine side chapels.

The other panels have nothing to do with Byzantine iconographic programs, and the placing of the Deesis on the west wall, the latest thirteenth-century addition to the program of the interior, is really an inversion of the Byzantine scheme in which the Deesis filled the tympanum above the main entrance outside the naos, in the narthex of the church. In San Marco, an Old Testament cycle was placed in the narthex, the most important addition to the program made in the thirteenth century. It is very doubtful that the stimulus for this could have come from Byzantium.

The San Marco program cannot be satisfactorily explained on the basis of Byzantine models and ideas alone; Western elements also had a decisive role. It must, however, be realized that the most important Western iconographic elements belong to the renewals of the later twelfth century, especially in the central dome, where the allegories of the virtues and the personifications of the rivers of paradise were added to the Ascension. The other Western elements that went into the making and arranging of the program are found not so much in the iconographic materials and principles of arrangement as in the realm of ideas that shaped the content and message of the whole. There are, nevertheless, some iconographic motifs and principles of arrangement for which a Western origin can be claimed. In several cases it is certainly difficult to choose between a Western and a Byzantine origin, especially those in which Western and Byzantine programs show strong parallelisms, for instance, the image of the Enthroned Christ in the apse. The two symbols in the eastern pendentives are seen as a unit together with the Christ of the apse and make this figure the center of what may be called a composite *maiestas,* which is much nearer to Western, especially Italian, apses than to either archaic Eastern Christian or Byzantine majesties. The lamb above the San Marco apse hardly ever occurs in Middle Byzantine monuments but is very frequent in the West, especially in the Adriatic region.

Western elements might also be seen in the placing of Gabriel and Michael bearing the icon of Christ near the precinct of the doge and in the icon of Michael painted on the marble revetment below on the pillar that was believed to have harbored the relics of Saint Mark. Both could be connected with the dynastic and governmental connotations of the veneration and representation of the archangels, especially Saint Michael.

Decidedly Western are the virtues in the central dome; Byzantine monumental art does not seem to have used the motif of female personifications of virtues in church decoration. Representations of the virtues are frequent, however, in Romanesque sculpture, especially as part of portal and facade programs, and it is, indeed, very likely that the Venetian figures were inspired by sculptural rather than by pictorial programs.

Prototypes for the representation of the rivers of paradise, a further addition of the late twelfth century, must also be sought in the West. These figures often occur in close conjunction with the allegories of the virtues and with the four evangelists; in Byzantium they are never imbued with allegorical meaning. In this case, too, it is likely that the impulse originated rather in the field of Romanesque sculpture or book illumination than in that of monumental painting.

Yet another motif may possibly owe its existence to the restoration campaign of the late twelfth or to the new Western wave of the thirteenth century, namely, the two figures of Ecclesia and Synagoga, found in baroque form at the foot of the vault with the *martyria* of the apostles. The two allegories were greatly in vogue in cathedral sculpture as well as in early Gothic wall painting. In San Marco they were probably meant to strengthen the ecclesiological aspect of the Pentecost in the cupola above.

The question of transmission has to be posed separately for every one of the various Early and Middle Byzantine elements of the program on the one hand and for the Western elements on the other. Earlier Byzantine iconography influenced the program of San Marco in the first place by the example of the Apostoleion in Constantinople and in the second by Ravenna. Most likely, in both cases, conscious revival rather than survival should be accepted. As for the transmission of Middle Byzantine principles of program selection and arrangement, these must have been known to the authors of the iconographic program through contemporary Byzantine decorations. Byzantine manuscript illuminations were also used as models but only for single cycles and scenes and not for the program and its arrangement.

The attitude was different with regard to Western ideas, principles, and motifs. In this respect, the authors of the Venetian program did not restrict themselves to monumental paintings as models, or even to painting in general: they had equally good use for elements taken from the context of sculptural decor and from the realm of minor arts.

Compared with the Byzantine elements of the decoration of San Marco, the contribution of the West would seem to be small; it is at any rate much less conspicuous. To the average beholder, San Marco certainly gives the impression of being essentially a Byzantine monument. The leading ideas, that is, the spiritual content of the decoration, are, however, decidedly Western or more specifically Venetian, even more so in the later parts of the decoration than in the earlier ones. To recognize this, the inscriptions are of great help. One of the most revealing of these is found in the Cappella di San Pietro, which reads, "This vault is the head, the godhead, hope, and future life. Through the middle you experience the past, the present, and the future." Although difficult to interpret, the inscription surely refers to the program and the arrangement of the twelfth-century decoration and enumerates four parts that it characterizes by the words *hope, past, present,* and *future*. It would seem that the first entity refers to the east dome with the apse, characterized by the words *godhead, hope,* and *future life*. And indeed, the message of the mosaics of this dome is the hope held out by the prophets who surround the image of the Emmanuel, the Logos to be made incarnate. The prophecies written on the scrolls of most of the prophets refer to the coming of the Messiah to be born of the Virgin, who is represented as orant in the main axis of the dome. The inscription that surrounds the dome leads from the dark prophecies of the Old Testament to the clear testimony of the Gospels, as indicated by the symbols of the evangelists.

The evangelists' symbols point forward to the second chapter in the sequence of the San Pietro inscription, which, under the heading of *the past,* deals with the historic life of Christ in the center of the church—with its apex in the Ascension of the central dome. In the pendentives appear the authors of the historical narrative, the evangelists, now in human form with an inscription that refers to the "unfigurative," "open" character of the New Testament in contrast to the *figurae* of the Old.

The third link in the chain, the *present,* could be interpreted as the life of the Church symbolized by the Descent of the Holy Ghost in the west dome, and the fourth—the *future*—might be connected with the eschatological representation of the Last Judgment in the westernmost vault of the church.

While the main sequence embraces the domes and vaults of the main axis, the transept domes with the Life of Saint John the Evangelist and with four saints represent side lines that continue or accompany the main theme— properly read as part of the "historical" sequence, from the time of expectation to the fulfillment of the prophecies in the Incarnation, the foundation and the life of the Church, and finally the Last Judgment. As regards the various parts of Scripture underlying the consecutive chapters of this history, the sequence would lead from the Old Testament to the Gospels, the Acts of the Apostles, and finally to the Apocalypse as a scriptural source for the Last Judgment.

The main elements of the program belong to the "old style" religiosity of Romanesque programs. Even the Christ of the original christological part of the program is not yet the gentle Savior of Gothic programs. The Virgin is introduced into this program not, as in the new cathedrals, as a figure of veneration in her own right but as a historical figure, a link in the history of salvation. Another characteristic feature of old-style Romanesque programs is the cosmological aspect, as it is contained in the combination of letters that appears in the apex of the north dome. Alternating with the letters alpha and omega, one finds in the outer ring of the central motif the letters ADAM, the name of mankind's first ancestor and also the initial letters of the Greek words for the four quarters of the earth. The second set of letters, AAOO, stand for the Latin words of the four cardinal points. The idea, although expressed in entirely different form, is the same as that embodied in the figures of the rivers of paradise. Thus, we find in the program of San Marco the time scheme of the ages of the world combined with the spatial scheme of the cosmos. In Byzantium, the idea of the cosmic universe combined with that of the Christian universe was expressed solely by the figure of the All-Ruler, the Pantocrator, without the help of other allegorical figures or symbols.

In this old-style program, the allegories of the virtues are definitely a foreign intrusion. This is also true of the figures of Ecclesia and Synagoga, which belong to the "new-style" programs that evolved in the decor of the great French cathedrals and were introduced into Italy in the later twelfth century. In San Marco they appeared, together with the rivers of paradise, as additions made during the great renewal campaign after the (hypothetical) catastrophe that destroyed the central part of the decoration. At the same time, there also

93

appeared a new element of direct appeal to the beholder in the scenes of the Passion with their "speaking" scrolls, which make these mosaics forerunners of the devotional image. Something of the new spirit can be found as well in the dramatic realization of the narrative in the mosaics representing the martyrdom of six apostles in the bay south of the Pentecost dome. The sequence of scenes shows a telescoping of events similar to that in the Passion scenes. It is as if a breath of fresh air from the great cathedrals of the West had found its way into San Marco.

The other main theme in the program is that of Venice itself, its church and its state. Next to the central theme of salvation, the political theme is therefore the strongest among the concert of themes that together make up the program of the mosaics. It is intimately connected with the central theme by Saint Mark, whose figure belongs to the religious as well as to the political sphere—perhaps more to the latter than to the former. In the apse it is indeed Saint Mark who is represented in full frontality. The apse figures also include Hermagoras, the first bishop of Aquileia and thus the founder of the patriarchate, and the "state saint" Nicholas, the patron of the Venetian fleet—the two representing the Venetian claim to ecclesiastical independence and to political, especially maritime, power.

The historical commentary on the statements of the apse is contained in the mosaics of the north vault of the Cappella di San Pietro, where the foundation of the patriarchate is represented in a number of scenes beginning with the consecration of Mark and Hermagoras and ending with Hermagoras's missionary activity. The transfer of the patriarchate from Aquileia to Grado is alluded to in the two figures of Pope Pelagius and Patriarch Helias of Grado, which bear inscriptions that state succinctly but clearly the Venetian claims to the patriarchate and to primacy over Istria and Dalmatia. From this, the narrative proceeds to the story of the relics of Saint Mark, the palladium of Venice—a political counterpart to the ecclesiastical history.

Assembled over a longish period, the cortège of the tutelary saint is vast and rather motley. The most important group of saints is, of course, that assembled in the presbytery, accompanying the earlier figures of the main apse. Peter was featured because of his connection with Mark and the foundation of the Aquileian church—sufficient reason, quite apart from the fact that there were in the altar relics to which the inscription of the main apse makes allusion. The reason for choosing Clement as patron of the southern choir chapel and its altar is to be sought in the fact that he was connected with Peter and Mark in the tradition of Alexandria, he was venerated in Aquileia, he was the patron of a monastery and a hospital on one of the Realtine islands, and he was, after all, a widely venerated tutelary saint of seafaring merchants.

For the representations of Sergius, Bacchus, Theodore, and Pantaleon, whose figures appear paired in the choir chapels, the possession of relics and the existence of early cults, in part directly connected with San Marco, may have been decisive. It is likely that the four apostles Matthew, Andrew, Philip, and James also owed their inclusion to the presence of relics and that some or all of the other saints whose relics were in the two altars were also originally pictured. The possession of relics was perhaps also the reason for the representation of the two holy bishops, Constantius and Epiphanius in the apse-like niches above the east doors of the upper stories of the choir chapels.

The two transept domes were also places of high honor. Their decor is connected with the *tituli* of the two transept altars dedicated respectively to Saint John the Evangelist and Saint Leonard. The pendentives of the Saint John dome show figures of four church fathers, probably because John was considered the theologian par excellence. In the dome of the south transept, we find Leonard (above the altar dedicated to him) and Nicholas, Clement, and Blaise, all saints of special significance in Venice. The four figures in the pendentives, Dorothea, Erasma, Euphemia, and Thecla were also venerated locally and Venice had possession of their relics.

Both Hermagoras and Julian were singled out for special treatment because of their connection with Aquileia and Grado, and it is very likely that some of the patriarchal saints now missing were originally represented in corresponding emplacements.

Thus, all the saints honored by being placed in the presbytery or in domes, pendentives, and top registers of the transept walls are state saints or saints closely connected with the Venetian church. It is a different matter with those whose images appear in the arches of the ground floor, where they are arranged in pairs. With few exceptions, these are Western and their names are mostly contained in the Roman Missal. Most of them were venerated in Venice itself or in its dependencies.

To sum up: the various groups of saints pictured in San Marco represent distinct categories. The oldest and most archaic group—consisting of state saints and figures intimately connected with the history of the patriarchate and the Venetian state church—is found in the presbytery. Also belonging to the presbytery group are those saints whose relics were contained in the presbytery altars, including, most probably, four apostles, so as to strengthen the character of San Marco as an apostles' church. The second group centered around the altars of Saint John and Saint Leonard. The third group is the most catholic; considered as a whole, it is neither very specific from the point of view of Venetian hagiography nor very original. It might be found in almost any large decorative system. The fourth group, perhaps never entirely realized and altered moreover in later periods, contained Roman martyrs and some Byzantine saints. There are no monks, hermits, or stylites among these groups, indicating that San Marco must be regarded as a specifically court church. The fact that all figures are clad either in patrician costumes or ecclesiastical vestments confirms this character. Certainly the program was to a large extent influenced by the individual ideas and wishes of the doge, the procuratori, and the clergy of San Marco itself.

To what extent and in what way did liturgy and rite influence the content and arrangement of the program in San Marco? The so-called Grado rite did not differ substantially from the Roman. The main differences between the rite of San Marco and that of Rome were, of course, caused by the fact that San Marco was the private chapel of the doge, a fact that influenced the liturgy, especially at those church festivals in which the doge took part. The most important of these feasts was the Ascension, which as Sensa became *the* state festival. Is it mere chance that the Ascension is represented in the central dome and that it dominates the entire program of mosaic decoration? And why was the Ascension represented as the only subject, as far as we know, in fresco in the portico on the exterior wall of the church?

Generally speaking, our information about the liturgy and ceremony of San Marco and especially about the role of the doge and the Venetian government in these rites is, of course, more plentiful with regard to later periods than with regard to the Middle Ages and this might be misleading. At all times, however, the participation of the doge was important. On most occasions, the

95

doge entered San Marco through the *porta media* of the south transept and took up his seat in the southeastern part of the church, in the chapel of San Clemente probably under the arch decorated in mosaic with the figures of Christ and the Virgin. The connection of these figures with the throne of the ruler is suggested by a number of other examples. The location of the throne was conditioned by two facts: first, the position of the main altar in the east rather than the center of the church and second, the situation of the ducal palace in the south. It is noteworthy that in Hagia Sophia in Constantinople, too, the emperor's throne stood on the ground floor, most probably beside the southeast conch.

There is good reason for assuming that a seat for the *primicerius,* the highest ecclesiastic official, was located opposite the doge's throne, under the corresponding north arch that connects the presbytery with the Cappella di San Pietro and, through a doorway, with the former *primicerius'* (now patriarchal) palace. Here, too, the mosaic decoration of the arch is conditioned by the special character of the location: it is the monumental statement of the Venetian claims to the patriarchate and to primacy over Istria and Dalmatia embodied in the figures of Patriarch Helias of Grado and Pope Pelagius. Thus, the two choir chapels of San Marco really represent two different domains, the north chapel the ecclesiastical domain, the south chapel that of the doge. This is also expressed in the mosaics of the great vaults above these chapels, which represent the foundation of the Venetian church in the north and the acquisition of the national palladium, the relics of San Marco, in the south. In other parts of the church, the ecclesiastic and governmental aspects interpenetrate. Thus, it may well be that the representation of the virtues and beatitudes in the central dome, with their admonitory inscriptions, was meant as an extension of the *speculum ducis* of the Cappella di San Pietro.

A fragment of the Deposition was discovered when the marble lining of the northeastern foot of the southeast pier of the central dome between the presbytery and the Cappella di San Clemente was removed in 1954. The emplacement and the small scale of the mosaic are so strange that we must look for a specific reason why the image was placed there instead of being included in the Passion cycle. Together with the Threnos, the Bewailing of Christ, the Deposition was the favorite devotional image of the period. Thus, it is as a devotional image that the mosaic was placed in the presbytery near the place of the doge. It is not impossible that it had a pendant on the corresponding face of the north pier, showing the Threnos.

Who were the authors of this program and its enlargements? One of the first problems that must be resolved in seeking to answer this question is whether the author of the inscriptions and the author of the mosaic program were one and the same. This is unlikely in the case of the inscriptions of the semicircular wall of the apse, which may not be of the same period as the mosaics. A similar doubt exists about some of the inscriptions of the main porch mosaics. The other inscriptions of the interior appear to be the product of two periods, namely, that of the grand decoration before the catastrophe and that of the restoration after this event. Some inscriptions of the later period may be simply copies of the original ones, and others may have been newly formulated together with the new iconographic compositions. With the exception of three groups—the Ascension dome, the Passion and Resurrection cycle, and the martyrdoms—and a few others, practically all the old inscriptions can be regarded as belonging to the time before the catastrophe, that is, to the time of the formulation and gradual execution of the grand program. In spite of certain

96

similarities with contemporary verse, the San Marco inscriptions form a peculiar and original body of medieval epigrammatic poetry.

The old inscriptions belong to several more or less distinct categories. The first category is made up of inscriptions with a very general content not connected with specific mosaics or groups of mosaics or if so, only in a very loose way. Those that are executed not in mosaic but in stone inlay are the most general ones; they were executed after the completion of the whole decoration and have nothing to do with the program. The ones executed in mosaic are somehow connected with the program as a whole or with certain parts. It may be taken as certain that these inscriptions, which are to be found around the apse and the domes and on the faces of the great vaults and which express the general ideas embodied in the program, are the work of the author or authors of the program. The explicative inscription in the Cappella di San Pietro, which is a starting point and key for the understanding of the program and its arrangement, may be an exception. Some of these inscriptions have a grandiose sound, especially those of the main axis. There are, however, others that show a lack of ingenuity similar to that manifest in certain parts of the program itself.

The second category is the largest. It includes those inscriptions that are firmly connected with specific mosaic figures or scenes, that give the names of saints and prayers addressed to them, and that explain the content of the scenic representations. All inscriptions that accompany scenic representations have an explicatory character: they are not just titles or one-word captions, but offer a kind of commentary. This practice is a departure from Byzantine usage, where simple headings giving the name of the feast are the rule, but is in accordance with Western cycles, which favor more detailed inscriptions, often in verse form, either in simple historical past or present tense or introducing a speaking figure, as in some of the post-catastrophe inscriptions of San Marco itself.

A third category comprises inscriptions on scrolls or books. The most numerous examples are offered by the prophets, which is quite in accordance with Byzantine practice, and by the allegories of the central dome. All these inscriptions are quotations from Scripture.

Difficult problems are presented by a few inscriptions that form a final category: these are riddles, composed of single letters, as in the apex of the north dome. Combinations of this kind are more frequent in the West than in Byzantium.

The language of all these inscriptions is Latin, with the exception of the Greek names of two apostles in the porch, of the Greek church fathers in the presbytery, and the title of the Anastasis. The form of most of the inscriptions is rather artificial and precious, to a certain extent because of the choice of the verse, the Leonine hexameter. Sparingly used in antiquity, this type of verse with its inner rhyme was eagerly taken up in the Middle Ages and brought to the height of its development in the eleventh and twelfth centuries. Even beyond the exigencies and temptations of this pretentious verse form the choice of words in the inscriptions is often peculiar or archaizing. The recurrence of certain words and rhymes and of thought motifs suggests that the greater part of the inscriptions were made at one time, at the beginning of the grand decoration. The bulk could, in fact, be the work of one author: supplements may have been added to them from time to time with the intention of imitating the style of the original core as closely as possible.

With all their artificiality, the San Marco inscriptions are certainly not great religious poetry. The core inscriptions are the product of an intelligent and moderately learned theologian, probably a cleric of the church itself. It is difficult to say whether he was also the author of the program and of its distribution. It is idle to guess at the identity of the author, but one name might be mentioned to indicate the category to which such a person might have belonged: we know of one Jacobus Veneticus Grecus, a translator of Aristotle and of other Greek authors, a learned canonist who took an active part in the discussion about the rank of the patriarchates and attempted to secure for Aquileia and Grado a second rank after Rome. Somebody like this man, equally well versed in Greek and Latin theology and literature, could have been the author of the main program of San Marco, and if we believe the Venetian tradition, Joachim of Fiore might have had a hand in adding the finishing touches in the later twelfth century.

The Greek mosaicists who worked in San Marco in the beginning must have felt they were treading on unfamiliar ground. The shape of the space they were called upon to decorate was completely different from the type of interior they were used to working in. The differences were in the number of domes and vaults, in the measurements and the shapes of all the vaulted parts, and in the extension of the mosaic crust to lower wall spaces and to insets on the lower walls and above the doors. Even before the additions of the thirteenth century, the interior of San Marco probably exhibited the largest unbroken expanse of mosaic in the Byzantine area in its time.

It is likely that the Apostoleion was the model for the great decorative scheme, for the treatment of the whole as a multiple golden baldachin in which the unbroken golden ground was the primary element. This is in contrast to Middle Byzantine mosaic churches, where there is an equilibrium between the quiet tones of the marble incrustation, which stretches high up (much higher than in San Marco), the flowery colors of the images, and the golden ground. There is also good reason for assuming that the odd way in which some scenes are arranged transversely in the zeniths of the vaults was copied from the Apostoleion.

The filling—or obscuring—of the golden ground with figures is strikingly different in the mosaics before and after the catastrophe of the late twelfth century. While the silhouetted patterns of the earlier parts are sparse and discontinuous, letting the golden ground dominate completely over the figural elements, the figural parts of the later mosaics are much denser and the compositions much more coherent, so that the gold recedes and becomes "background" on the sides and above the massed figures.

Even in the relatively later mosaics, the hemming in of the scenes is effected without any framing device. Prior to the thirteenth century there are no framed pictures in San Marco, but the post-catastrophe mosaics of the west central vault are, so to speak, on their way to becoming "pictures," that is self-contained formal units. And it seems that the Deposition in the presbytery had already reached this goal: this would be connected with the special character of the scene as a devotional image. The scenes of the Life of the Virgin are a somewhat different case: their picturelike entities are due to the fact that they are copies from manuscript illumination. But even these latter picturelike scenes have no frames, not even horizontal partitions. As a matter of fact, the only framing devices that occur in San Marco before 1200 are the framing and accentuating of architectural units themselves. This framing of architectural units, stronger in the presbytery than in other parts of the church, is essentially a Greek principle.

Thirteenth-Century Mosaics
of the Interior

17

ALTHOUGH THE SAN MARCO MOSAIC PROGRAM was essentially complete by the end of the twelfth century, work continued during the thirteenth century, largely as the result of architectural changes. For the sake of clarity, the mosaics will be presented in groups according to the places they occupy, beginning with the highest, (1) the great panels of the side walls, (2) the cupolas of the tribunes, (3) the smaller panels on the walls of the west arm, (4) the arches, and (5) the lunettes.

THE GREAT PANELS OF THE SIDE WALLS

The large surfaces of the zone between the two cornices, at the height of the tribunes of the main pillars, were left undecorated until the gallery floors were removed, making these areas visible from the ground. They are the largest flat surfaces and were filled with cyclic representations—six in two stories and three in single-story format. There is no unified and consistent program for the six large panels of the west arm and the transept. As far as can be made out, their execution was spread over at least a whole generation and it is unlikely that they were planned together. The moving force was, primarily, the desire to decorate the newly gained wall spaces.

In the individual cases, the only determining motive was the functional position of the individual wall space or, if no such functional position could be found, the neighborhood of existing subject matter. Thus, for the wall space in the south bay of the west arm the mosaicists introduced the Agony in the Garden because of the proximity of the pre-Passion and Passion cycles on the nearby vault. On the opposite wall in the north bay of the west arm, they chose to continue the cycle of the Last Judgment, with the result that a representation of paradise was included. The placement of a cycle illustrating the story of Susanna—more precisely, the Judgment of Daniel—may have been determined by the propinquity of the north arm of the atrium, where the ecclesiastic tribunal seems to have had its seat. In all likelihood, the panel containing representations of the Communion of the Apostles and the Emmaus story on the east wall of the north transept was placed there, next to the presbytery, because of the eucharistic connotations of the imagery. The story of Saint Leonard, occupying the corresponding panel on the east wall of the south transept, was suggested by the dedication to the saint of the altar immediately underneath. More involved

+DVMMODOREXORATSVPPLEXSVATVRBASOPORAT·ADQVOSMOXTENDITETEC

Fig. 48. West arm, south wall: Agony in the Garden

is the problem of the placing of the *apparitio* of Saint Mark's relics on the west wall of the south transept, apparently the last of the panels to have been filled. Its legitimate place would have been the east wall, which, however, had already been taken up with the story of Saint Leonard.

The Agony in the Garden

The framed picture surface is filled with three units, each containing a standing figure of Christ speaking to one or several apostles plus, on the slope of a hill, a kneeling figure of Christ in prayer; the Christ figure on the right is approached from the back by a flying angel (figs. 48–49). The mosaic is one of the best-preserved of the entire mosaic decoration of the church.

All the motifs narrated in the synoptic Gospels appear in the mosaic; although the representation of the story in several phases did exist in both Byzantium and the West, it is doubtful that the designer of the mosaic had a complete model for his tripartite composition. All the figures could easily have been developed from the dominating type of composition having one figure of Christ praying and another reproving Peter amid the group of sleeping apostles. The Byzantine prototype of the core of the mosaic must have been an approximately contemporary Constantinopolitan composition. None of the figures is a faithful copy; each is drawn and grouped with a perfect knowledge of the Byzantine repertoire, freely interpreted.

This facility for free variation makes it probable that the author of the model that formed the basis for the design of the group of sleeping apostles was Greek, and it is very likely that the designer himself, if not Greek, was in any case thoroughly conversant with the principles of Greek design. Although he

Fig. 49. West arm, south wall: Agony in the Garden

must have laid out the composition of the entire panel, he was only responsible
for the mosaic work of the group of eight sleeping apostles (beginning at the
left); the rest is the work of other masters. In arranging the scenes from left to
right, the designer may well have been influenced by the composition of the
Temptation, with its threefold repetition of the standing Christ and Satan. He
also followed the lead of earlier mosaics in San Marco by avoiding any cutting
off of forms by the newly introduced frame. This is most conspicuous on the
extreme left, where the perpendicular contour of the cliff runs parallel to the
frame; the gap at the upper edge is narrower, but there, too, an empty strip of
golden ground intervenes. A similar attitude is found in the vertical limitations
of the figure groups at the edges of the pre-Passion and Passion scenes of the
west vault, even though there is no framing border. It is also in these latter
mosaics that we find a continuous strip of vegetal ground stretching from one
end of the composition to the other, accentuating the horizontal extension and
the coherence of the whole.

It is quite obvious that no fewer than three, perhaps even four mosaic
masters had a hand in making the large panel. The first and chief master is
technically the most skillful and artistically the finest. He produced the greater
part of the group of sleeping apostles in the first unit on the left (fig. 50). The
three apostles at the right, Peter, Andrew, and John, and the standing and
kneeling Christs of the first unit are the work of a second master who also did
parts of the rocky landscape (pl. 29a). All the rest, from the right-hand contour
of the first standing Christ to the right edge of the panel, is the work of a
workshop consisting perhaps of two mosaicists (pl. 29b).

Technically the only works in San Marco that come anywhere near the

Fig. 50. West arm, south wall: Agony in the Garden,
sleeping apostles, central section

CHAPTER SEVENTEEN

materials and manner of the Agony panel masters are those of the central dome. In general, though, the technique is closer to that of portable mosaic icons made more for close inspection than for the long-distance effect of monumental mosaics.

The group of works around the mosaics of the central dome, which shows some technical affinities with the Agony panel, is also the only one in San Marco that is in some way related stylistically to the first master. Some of the types are reminiscent of those in the martyrdoms directly above and the handling of drapery and modeling is similar. Nonetheless, the general conception is quite different. The figures in the Agony are less elongated, more substantial, in fact, quite normally proportioned. The relief is less deeply furrowed and cut up, much quieter. Foreshortening does not seem to have presented great problems: the figure seen head on, while convincingly foreshortened, is fitted in without breaking the relief of the entire group.

With all the differentiation of postures and attitudes, the general character of the group is quiet. The sleeping apostles seem almost classical, and there is no trace here of the restlessness, the agitation, the movement for its own sake of the typical dynamic-style work (pl. 30). The San Marco Agony belongs to the earlier manifestations of a return to a monumental style after the overheated mannerism of the second half of the twelfth century. The immediate model of the group of figures must have been a Byzantine model book of the last years of the twelfth century or early years of the thirteenth—one that contained the composition as a whole and the schemata of the figures in their individual attitudes, and another that furnished details of drapery, design, and modeling.

In addition to those features of the first group of figures that can be connected with the Byzantine development, there are some that show an awareness of contemporary movements at work in Western art. The covering of the figures with thin folds in form-designing lines is a parallel to the Western *Muldenfaltenstil* of the late twelfth and early thirteenth centuries, a style that grew from conditions similar to those of the Venetian apostles. Nonetheless, the style of the first master of the Agony is first and foremost Venetian. It must be connected to a continuous development, the intermediary phases of which are now lost.

The style of the second master of the mosaic is so different from that of the first that the two artists seem to have come from different worlds. The features of the figures correspond roughly to the current Middle Byzantine types, but they are rendered more summarily. It is as if the second master was imitating the technique of the first without a real understanding of its intricacy (pl. 31). As a result, many elements are almost clumsy. Where this master attempts detailed rendering, he is clearly unsuccessful, and he does not achieve adequate spatial projection. Only the figure of the standing Christ shows few traces of the uncertainty, the almost amateurish ineptitude in the design of the entire figure as well as of the drapery. As a matter of fact, this figure is perhaps the most commanding in the entire mosaic (fig. 51). Most likely, the mosaicist was able to use a good model drawing for the standing figure as a whole, while he was unable to follow the models of the other figures in their entirety because of lack of space. Even here, however, the execution does not do justice to Christ's monumental grandeur of stance and gesture. The function of the left hand, for instance, gathering and lifting the upper garment, is not fully understood and rendered. The hands are as clumsy and as little differentiated as those of the apostles, although there is considerable improvement, as if the mosaicist were

103

Fig. 51. West arm, south wall: Agony in the Garden,
standing Christ at left and apostles

gradually becoming familiar with the technique of mosaic-making in general
and with that of San Marco in particular. New is the technique of chrysography
in the pink undergarment, as well as the use of tinted gold in the zigzag seam.
What is true of the standing Christ applies also to the figure kneeling in deep
prostration on top of the rock. For this figure, too, the mosaicist must have had
a good prototype, of which a shadow is preserved in the Wolfenbüttel
sketchbook.

The fluctuation of artistic quality, even of competence, within the
comparatively small oeuvre of the second master, the contrast between concept
and execution even of the best figures, boldness and timidity existing side by
side—all this strongly suggests that the master was a young artist, gifted but not
sure of himself or his craft and, in any case, not fully conversant with the
traditions of San Marco. He learned as he went along but disappeared before he

104

mastered his craft. The new monumental style, which the first master of the Agony had adopted only hesitantly, without breaking away from the tradition of Late Comnenian art, the second master attempted to realize without reserve. It is difficult to say where this artist came from, but it is unlikely that he came directly from the Byzantine area, for he must have known some of the most recent monumental paintings, such as those in Serbia. Most likely, he was a Venetian only recently schooled in the technique of mosaic.

The workshop that took over and brought the mosaic to completion was certainly well equipped for its task. It must have been so well directed and organized that even a change of hands is hardly noticeable. But how is the odd sequence of three chief masters to be understood? That they were not working side by side, having divided the work within the long strip, is proved by the odd partition of the area. Moreover, a strictly concurrent working of the three masters would surely have produced a more homogeneous result, at least in the size of the figures and the general structure of the landscape. The sudden breaking off of the shares of the first and second masters and their continuation by artists of such different training suggests some external interference. It is exceptionally fortunate, therefore, that there is, in fact, sufficient documentary evidence of such interference—a case in a thousand! A letter from Pope Honorius III is preserved, thanking the doge Pietro Ziani for having sent him a mosaic master for the work in the church of San Paolo fuori le mura in Rome and asking him, with reference to the extent of the work, for two more mosaicists. The date of the letter suggests that the first mosaic master may have been dispatched from Venice to Rome in 1216 or 1217, and it is very likely that the second (and perhaps third) was sent in 1218. The question is now, could the first Venetian master sent to Rome in 1216–17 have been the first master of the Agony mosaic, and one of the two requested in 1218 the second? Any answer to this question would be doubtful were it not for the fact that the Roman mosaic of San Paolo shows quite unmistakable similarities with mosaics in San Marco. Not only does the "Roman hypothesis" explain the sudden disappearance of the first and second Agony masters, one after the other, it provides an exact date for their respective activities.

Two observations should, perhaps, be added. First, the fact that three artists working, one after the other, at the execution of one uniformly planned mosaic should have used three different styles suggests that at this moment there existed no firmly established stylistic tradition in Venetian painting, that it was an "open" situation, in which every master had to feel his own way. Second, the share of the second master must have been striking if only for the much larger scale of the figures and their coloristic disparity. This may account for the return to a more normal style in the share of the third master (pl. 32). The accepted styles of the first and third masters—in other words, the dominant styles of the entire mosaic—are rather conservative and represent a phase that does not go much beyond late twelfth-century work. The force of the Venetian tradition, especially that of the fully developed style of the central dome, was apparently so strong that the intrusion of the modern monumental style in the work of a young and comparatively inexperienced artist, the second master, did not succeed in deflecting the Venetian development from its traditional course.

Nevertheless, the Agony represents for Venice the beginning of a new phase in the development of the mosaic style. Its pliable style or, rather, that of its third master, became the point of departure for a school of mosaicists that dominated Venetian art for quite a long time.

105

The Paradise

The seventeenth-century composition opposite the Agony on the north wall of the north aisle is compositionally and iconographically unrelated to the original representation in this place. Were it not for the fact that the theme of paradise is attested independently, one would doubt that the subject itself was part of the program.

On the basis of the surviving inscription and a description, it is even possible to venture a reconstruction of the original mosaic. It would have consisted of Abraham, Isaac, and Jacob seated on thrones with the souls of the deceased on their laps, then the Virgin, surrounded by the choirs of angels, then the apostles, martyrs, confessors, and virgins, with an angel above their heads, holding a scroll with the words, VENITE BENEDICTI. With the exception of the inscription, the reconstructed mosaic conforms on the whole with the normal, complete, Middle Byzantine type of representations of paradise within the context of the Last Judgment, somewhat enriched, even inflated, to fill the given space. Thus, it was a parallel of its pendant, the Agony, which is also a normal Byzantine type enriched and enlarged to the greatest possible extent.

The Story of Susanna

The present mosaic of the Judgment of Daniel was made after cartoons of Jacopo Palma (il Giovane) and Jacopo Tintoretto. Nothing is known of its medieval predecessor and the question whether it perpetuates part of the original program cannot be answered with absolute certainty, though a number of factors speak in favor of the assumption that it was. The arrangement of the scenes in two tiers is thoroughly in keeping with thirteenth-century practice, and the present mosaic preserves the divisions separating the six compartments, which continue the divisions between the scenes above illustrating the Infancy of Christ. The lack of symmetry may also have been conditioned by the overall composition of the old mosaic, which, in analogy to similar thirteenth-century compositions, would have relied more on repetitive rhythm than on symmetry. In addition, one of the compositions, the first of the cycle, mirrors the scheme of Christ among the Doctors, in the cycle above. As a matter of fact, the young Daniel sitting in judgment among the older councilors has often been taken as a *typos* of the twelve-year-old Jesus in the Temple. The form and content of the inscriptions do not contradict this hypothesis. If the scenario is authentic, its source can only have been a Western, not a Byzantine work: the story was little known in Byzantium.

The subject above the doorway communicating between the transept and the north wing of the atrium was chosen because of its judgment aspect, the meting out of justice by the impartial judge. The ecclesiastic tribunal seems to have been installed in that part of the atrium. The Susanna story is thus one of a number of motifs, representations, and inscriptions that refer to this function, all found in close vicinity of the Porta Sant'Alipio, which served as an entrance from the piazza into this part of the atrium.

The Communion of the Apostles and Christ at Emmaus

With the panel opposite the Susanna story, we are on much firmer ground. We know that the seventeenth-century mosaic reproduced the subjects and the inscriptions of the thirteenth-century original, as well as the arrangement of the two themes in two stories, similar to the Susanna mosaic. What is more, a drawing made in 1611 contains a fair amount of information about the destroyed original.

Why the two themes were combined in one composition and placed on the east wall of the northern transept is fairly clear from the nature of the subject matter: both representations refer to the Eucharist and were therefore placed together, as close as possible to the presbytery and the main altar. The original composition of the "Liturgy" can be reconstructed as a symmetrical arrangement on either side of the altar with a cross decorating the front and with a chalice and a ciborium in the center. To the left and right of it is a figure of Christ standing on a footstool, handing the bread to Peter on the left and offering the chalice to Paul on the right. The leaders of the apostles are followed by eleven figures on each side. That the full number of apostles was represented twice instead of in the usual division into two groups of six figures was probably suggested by the comparatively long strip to be filled: as in the Agony, the fullest possible version was chosen. The composition follows a nondescript Middle Byzantine type. The representation of all twelve apostles on either side could be regarded as a modern feature, since it became frequent only in the fourteenth century, but it may have been suggested primarily by the format. What little can be deduced about style from the drawing would point to a date prior to the middle of the thirteenth century.

The story of Christ at Emmaus was told in the lower part of the panel in four episodes. The scenario, the number and attitudes of the figures, their costumes, and the compositions of the scenes can be made out in the drawing. The San Marco cycle is one of the few that consist of four scenes: Christ meeting the disciples, the disciples insisting that he remain with them, the supper, and the report to the apostles. The iconographic principles governing the rendering of the Emmaus story in our mosaic are the same as in all the panels hitherto considered: namely, an extension of the scenario to embrace as many phases as possible with the concomitant reduction of the single units to their most elementary forms. All details are derived from Byzantine prototypes of unspecific character and there is no attempt at original interpretation let alone iconographic inventiveness.

The Legend of Saint Leonard

The mosaic on the east wall of the south transept, with scenes from the story of Saint Leonard, is also divided into two tiers, each of which contains three scenes, as in the Susanna story. The theme of the seventeenth-century mosaic is authentic:

1. The baptism of Leonard with King Chlodovech as godfather
2. The saint's prayer assisting the delivery of the queen
3. Leonard healing the sick and giving alms to the poor
4. The saint's prayer making a spring flow
5. Leonard freeing slaves
6. The saint appearing to and liberating a prisoner

The cult of Saint Leonard, who died in 559, became widely diffused after the elevation of his relics in Noblac in the early eleventh century; the first *vita* was written at that time. Venice had special reasons for taking up the cult of the saint: her enterprises and wars, especially in the eastern Mediterranean, caused many Venetians to become prisoners whose liberation might be effected by Saint Leonard's intercession.

Fig. 52. South transept: *Apparitio Sancti Marci,* Discovery of the Relics

We do not know whether the seventeenth-century mosaics perpetuate the thirteenth-century scenario, only that there was in San Marco a cycle of scenes from the legend arranged in two tiers. It may be more than mere coincidence that a man called Leonardo Querini was *primicerius* of San Marco until 1229.

The Apparitio Sancti Marci

Opposite the story of Saint Leonard, on the west wall of the south transept, the last in the sequence of the great panels represents the rediscovery of the patron saint's relics, in two scenes, the *preghiera* (prayer; pls. 33 and 34a) and the *apparitio* (apparition; fig. 52). The panel has been cut off on both ends and must originally have extended around the two corners, filling the narrow wall spaces adjoining on either side. Unfortunately, this was not the only injury that the panel suffered. Some details point to early "restorations," and there have been extensive modern repairs. Nevertheless, the mosaic can be regarded as authentic, including even some original parts.

The subject is highly complex. It purports to represent the miraculous self-revelation of the relics of Mark in their hiding place, the location of which had been forgotten during the building of the present church at the end of the eleventh century. The historical nucleus of this legend was most likely the *collocatio* (elevation) of relics in 1094, which was later turned into an *inventio,* and finally into a miraculous *apparitio.* According to this legend, the lost relics reappeared after three days of fasting and prayer in which the entire Commune Veneciarum, with doge and the clergy, took part. A pillar or column of the church then opened miraculously, revealing the saint's sarcophagus.

Venetian tradition has it that the lost relics reappeared in the southeast pillar of the central dome, more precisely, in the southwestern support of this quadripartite pier. The fact that an Early Byzantine pattern was chosen for the pavement of this part of San Marco suggests that it was singled out as having special importance and as being the "oldest part of the church." One might well ask, then, why the representation of the alleged miraculous apparition was not placed within this sacred precinct, on the east wall of the south transept, instead of on the wall opposite. The most probable explanation of this is that, when the decision was made to have the *apparitio* represented, the east wall was occupied by the Leonard panel, that is, before the "miracle" was invented. Thus, the next-nearest emplacement had to be adopted, the one opposite, on the west wall.

To identify and characterize realistically the exact place of the alleged miracle was, of course, not within the range of possibility of either the designer or his time. While he was able to depict the scene of the *preghiera* "correctly" in the nave of the church along the main axis from the west door to the main altar of the apse, with the chancel barrier and the double lectern in its actual place next to the northeast pier of the central dome, it was beyond his means in the way of spatial representation to "portray" the south transept, with the "miracle pier." The only detail of spatial identification that he could and did employ was the large pulpit which stands next to the southeast pier and thus belongs to the south transept. It is, however, employed only as an attribute and does not clarify the spatial situation. The design does, however, make clear that the location of the miracle is different from that of the prayer.

Such an arrangement fittingly reflects the difference of the two events. The first is without doubt a Mass celebrated on the high altar by a priest in full episcopalia. The event represented in the second half of the mosaic is either the miracle itself, that is, the moment when the wall of the pier opened to reveal the sarcophagus of the saint or the thanksgiving ceremony after the miracle. The "ideal" character of the representation seems to militate against too precise and realistic an interpretation. The performers in both scenes are the clergy, the doge and his advisors, the nobility, and—perhaps—the people. It seems possible to go even further and to identify certain groups and perhaps even individuals. This is provided by the dual nature of these (and many other, especially Venetian) "historical" representations. They relate not only to the historical time of the event they depict but also to the actual "present," the time in which the image was created. In our case, this signifies that what is meant is the

109

"event" of the *apparitio* of 1094, but what are actually represented are ceremonies that would have been performed at the time of the making of the mosaic, in the thirteenth-century ambient, with the two pulpits brought from Constantinople after 1204. At the same time, the setting is understood as the church at the end of the eleventh century. The twofold fidelity goes even further: the doge who leads the prayer and the thanksgiving is at the same time Vitale Falier (1084–96), under whom the miracle was alleged to have taken place, and the doge reigning at the time when the mosaic was made. This is probably true of a good many other figures, beginning with the clergy.

The officiating priest in the prayer and the mitered figure in the miracle are certainly meant to be the patriarch. This is, of course, an anachronism, since in 1094, the date of the alleged *apparitio,* the patriarch of Grado would hardly have led the prayer in the ducal chapel. This did, however, fit the situation in the thirteenth century, when the patriarch resided in Venice, and it would fit especially well the patriarch Jacopo Belegno, who, prior to his elevation to the patriarchal see in 1255, was in fact *primicerius* of San Marco. The attempt to identify some of the secular dignitaries in the two scenes may be more successful than the attempt to identify clerics. The doge in both ceremonial representations is probably Ranieri Zen, who reigned from 1253 to 1268. He was the doge who "reintroduced" the feast of the *apparitio*—which means, most likely, that this motif of the state myth was invented in his time and under his auspices. Thus, we may exclude a date prior to his election in 1253. Ranieri is also known to have been a great believer in miracles, especially if their acknowledgment added to the glory of Venice and its church. A substantial part of his great wealth went into the embellishment of San Marco: he had the piazza paved, and mosaicists were employed in the atrium, where part of the north wing was decorated under his auspices. Ranieri Zen's concern for San Marco also led to the increase of the number and importance of the procuratori and there is a strong possibility that the procuratori are represented in the mosaic of the miracle, behind the doge. These three figures indicate a date of sometime before 1266 when a fourth procurator was installed.

The most interesting and, at the same time, most difficult problems are posed by the two small figures that appear in close connection with noble ladies in front of the group to the left in the miracle. That these are children is clear from the manner in which they attach themselves to two noble Venetian ladies. The only hypothesis that seems to fit the date and evidence is that the crowned youth represents Philip of Courtenay, only son of the Latin emperor of Constantinople, Baldwin II (reigned 1237–61). The child was given by his father to Venetian merchant nobles as security for a substantial loan and taken to Venice. Since in the mosaic he seems to be under fifteen years old, the date of the representation could be tentatively fixed between 1250 and 1255/56. The Venetian lady whose girdle he holds could be one of the members of the Cà Ferro family, in whose house he lived. The other lady who takes precedence could be the dogaressa with a girl of her family. Whether or not this identification is accepted, a date around the middle of the thirteenth century can hardly be doubted.

The religious element is stronger in the first of the two scenes offering two different aspects of this theme. On the left are the clergy, government, and people in intense and humble prayer, all necks bent, half the figures on their knees, some in deep *proskynesis,* others with hands raised. The ranks are intermingled, and the foreground is dominated by canons and choir boys.

Though colorful, the costumes are not rich or elegant. The dominant impression is that of a people united in prayer. In the *apparitio,* or the thanksgiving after the miraculous appearance of the relics, we find not the people, but only the aristocracy, the representatives of the ruling class, divided in groups according to their ranks and clad in their most splendid costumes. Only the patriarch and the doge lift their hands in adoration, and not all heads are turned toward the "miracle pier." With its groups conversing, the mosaic portrays the atmosphere of an exclusive party rather than a scene of religious fervor (pl. 34b). Even in the festive atmosphere of the *apparitio,* however, the doge appears as first among equals, not as a ruler by the grace of God but as the elected head of an aristocratic oligarchy. The two themes, collective prayer and festive assembly in a church, also existed, of course, in Byzantine art, but they lacked the dramatic and supernatural elements of prayer and miraculous fulfillment and offered copious and graded representations of the clergy and of the princely family, but not of the people. The Byzantine dynastic images lack the compositional tension of the Venetian mosaics and also their differentiated, rhythmical grouping. In spite of the lack of true analogies in Byzantine art, the roots of the species that our mosaics represent must be looked for in Byzantium and, more precisely, in Byzantine dynastic art. It is in Byzantium that we find, on a much larger scale than anywhere else, the interpenetration of the religious, the social, and the dynastic elements as a constitutive principle, not only in fact, but also in artistic representation. Wherever we find it in the West, we can be sure of Byzantine influence; moreover, in most Western representations of *translationes* or other religious ceremonies, the social and dynastic elements are lacking. In Venice, at any rate, the indebtedness to Byzantine ideas cannot be doubted. The specific transformation that the Byzantine scheme underwent there is thus all the more impressive.

Stylistically, the mosaics are the work of two teams. It certainly cannot be overlooked that the compositional designs are profoundly different in the two mosaics. It is also patent that the artistic quality and the technical refinement of the second mosaic, the *apparitio,* is considerably higher than that of the *preghiera* even if the ill effects of restoration, which are much stronger in the latter, are discounted. The composition of the prayer is not only broader, it is more prolix. Compared with the firm and at the same time subtle rhythm of the isocephalic groups in the *apparitio,* which pervades and unifies the whole extent of the picture surface, the grouping of the figures in the *preghiera,* which differ greatly in size among each other, lacks logic and cohesion. It is actually divided into three parts—the people, the "government" and clergy, and the officiating priests at the altar; and each of these units is again subdivided horizontally, the lower parts being made up respectively of the triangular group of kneeling people, the clergy in the precinct of the sanctuary enclosed by the chancel barrier, and the block of the altar. The first of these lower units, the triangular group with the rising and descending garland of praying hands, is clearly inspired by the chain of imploring gestures in the Anastasis, a rather unsuccessful attempt at borrowing an earlier motif (fig. 53). No more successful is the experimental introduction of spatial motifs, of such clues to depth as the tract of tiled flooring between the first and second units. Finally, the purely additive stringing up of the domes cannot compare with their ingenious grouping in the *apparitio.*

The technique of the *preghiera* is somewhat bold, with flashing highlights and an almost impressionistic mixing of colors, but also coarser than that of the

Fig. 53. South transept: Prayers for the Discovery of the
Body, kneeling figures in foreground

miracle. Although the palette of the two mosaics is very similar, there are a few
colors that appear only in one or the other. It is a little richer in the *apparitio,* with
a few more translucent colors, and the texture is a little finer, more regular, less
painterly and impressionistic (pl. 35). The organization of labor in the miracle
must have been different from and much more unified than that in the prayer,
where at least four and possibly five different hands can be distinguished in the
heads of the figures alone. It seems almost as if the division of labor was
"horizontal" there and "vertical" in the *apparitio.* The work of one of the
masters in the *preghiera,* the one who set the faces of the female group at the left,
is so closely related to the style of the miracle that the two groups could be the
work of the same or of closely related artists—which means that the chief
master of the *apparitio* or one of his assistants or pupils could have collaborated
in the *preghiera.*

   This partial collaboration in execution links the two representations closely
together, as do, of course, the common frame, the inscription, and especially the
technique. Within the limits of a common style, somewhat parallel differences
can be observed in the other formal qualities: in the *apparitio* everything is more
formalized, refined, even sophisticated, compared with the rougher mode and
attempted realism in the *preghiera.* Although the designer of the latter and his
team were less accomplished artists and craftsmen, they were certainly bolder
and more modern. The style of this team has no visible roots in San Marco itself,
whereas the *apparitio* master can, to a certain extent, be traced back, in the last
analysis, to the great panel of the Agony. The links are provided by some figures
of saints in which the art of the first master of the Agony seems to have been

further developed. Some other elements, such as the clumsy hands and the large forms of the draperies with their cushionlike volumes and sharply indented folds, seem to hark back to the share of the second master of the Agony, especially to the kneeling figure of Christ. The discrepancies between the styles of the Agony and that of the *apparitio,* however, are stronger than the similarities. The gothicisms have disappeared completely, and the graphic element, which is so marked in the first phase of the Agony mosaic, is much less noticeable in the *apparitio.* There is little left of those Late Comnenian forms that still survive in the style of the Agony.

There is evidence that the style of the miracle mosaic was the product of an organic development that took place in San Marco itself during the second quarter of the thirteenth century. If we cannot follow this growth step by step, it is because of the large gaps caused by the destruction, among other works, of four large panels between the Agony and these mosaics. The situation is different with regard to the style of the *preghiera;* we do not have in San Marco a single work that could be regarded as a forerunner of the style of this mosaic. Of course, the possibility that such stylistic predecessors existed among the destroyed mosaics cannot be excluded, but as far as the extant mosaics are concerned, all those that are in some way related are later works, and are in part directly derived from the *preghiera.*

The Venetian element is very strong in both mosaics, in such costume details as the men's fur caps, bonnets, colored stockings and cut-out shoes, and mantles lined with two different kinds of ermine and the women's fillets, diadems, toques, turbans, and strings of pearls. The architectural background, too, representing the interior of San Marco is in a way the sophisticated product of a development which began with the domed arcades of the Clement story in the southern choir chapel. Also Venetian are the technique and the use of certain materials, as are the essential qualities of the style, such as the preponderance of rhythm with a pronounced direction from left to right rather than a centered composition, and the repetitious pattern of hands as an expressive motif.

Several other qualities and tendencies that appear in the style of the *preghiera* mosaic and, to a lesser extent, in that of the *apparitio,* however, are not traceable to earlier Venetian mosaics: the increased volume of figures and plastic details; the modeling by means of sharp "impasto" highlights; the tendency toward physiognomic realism; and finally, the attempt at the representation of space. The increase in volume is essentially characteristic of the stylistic development of the thirteenth century, in Byzantium as well as in the West— indeed perhaps its most important single characteristic. The specific form of the volume style in both mosaics is much nearer to Byzantine than to Western examples: it is more painterly, less exact and sculptural than the Western variety. Some of the plastic modeling is still restricted to details, but some figures already show a pronounced feeling for plastic totality; others even look rather bloated, inflated, as it were, by some internal pressure. In these, all linear patterns that still survive in the others have disappeared or been reduced to parallel ridges and grooves.

Seen from the point of view of Byzantine developments, our two mosaics represent a critical stage, a phase of transition from post-Comnenian to Palaeologan art, with the master of the *apparitio* belonging more to the earlier phase and the workshop of the *preghiera* to the later. However, our mosaics are far from being purely Byzantine works. The tendencies toward physiognomic realism and spatial projection must be sought in the Italian ambient. It is surely no mere chance that physiognomic realism is most noticeable in the kneeling clerics of the prayer; it is as if the monotony of the costumes had suggested to the painter the necessity of facial differentiation. This "intentional" realism seems to have evolved around the middle of the thirteenth century in Tuscany. The Venetian movement was part of a larger Italian development. The representation of space is another aspect of this nascent realism. Two details of the floor, the threshold at the open door at the extreme left and the lower corner of the right-hand leaf of this door at the feet of the girl, also testify to this awareness, as does the daring experiment with the tiled floor.

All in all, the styles of the two mosaics are both genuine Venetian growths. Although the two masters took cognizance of certain new tendencies in both Byzantine and Italian art, their work shows little direct influence from outside.

THE CUPOLAS OF THE TRIBUNES

The six large panels were not the only mosaics made in the thirteenth century for the decoration of the vaults and wall spaces that had become visible from the ground when the gallery floors were removed. Remains of cupola decorations in the northwest and northeast tribunes are preserved, and it seems possible to reconstruct ideal versions of the original programs of all six tribune cupolas.

The southwest tribune of the west dome, above the Porta San Clemente, shows with one exception only baroque mosaics: the exception is the fourteenth-century ornamental motifs of the west lunette and arch, which are so close to the mosaics of the baptistery that they can with certainty be ascribed to the same workshop. The only part of the rest that may still preserve a reminiscence of the thirteenth-century decoration is the calotte of the little dome and its pendentives: it contains an image of Christ with two cherubim and four medallions with busts of the evangelists in the spandrels. The corresponding cupola on the north side, above the Porta San Pietro, has a similar program: the Holy Wisdom between two angels, and again the four evangelists in the pendentives. That this program may indeed be authentic is suggested by the similar scheme in the northwest tribune of the central dome, which is the only iconographically complete cupola decor of the six tribunes (fig. 54). It is treated like a cross-groined vault with a central medallion and four decorative bands dividing the gold surface in four equal sectors. The pendentives are filled with busts of archangels in medallions, wearing classical and imperial costumes alternatively, in a diagonal arrangement. The iconographic scheme, a bust of Christ Pantocrator in the center and archangels in the four pendentives, is a classical Middle Byzantine type.

Insofar as the style of the mosaic can still be regarded as authentic, it seems to precede the *apparitio* and so the date of this part of the decoration is most likely the late second quarter or middle of the thirteenth century.

The fourth little cupola in the series, that of the northeast pier of the central dome seems only to have had a wheel-shaped ornament in the zenith, with rosettes. However, there was in the golden ground of one of the pendentives a distorted, bearded head composed only of golden cubes, that is, realized by texture alone without the help of color. In addition, there were in the gold ground, stars and concentric circular patterns, in part made with specially shaped golden particles—all of it doodles, so to speak, made by a bored mosaic worker.

Fig. 54. Northwest pier of central dome, cupola (Tribuna del Capitello), view looking east *(Böhm)*

The fifth cupola in the southeast pier of the central dome has the same aniconic decor as the fourth. The seventeenth-century cupola decor in the sixth tribune in the southwest pier of the central dome shows Christ, two angels, the Virgin, and a female bust. Thus, in iconographic pattern the six cupola decorations are not much varied. The two easternmost domes have no figural decorations; the middle pair showed Christ Pantocrator, with medallions of angels in the pendentives; and the western pair again Christ, most probably with medallions of the evangelists.

SMALLER PANELS OF THE WALLS OF THE WEST ARM

The main walls of the aisles in the western crossarm of the church are decorated in a more sumptuous manner than those of the transept. These are encrusted with precious and colorful marbles in combinations of veining patterns, the symmetrical arrangement of which makes them appear as so many framed ornamental carpets. In addition, these panels alternate, in the space between two plastic cornices, with mosaics, framed icons of single figures. The latter are not set in niches but flush with the framed marble panels; the two elements of wall

115

decoration are, so to speak, aesthetically equivalent. There can be no doubt that the entire decoration of these side walls was planned and executed as a whole, using the techniques of figural and ornamental sculpture, marble revetment, and mosaic to produce the most opulent effect. On the other three walls of the aisles we find, in addition, *opus sectile* in ornamental and vegetal shapes.

There are five mosaic panels on either wall: on the north wall we find Christ Emmanuel flanked by Hosea, Joel, Micah, and Jeremiah (fig. 55); on the south wall is the Virgin, accompanied by Isaiah, David, Solomon, and Ezekiel. With regard to the representation of prophets, this is surely the richest iconographic program in existence that is not an extension of or supplement to another cycle. Its message is a repetition of that of the east dome, divided into two parts, Christological and Marian. The figures are pure additions, motivated exclusively by the desire to enrich the decorative ensemble.

In spite of certain differences in design and execution, the two series of panels must have been conceived as a unit. They share not only a general arrangement, with four prophets grouped around a central figure toward which they are turning, but also general attitudes, the ornamental frames and flowered meadows, the arrangement and paleographic character of the inscriptions, as well as palette and technique, with mother-of-pearl in the light-colored undergarments and the tablets, and even, to a certain extent, the facial types. The costumes and types in both series are those current in Byzantine and Veneto-Byzantine art, with the exception of the coloristic treatment, especially of the figure of the Virgin. All the prophets are bearded, and most of them of advanced age. Solomon, of course, is young and beardless; he and David are crowned and wear royal garments. The general attitude of the prophets, with right hand raised and left holding a rectangular tablet, is also that customary in Byzantine representations.

Three entire figures, Joel (from Zephaniah), Isaiah, and David, seem to

Fig. 55. West arm, north wall: Joel, Christ Emmanuel, Micah, Jeremiah

have been copied directly from their equivalents of the east dome and Micah and Jeremiah are also related to figures or parts of figures in the same dome. The figure of Christ Emmanuel in the center of the north wall conforms to the current Byzantine type (pl. 36); the special interpretation, however, that was applied to the Byzantine model points in a different direction. The Virgin on the south wall differs from the Orant Virgin of the east dome: her hands are not spread out but held in front of the breast, in a type which in San Marco appears in the central dome (pl. 37a). This latter figure may in fact have been the model of this panel.

Not only were the general types and attitudes of the figures copied from earlier Venetian mosaics but most of the style of the panels is also, so to speak, home-grown. The immediate predecessors of these mosaics were the two large panels above, of which only one, the Agony in the Garden, survives. Most of the plants and blossoms at the feet of the prophets are derived from those in the second and third mountain units of the Agony mosaic; the stars in the background of the Emmanuel panel are in form and technique identical to those in the segments of heaven in the Agony; the weighted tips of hanging folds occur in both works; mother-of-pearl and tinged gold are used in the large and small panels; and white disks or buttons are placed in the middle of concentric arrangements of tesserae. Facial features are also the same, as is the shape of hands and feet. As regards drapery style, the pattern of the Emmanuel figure is a sophisticated variant of the drapery of the second standing Christ in the Agony; more generally, the linear, form-designing drapery style of the prophets is, in fact, an elaboration of the style of the Agony.

At this point, it is necessary to discriminate between the two series of panels, which so far have been treated more or less as a homogeneous whole. The palette and technique show such palpable differences that the two must have been executed by two different mosaicists. The similarities in the design must be explained by these two designers borrowing independently from the mosaics of the east dome. Both adapted their models in their individual ways to the sophisticated, elegant, and decorative style of their period. The adaptation concerns first the proportions: from massive and stocky figures with large heads they have become slender and small-headed (fig. 56). In the second place, the relief of the drapery has changed materially and characteristically: the comparatively few, heavy, and clumsy motifs have been transformed into a multitude of small, smooth forms, thin ridges, and incisions (pl. 37b).

Thus, the two series are certainly the work of two masters working with their assistants under the general leadership or after the master plan of a supremely gifted decorator, who may actually have been one of the two masters. The characteristic differences between the two groups suggest that there was also a certain difference in the dates of their execution. There can hardly be any doubt that the north series preceded the south series at least by a few years. The north group is much closer to the style of the Agony panel, the execution of which must have preceded the decoration of the wall space below. Its figures are more organic in build and attitude and modeled in a more convincing relief (pl. 38a and figs. 57 and 58), while those of the south series tend toward the abstract, the decorative. This and the change of the palette from the north to the south series correspond to general tendencies within the development of Venetian mosaic work. Another argument for the somewhat later date of the south series is a characteristic and irreversible change in the attitude of the two masters toward the Byzantine heritage and the introduction

Fig. 56. West arm, north wall: Hosea

CHAPTER SEVENTEEN

Fig. 57. North transept:
Anthony *(Böhm)*

Fig. 58. North transept:
Macarius *(Böhm)*

of Western elements. So far, only the Venetian components of the styles of the
two series have been considered, but now the question arises whether the style
of these figures can be explained on the basis of the Venetian development alone
or whether they also contain new and foreign elements, Byzantine as well as
Western.

Most if not all the Byzantine features of the two series were certainly
already endemic in Venice at the time. This could apply even to the format as
such, although it is not impossible that Byzantine templon icons, framed
wooden icons, or even manuscript illuminations played a certain part. It should
be kept in mind, however, that the Byzantine one-figure icon had already been
adopted in Italian painting by about 1220 and that even the overstepping and

119

overlapping of the frame occurred in the earliest Italian examples. It cannot be excluded that the framed, high, rectangular, one-figure icon was already known in Venice and thus need not have been a recent import from Byzantium.

More important still: neither the north nor south series shows any new influence of the monumental style that developed in Byzantium at the turn of the century and of which an intimation appeared in Venice in the work of the second master of the Agony, only to vanish again with the disappearance of this artist. Neither this Venetian version nor any other offshoot of this movement seems to have made any impression on our mosaicists. It goes almost without saying that there is not the slightest trace to be found, in our figures, of the subsequent Byzantine development, that of the volume style. In brief, there is nothing here that goes beyond the stage of the third master of the Agony, as far as the reception of Byzantine influences is concerned: the basis of the style is, in the main, still the Late Comnenian style, with even a certain tendency to revert to the style of the central dome or the Anastasis.

The situation is quite different as regards Western features and influences. To ascribe the strong decorative tendencies in the style of the panels to direct Western influence would perhaps be saying too much and too little at the same time: this trend seems to have been generally part of the Venetian atmosphere, which, in the thirteenth century, became increasingly tinged with Western elements. It is, therefore, not necessary to assume specific Western influences to explain this general decorative quality. Whether the inclination toward a kind of zigzag style noticeable in a number of our figures is to be ascribed to Western influence or whether we are confronted here with an evolutionary parallel can hardly be decided yet. For the rest, the entire question of Western influence in Venice is complicated by the fact that most of the Western phenomena that can be adduced as analogies themselves originated under strong Byzantine influence, so that some features in our mosaics that can be paralleled in Western works are, in the last analysis, of Byzantine origin—and, vice versa: some Byzantine-looking features may have been transmitted to Venice by Western models. If we add to this the manifestations of the mixed West-East atmosphere of Venice itself, the complexity of the problems will be apparent.

There are, however, a few more specific features that must be regarded as being due to definable Western influence. Among these is the gothicism in the shapes of hands and feet. Good parallels can be found in France, the Meuse country, and western Germany, where these fashionable forms appear as early as 1180. The ornamental background of the Virgin panel, which points in the same general direction, is reminiscent of French miniatures, stained glass, or enamels. Western influence is certainly apparent as well in the tendency toward the simplification of contours and toward surface flatness as against high relief.

Since the north group is stylistically dependent on the Agony, which must be dated between 1215 and 1225, it probably originated around 1225–30, with the south series following at about 1230–35.

THE ARCHES

The series of standing figures of saints added to the hagiographic pantheon of San Marco in the thirteenth century fills those arches of the cupola piers that connect with the side aisles and are not visible from the main space of the nave and transepts. These arches, which before had been in the dark, became available for decoration only after the removal of the gallery floors; the same applies to the narrow arches on the outer walls of the aisles. In addition to four saints without names, the saints include:

Gerardus Sagredo, one of the few saints of Venetian extraction, is the Venetian protomartyr so to speak (pl. 38b).

Opposite Gerardus is Paul Martyr, who died in Constantinople as a defender of images. His relics were brought to Venice in 1222 and were deposited in San Giorgio. It is quite clear that this *translatio* was the reason he was represented.

Bassus was bishop and martyr under Decius. His cult was observed in the church next to San Marco. His companion is Ubaldus, bishop of Gubbio, who was canonized in 1192 and was invoked for protection against evil spirits.

Julian and his wife Basilissa were fourth-century martyrs of Antinoë (pl. 39a). They had a church in Venice at least from the eleventh century.

Homobonus, merchant of Cremona, a benefactor of the poor and founder of pious societies, was canonized in 1199. His companion is Bonifacius, who could be either the "apostle of the Frisians" or the bishop of Ferentino. The latter would fit better as the counterpart to Homobonus.

Catarina is, of course, the legendary martyr of Alexandria, whose feast was one of the great Venetian festivals. Her companion is Mary Magdalen; she, too, had an early cult in Venice.

The recent acquisition of their relics may have been the reason for the representation of two nameless saints in one of the arches of the southwest pier of the central dome. Whether the translation of relics was also the cause for the inclusion of Paul the Hermit, whose relics were brought to Venice in 1240 is not certain; his cult in Venice preceded the translation of his relics. He is accompanied by the hermit Hilarion, the fourth-century founder of Palestinian monasticism. In most representations, Paul's companion is the holy abbot and hermit Anthony, who, however, is represented outside the central group in the north transept, together with Macarius. Both are connected with Alexandria.

The corresponding pair includes Saint Sirus, who, according to Aquileian legend, was consecrated by Saint Hermagoras as the first bishop of Pavia. This makes it very likely that the corresponding figure, mysteriously labelled "Henhoc" is Hermogenes, another saint related to Hermagoras.

One of the unnamed figures in the narrow arch above the treasury undoubtedly represents Saint Francis of Assisi. He shows the stigmata and is clad in the distinctive garments of the Friars Minor (fig. 59). The other figure, usually regarded as representing Saint Dominic, in fact portrays Saint Benedict (fig. 60). The idea behind the coupling of the figures was apparently that of paralleling the founder of the new mendicant order with the founder of Western monasticism par excellence. It is very likely that these figures were among the latest additions to the pantheon of saints represented in the interior of San Marco. They probably originated about the middle of the thirteenth century and mark the appearance of a contemporary movement that was to transform religious thought and feeling even in conservative Venice.

If the saints of the earlier arcade series are little more than names in a litany, those of the thirteenth-century cycle are mostly individuals selected for very specific reasons. The series not only has a distinctive character, it must have also had a certain actuality for contemporary beholders. Some figures represent contemporary saints; others are connected with recent acquisitions or translations of relics; some testify to the newly awakened interest in monasticism;

121

Fig. 59. South transept: Francis
of Assisi *(Böhm)*

Fig. 60. South transept: Benedict
(Böhm)

others, such as Homobonus and Bonifacius, are connected with the rise of
charitable institutions.

With regard to placement, the series of saints divides into three groups.
The western group occurs on the two arches of the aisles, facing the Porta San
Clemente and Porta San Pietro, respectively, and also on the narrow arch of the
south wall next to the first of these doors. The central group comprises ten
(originally twelve) figures. These are not framed but are richly attired. The third
group originally included eight or even twelve figures, of which six are preserved; they are placed in the eastern part of the church. All have been restored
repeatedly. The decorative framing of several of the saints with canopies is
derived from Byzantine templon icons. Venice itself has an important relief
icon, the marble icon in Santa Maria Mater Domini, which was most likely part
of the Constantinopolitan booty of 1204 and may, with others, have influenced
the frames. Also of Byzantine origin are most of the other decorative elements
and motifs.

The types of the two hermit saints conform in the main to those current in

122

Byzantine painting, except that Hilarion is shown nude (pl. 39b). These show that no new Byzantine models were employed for the figures or ornamental frames, or for the style, the palette, and the technique of the mosaics. In all these respects, they are simply the continuation of the prophets nearby, more particularly of the style and technique of the south series. The two arches are certainly the work of two masters, and it is possible to detect in the north pair the first signs of a certain simplification. The two figures on the narrow arch of the south wall next to the Porta San Clemente are, so to speak, the poor relations of the two hermits.

The series of the prophets and saints bridges the gap between the Agony panel and the twin mosaic of the *preghiera* and *apparitio*. Work on the saints seems to have proceeded from west to east, the line of development going from a highly decorative, linear, and flat style toward a stronger relief, an indication of volume, and a more painterly treatment of details.

In connection with the series we have a few termini; Ubaldus was canonized in 1192, Homobonus in 1199; the relics of Paul Martyr were taken to Venice in 1222. Work on the figures in the transept and the east part of the church may have lasted well into the early fifties, close to the date of the *apparitio,* to the style of which the latest figures of the series are intimately related.

THE LUNETTES ABOVE THE DOORS

Four doors of the interior are decorated with lunettes consisting of elaborate frames around figural mosaics. The one above the treasury door has a terminus post quem of 1231, the date of the burning of the old treasury. According to documents and chronicles, the fire spared a reliquary with a fragment of the True Cross; this was considered a miracle, and the mosaic that fills the ogee of the frame alludes quite clearly to the event by showing two angels holding the reliquary, a golden rectangle with a cross (fig. 61). The mosaic can hardly have been made before 1235, which brings us to about the same date as that of the series of prophets on the south wall of the western crossarm. As a matter of fact, there can be no doubt that the lunette is the work of the artist who set the south series of prophets. The iconographic scheme of two angels guarding a cross between them is indeed an old one. The most interesting feature of the mosaic is perhaps its restricted palette. Together with the gold of the relief frame, the lunette gives the impression of being itself a kind of reliquary.

The lunette of the south door shows only the nimbed half-figure of Saint Mark. The simplicity of the decor is hardly in keeping with the ritual importance of the door, which leads into the courtyard of the doge's palace and which played a major part in the ceremonies of the ducal liturgy. Although restored in the second half of the nineteenth century, the mosaic should be dated on stylistic grounds around the middle of the thirteenth century.

With its brilliant colors and elaborate marble frame, the Deesis above the main door dominates the west wall (fig. 62). It comprises three figures: an Enthroned Christ flanked by two standing figures, the Virgin on the left and Saint Mark on the right. Christ's head is surrounded by a cruciform halo with a checkered contour in black and white. The painterly technique of white highlights dominates the incarnadine of Christ's face, hands, and feet. The figure of the Virgin is considerably less colorful than that of Christ, but the

123

Fig. 61. South transept, door to tesoro: angels *(Böhm)*

CHAPTER SEVENTEEN

Fig. 62. West door: lunette with Deesis *(Alinari)*

painterly approach may be seen there too. The white lights in face and hands are even more conspicuous. The painterly technique is still bolder in the figure of Mark, and, indeed, the whole mosaic is coloristically very bold but at the same time so richly differentiated that no single color covers a large area without being energetically graded in itself or shot through with other colors. The master, though perhaps not a great designer or draftsman, was certainly a great colorist and able technician.

The placing of the Deesis on the inner west wall had nothing to do with the fact that in the vault above there was a representation of the Last Judgment. Actually, the mosaic is not a true Deesis at all, since John the Baptist is here

125

replaced by Mark. Rather, it is a special Deesis, fashioned especially for the church of the evangelist. The substitution of the male figure is, in fact, not too rare, and the theological content is intercession, the same as that of the traditional Deesis. It is not surprising that in Venice, Mark's intercession was thought more effective than any other saint's.

Along with the theological meaning, the compositional scheme of the regular Middle Byzantine Deesis was retained in our mosaic. The arrangement with the Enthroned Christ in the center was certainly the most frequent scheme, but it was not the only one: San Marco itself has an example of the other important type, that with the standing Christ, in the relief set into the south wall of the west arm, next to the door that leads into the baptistery. San Marco also followed the current Middle Byzantine scheme as regards the format, which permits a well-balanced filling that is neither empty nor overcrowded.

The Deesis is connected with the *preghiera* in a number of ways, beginning with the types of the figures, the bold colorism, and a certain emptiness in the faces. There can be no doubt that both mosaics are the work of the same master, although the Deesis would seem to be slightly later in date because of the bolder use of white highlights, the stronger volume of the figures, and the adoption of forms that must already be classed as Early Palaeologan. Seen as a whole, the style of the Deesis is more strongly Byzantine than that of the *preghiera*. Some of this may be due to the fact that the Deesis is a Byzantine theme while the *preghiera* is not and that more "modern" prototypes would probably have been available for the former. This would not, however, explain the more strongly Byzantine character of small details and especially of the technique. In view of these traits we must assume that the mosaicist had an opportunity, between the *preghiera* and the Deesis, to see contemporary Greek works or works under strong contemporary Greek influence.

The half-figure of the evangelist John above the door leading from the north transept into the north wing of the atrium is connected with the original dedication of the altar directly opposite in the east bay of the north transept and with the theme of the cupola mosaics above. The style of the sculptured frame already shows the influence of Palaeologan decorative sculpture and must be dated to the last quarter of the thirteenth century. This must also be the date of the mosaic within the frame which belongs in the orbit of the latest mosaics of the atrium.

126

The Mosaics of the Atrium:
Setting and Subject Matter

18

THE INCENTIVES that led the Venetians to extend the mosaic decoration of the atrium to incorporate a vast series of Old Testament scenes were threefold: (1) jealousy of Sicily and Rome and a desire to emulate them, (2) "imperial" propaganda coupled with the well-known archaistic tendencies of the Venetian "proto-Renaissance," and (3) the influx of riches from occupied Constantinople, in money, material, and models. Another incentive may have been the need to carry out some repairs after the earthquake of 1223, architectural repairs that, once begun, may have suggested the extension of the vaulting system to include the north wing, which was either built or enclosed at that time. The north wing of the atrium surely must have been at least planned in detail at the time when its program of decoration with scenes from the Old Testament was worked out, but the stylistic gap between the first and second Joseph cupolas suggests that the vaulting of the north wing as a whole was not yet complete when the mosaicists finished the first chapter of Joseph's history. Whether the vaulting of the entire west tract including the corner cupola was also carried out only in the thirteenth century or at an earlier period can hardly be made out without extensive soundings. In any case, it must have preceded that of the north wing by a considerable margin, a fact that can be deduced from the differences in the shape of the vaults—those of the north wing being strongly pointed—and the decor of the stone cornices of the cupolas. Although examples of an enfolding narthex were known in Byzantium, the idea of extending the atrium in San Marco need not have been suggested by any foreign model.

Prior to 1200, the present Cappella Zen, which continued (or preceded) the west tract of the atrium in the south, existed as an entrance hall, a south vestibule. Originally, it seems to have terminated in an apse, suggesting perhaps the row of "apses" of the north wing. This feature may have recommended itself for technical reasons: by this artifice an essential part of the buttressing system was transferred from the north facade, which lacks the deep recesses of the west front, into the interior. It also had important consequences for the layout of the mosaic program.

The doorways that lead into the atrium from outside and from the atrium into the interior provided several axes important for the iconographic arrangement and visual composition of the decor. The west wing has no fewer than three of these axes pointing from west to east and corresponding to three

Fig. 63. Atrium, north wing, view looking east *(Alinari)*

CHAPTER EIGHTEEN

doorways of the facades, almost in line with the three doors of the church's west wall, and another axis, from south to north, that extends from the doorway of the Cappella Zen to the apsidal niche of the corner of Sant' Alipio. This niche thus became the focal point of the vista from the sea entrance and, consequently, lent itself to a special treatment in the context of the atrium decoration.

The north wing has only one axis, that from west to east, from the Porta di Sant' Alipio to the Porta della Madonna, again with an "apse" as focus (fig. 63). This apse was also singled out for special treatment.

Generally speaking, only the entrance vistas, not the exit vistas, are especially accentuated. This may have had psychological as well as practical, that is optical, reasons: the exit vistas are adversely conditioned by being directed against the light, and the mosaics in these places (above entrance doors) are therefore hardly visible. The most important vistas were, and still are (apart from the central doorway), the two of the most frequented entrances, the south entrance and that through the Porta di Sant' Alipio. The first gave the complete view of the west wing, the second that of the entire length of the north wing. Both terminated in "apses" with iconographic content that sets them apart from the rest of the decoration.

There was, of course, one part of the atrium that was already decorated, namely, the entrance bay. This bay (the later *pozzo*) had to be exempted from the new scheme and was, in fact, treated as a foreign body, with the Old Testament narrative jumping from the barrel vault south of the entrance bay to that north of it.

Because the program was planned from the very beginning to fill the entire extent of the atrium, it had to provide for the filling of six cupolas, two broad barrel vaults, five transversal and several longitudinal arches, six flat lunettes, five apsidal niches, the latter all in the north wing, and some odd spaces above the doorways of the west wall. This rich decoration, with its innumerable small-scale figures, has, of course, not come down to us in its original form. There are significant replacements, particularly of the seventeenth century, but during the nineteenth century there was destructive restoration, including a great deal of removal of the mosaics and reapplication after the repair of the masonry and the cleaning of the mosaic crust. In view of its tormented history, one can hardly expect any part of the mosaic decor of the atrium to have escaped restoration and to present itself today in its original freshness.

DESCRIPTION

Given these circumstances, one might well ask how far the mosaics of the atrium can be trusted iconographically. This question must certainly be answered in the negative with regard to the baroque compositions in the "apses" and lunettes of the north wing. It seems, though, that in those cases in which the restorers were intent on preserving or simulating the medieval aspect of the scenes, they would certainly have retained the original compositions and, as far as possible, the original attitudes, costumes, and types of the figures as well. Thus, there are no grounds for doubting the iconographic authenticity of the "restored" mosaics. The question of their stylistic authenticity is much more complicated.

An entirely different problem is that of accuracy on the part of the original mosaicists in following the preparatory drawings, the *sinopie*. Soundings by F.

Forlati have shown a marked difference in the relation of figures and building between the *sinopia* and the finished mosaic in the scene preceding Cain slaying Abel. It seems that we are confronted with a last-minute adjustment on the part of the mosaicist, made probably for compositional reasons, which shows that there existed a certain margin of freedom in the interpretation of preparatory drawings.

First Bay of the West Wing (Pl. 40)

The mosaic is very dirty, neglected, and patched, and many cubes are missing. There is some foreign material. Many of the details are almost caricatures of the original.

The scenes of the Creation are arranged in three rings around a central motif. Cherubim are represented in the four pendentives (pl. 44a), with decorative trees filling the spandrels. The episodes are:

First ring
Spirit above the Waters
Separation of Light from Darkness (pl. 41)
Creation of the Firmament
Separation of the Seas and the Dry Land
Creation of the Plants (fig. 64)

Second ring
Creation of the Heavenly Bodies
Creation of the Birds and the Marine Creatures (pl. 42)
Blessing of the Birds and the Marine Creatures
Creation of the Terrestrial Animals
Forming of Adam (fig. 65)
Blessing of the Seventh Day
Animation of Adam
Introduction of Adam into Paradise

Third ring
Naming of the Animals
Creation of Eve
Introduction of Adam and Eve
Temptation of Eve
Eve Plucking Fruit and Bringing It to Adam
Covering with Fig Leaves
Adam and Eve Hiding from the Presence of the Lord
Denial of Guilt
Punishment of Adam and Curse of the Serpent (fig. 66)
Clothing of Adam and Eve
Expulsion, Adam's and Eve's Labors (pl. 43)

East Lunette of South Bay

Begetting of Cain (pl. 44b)
Birth of Abel
Sacrifice of Cain and Abel

South Lunette of South Bay

Wrath of Cain
Lord Speaking to Cain

Fig. 64. Atrium, Creation cupola: Creation of the Plants

Fig. 65. Atrium, Creation cupola: Forming of Adam

Fig. 66. Atrium, Creation cupola: Punishment of Adam and Curse of the Serpent

CHAPTER EIGHTEEN

Ham Beckoning His Brothers Shem and Japheth
Shem and Japheth Covering Noah
Noah Cursing Canaan
Burial of Noah (pl. 47a)

West Half of Vault North of Entrance Bay (Fig. 72)

Building of the Tower of Babel
Appearance of the Lord at Babel and the Confounding of Languages (pl. 47b)

Second Cupola, West Wing (Pl. 48)

The mosaic was repaired and greatly restored in the nineteenth century. The
present seemingly good state of preservation is deceptive.

Lord Speaking to Abraham
Departure to Canaan (pl. 49a)

Fig. 67. Atrium, entrance bay, south vault, west half

Fig. 68. Atrium, entrance bay, south vault: Noah Ordered to Build Ark, right section

Fig. 69. Atrium, entrance bay, south vault, east half

Fig. 70. Atrium, entrance bay, south vault: Noah Sending
Forth the Raven and the First Dove, Noah, dove

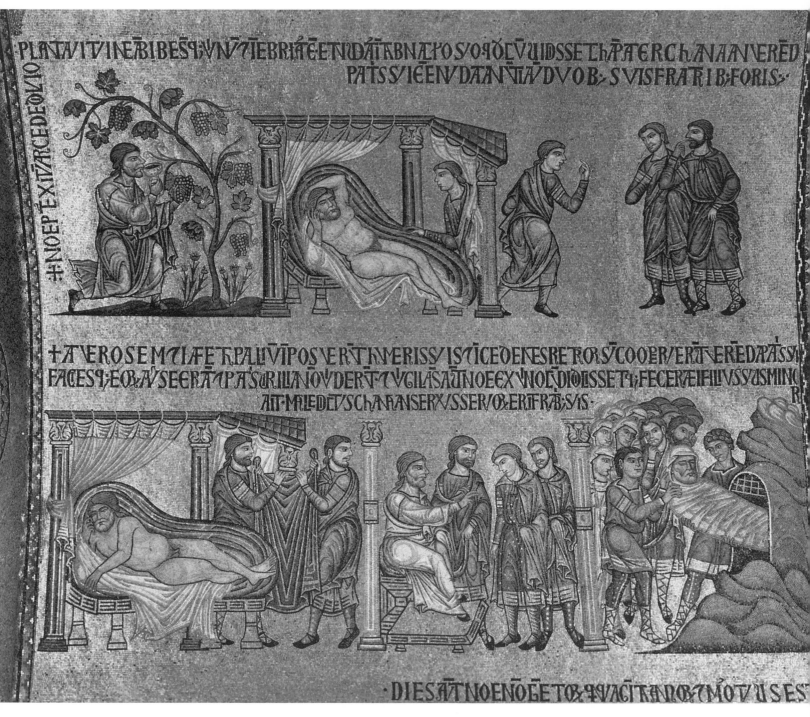

Fig. 71. Atrium, entrance bay, north vault, east half

CHAPTER EIGHTEEN

Fig. 72. Atrium, entrance bay, north vault, west half *(Alinari)*

Journey to Canaan (fig. 73)
Abraham Speaking with the Lord
Abraham Arming His Servants for the Liberation of Lot
Meeting of Abraham and Melchizedek and Men of Aner, Eshcol, and Mamre
Taking Their Portion (fig. 74)
Abraham and the King of Sodom
Lord's Covenant with Abraham
Hagar Given to Abraham
Abraham Handing Hagar over to Sarah
Discourse between Hagar and the Angel (fig. 75)
Birth of Ishmael
Lord Speaking to Abraham
Circumcision of Ishmael
Circumcision of All the Men

East Lunette

Abraham Meeting the Angels (fig. 76)
Hospitality of Abraham (pl. 50)

West Lunette

Birth of Isaac (pl. 49b)
Circumcision of Isaac

Pendentives

Isaiah
Ezekiel
Jeremiah
Daniel

Niche above Porta San Pietro

St. Peter

Corner Bay

The ornament on the arch preceding the bay and some on the adjoining arch date to the eighteenth century. Numerous, and in part clumsy, repairs were carried out in the nineteenth century. The bay was completely restored in 1909/10. On the whole, the state of preservation seems fair.

Arch between Second and Third Cupolas

Justice
St. Alipio
St. Simeon

Cupola with the Life of Joseph, 1 (Pl. 51)

Joseph's Dream of the Sheaves and of the Stars
Joseph Telling His Dreams to His Brethren
Joseph Telling His Dreams to His Father and Brethren
Man Showing Joseph the Way to Dothan
Brethren Seeing Joseph Coming
Joseph Thrown into the Pit (pl. 52)
Brethren Feasting (pl. 52)
Lifting of Joseph from the Pit

Fig. 73. Atrium, Abraham cupola: Journey to Canaan

Fig. 74. Atrium, Abraham cupola: Meeting of Abraham and Melchizedek,
Men of Aner, Eshcol, and Mamre Taking Their Portion

Fig. 75. Atrium, Abraham cupola: Discourse between Hagar and the Angel

140

Fig. 76. Atrium, Abraham cupola, east lunette: Abraham Meeting the Angels

141

Joseph Sold to the Midianites
Midianites Bring Joseph to Egypt
Reuben Returning to the Pit
Jacob Rending His Clothes (fig. 77)

Pendentives

Samuel (fig. 78)
Nathan
Habakkuk (fifteenth-century replacement)
Eli

Lunette, West Wall

Tree with two magpies (left), fountain with two egrets (right)

North Apse

Judgment of Solomon (sixteenth century)

Arch between First and Second Cupolas

Charity
St. Phocas
St. Christopher with Christ (sixteenth century)

North Wing, First Bay

The mosaics of this bay have suffered more from destruction and bad restoration than those of the preceding ones. Extensive restorations were completed during the nineteenth century and again in 1910–15.

Cupola with Life of Joseph, 2 (Pl. 53)

Joseph Sold to Potiphar
Potiphar Making Joseph Overseer
Potiphar's Wife Casting Eyes on Joseph
Potiphar's Wife Catches Joseph's Garment (fig. 79)
Potiphar's Wife Displays Garment to the People of Her House (pl. 54a)
Joseph Thrown into Prison
Pharaoh Throwing the Butler and the Baker into Prison (pl. 54b)
Dream of the Butler and Dream of the Baker
Joseph Interprets the Dreams of the Butler and the Baker

Pendentives

Butler Serving Pharaoh (pl. 55)
Baker Crucified
Pharaoh Dreaming
Pharaoh's Dream of Seven Fat and Seven Lean Kine (nineteenth century)

South Lunette (Fig. 80)

Pharaoh's Dream of the Seven Ears of Corn
Pharaoh and the Egyptian Magicians
Butler before Pharaoh

Fig. 77. Atrium, first Joseph cupola: Jacob Rending His Clothes

North Apse

According to an early description, the narrative cycle was continued on the north side with three scenes: Joseph groomed and brought before Pharaoh, Joseph interpreting the dreams of Pharaoh, and Pharaoh making Joseph governor of Egypt. The three scenes were replaced in the seventeenth century by one composition showing Joseph interpreting Pharaoh's dreams.

Arch between Second and Third Cupolas of Joseph Story

Hope
St. Agnes
St. Catherine (sixteenth century)
St. Silvester
St. Geminianus (sixteenth century)

North Wing, Second Bay

No wholesale repairs or replacements seem to have been carried out before the general restoration campaign of the atrium in the 1880s and 1890s. All the mosaics are very dirty, and there is a good deal of damage. The original mosaics

143

Fig. 78. Atrium, first Joseph cupola, southeast corner *(Strempel)*

CHAPTER EIGHTEEN

Fig. 79. Atrium, second Joseph cupola: Potiphar's Wife Catches Joseph's Garment

Fig. 80. Atrium, second Joseph cupola, south lunette

of the north niche were destroyed in the fourteenth century when the "apse" was transformed into a barrel-vaulted niche.

Cupola with the Life of Joseph, 3 (Pl. 56)

Joseph Gathering Corn (fig. 81, pl. 57)
Birth of Manasseh and Ephraim (fig. 82)
Egyptians Crying for Bread
Joseph Selling Corn (pl. 58)
Jacob Sending His Sons to Egypt
Joseph Orders One of the Brethren to Be Bound
Joseph Turning and Weeping
Joseph Having Simeon Bound (fig. 83)

South Lunette (Fig. 84)

Emptying of the Sacks before Jacob
Jacob Giving Benjamin to His Sons
Brethren Load Their Asses
Brethren Brought into Joseph's House

Arch around the South Lunette

St. Cecilia
St. Cassianus
St. Cosmas
St. Damian
St. Gaudentius
St. Marinus

Pendentives

St. Matthew
St. Mark
St. Luke
St. John (pl. 59)

North Apse

The original north apse was replaced in the fourteenth century by a rectangular niche and barrel vault. In the vault are mosaic figures of Sts. Apollinaris, Sigismund, Francis of Assisi, and Anthony of Padua, all of the seventeenth century. The figures do not seem to belong to the original program, although the existence of two of them is attested as early as 1381.

Arch between the Fifth and Sixth Cupolas

Queen of Sheba
St. Blaise
St. Nicholas
St. Peter Martyr
St. Dominic

North Wing, Third Bay

The state of preservation of the sixth cupola and its north apse is the result of several nineteenth- and twentieth-century campaigns. The south lunette is a seventeenth-century work; the east apse is a bad but iconographically depend-

146

Fig. 81. Atrium, third Joseph cupola: Joseph Gathering Corn

147

Fig. 82. Atrium, third Joseph cupola: Birth of Manasseh and Ephraim

CHAPTER EIGHTEEN

Fig. 83. Atrium, third Joseph cupola: Joseph Having Simeon Bound

149

Fig. 84. Atrium, third Joseph cupola, south lunette

CHAPTER EIGHTEEN

able nineteenth-century copy. In the apse and in the cupola and its pendentives, the main damage was done during the restoration campaign of the late 1880s, when the mosaics were taken off and radically restored. The whole is much discolored by dirt.

Cupola with the Life of Moses (Pl. 60)

Basket with Infant Moses Put into and Taken out of River
Moses Presented to Pharaoh's Daughter
Ordeal of Moses (fig. 85 and pl. 61a)
Egyptian Maltreating an Old Hebrew (fig. 86)
Moses Looking Around (fig. 86)
Moses Slaying the Egyptian (fig. 86)
Moses with Two Hebrews
Moses Wandering (Flight of Moses)
Moses at the Well
Moses and the Daughters of Jethro at the Well (pl. 62)
Moses Driving Away the Shepherds (pl. 61b)
Moses Received by Jethro, Priest of Midian
Moses at the Burning Bush (fig. 87)

South Lunette

Crossing the Red Sea (seventeenth century, after destroyed original)

Arch around South Lunette

Medallions of Sts. Paternianus, Fantinus, Juliana, Augustine, Magnus, and
    Lucia

Apse above the North Door (Pl. 63)

Miracles of the Manna and the Quails
Miracle of Water from the Rock

Pendentives

Zechariah
Malachi
David
Solomon

Apse above the East Door

The Virgin Enthroned between St. John the Evangelist and St. Mark

The iconographic authenticity of this nineteenth-century copy of the lost original is confirmed by an early description.

Fig. 85. Atrium, Moses cupola: Ordeal of Moses

CHAPTER EIGHTEEN

Fig. 86. Atrium, Moses cupola: Egyptian Maltreating an Old Hebrew,
Moses Looking Around, Moses Slaying the Egyptian

153

Fig. 87. Atrium, Moses cupola: Moses at the Burning Bush

PROGRAM

The most conspicuous foreign body in the program of the atrium mosaics is the sixteenth-century representation of the Judgment of Solomon. Inasmuch as no alternative theme comes to mind for this spot, however, the authenticity of the subject must be considered. Together with lost inscriptions, the theme served as an admonition to judges, and the themes of justice, just conduct, and righteousness are also sounded in the scrolls of Habakkuk and Samuel. Another inscription placed above the Porta Sant'Alipio continues the theme with words that recall verses on the Bridge Gate at Capua erected for Emperor Frederick II between 1235 and 1240. The two inscriptions may have been connected, not only as regards their message—the threat to criminals and unbelievers and the glorification of justice—but even historically. Frederick, who came to Venice in 1232, officially to worship the evangelist and to bring precious gifts for San

Marco, may actually have seen the inscription in the atrium and been so impressed by it that he modeled the Capuan inscription after it. It would, however, be rash to take this as a fact and to construe on the strength of it a terminus ante or ad quem of 1232 for the mosaics of the corner bay.

The theme of justice and judgment is strengthened by the bust of Justitia on the south arch; furthermore, it should be noted that the Porta della Madonna, which is approached in a straight line east from the Porta Sant'Alipio, leads into the north transept, where we find, above this entrance, another Old Testament theme displayed in a sequence of scenes in mosaic, namely, the story of Susanna and the Judgment of Daniel. It is, therefore, perhaps not too daring to assume that the stretch of the atrium between these two representations of the Good Judge—that is, the north wing or part of it—was used as a tribunal, perhaps of an ecclesiastic court. The seat of the judge may well have stood in the "apse" below the Judgment of Solomon.

Another foreign body in the decoration of the atrium appears in the last but one vaulted niche of the north wall, namely, the seventeenth-century representation of four saints in full figure. This does not belong to the original program.

Some sixteenth-century mosaics in the tomb niches of the west wing were supplanted by simple golden ground in 1885, but it is not known whether there existed originally any medieval mosaics in these places.

Thus, the program of the atrium consists of several elements: first, the Old Testament cycle, accompanied by prophets and angels; second, a series of saints, including the Virgin and the evangelists; third, a representation of the Judgment of Solomon, and fourth, three allegories of virtues.

The Old Testament Cycle

Quite a number of reasons can be imagined why the Old Testament was chosen for extensive illustration. One powerful motive may have been the desire to draw level with, or even to surpass, the Norman rivals by imitating the extensive narrative programs of the Sicilian churches, programs that were conceived and in part executed later than the great program of the interior of San Marco. Next to Sicily, Rome may have provided an incentive for the choice of an extensive Old Testament cycle for the program of the atrium. Old Testament cycles were much favored in Rome from the late eleventh century, most in connection with the revival of the Early Christian cycles of Saint Peter's and Saint Paul's. From Rome, the vogue spread over central and southern Italy in both monumental and miniature painting. Independent of the Roman movement, Old Testament cycles became important parts of church decorations in France and England, partly as adaptations of Early Christian and Early Byzantine manuscript illustrations. In the thirteenth century, Old Testament cycles became not only more numerous but also more comprehensive, especially in French stained glass and in the gigantic series of the *Bible moralisée*. Early Christian and Early Byzantine recensions of Old Testament cycles, especially Genesis, exerted a profound influence on the monumental decoration in Italy and the West, an influence that was perhaps stronger in Venice than anywhere else, with the possible exception of Rome. The cause of this strong influence was the fact that a representative of one of the most important Early Byzantine redactions, the Cotton Genesis, was in Venice at the crucial moment, as was almost certainly the Vienna Genesis. Venice was thus not merely influenced by the contemporary vogue of Old Testament illustration but was surely one of the centers to receive and even propagate this influence.

155

Contemporary Byzantine monumental painting cannot have played a decisive part in this vogue. Large Old Testament cycles, although of great importance in Middle Byzantine book illumination, hardly occupied an important place in Middle Byzantine church decoration. The recommendation of Canon 82 of the Quinisextum (the Synod *In trullo,* 692) to represent in the churches not the "shadows" of the history of salvation in the Old Testament but the realities of the New Testament was, by and large, followed until about 1300.

The likelihood is that the impulse to represent a large Old Testament cycle in San Marco did not come from Byzantium but from the West, in the first place, from Italy—the more so since in Italy the place of Old Testament representations was also the western part of the church building, the atrium, as in San Marco, or the nave (or aisles). Thus, there existed a strong incentive for choosing an Old Testament cycle for the decoration of the atrium of San Marco. In fact, one might feel inclined to ask what other subject matter the author of the atrium program might have chosen or found for filling the large spaces of the L-shaped atrium: the New Testament had already been used up in the interior.

It has been known for a century that the model of the Old Testament cycle of San Marco was the so-called Cotton Genesis in the British Library or, less likely as several authors would have it, a close relative of that codex. It goes without saying that the subject of the last cupola, the life of Moses, was not contained in the Genesis model, and so there must have been a second source quite different in date and style. This was, however, clearly used only as a supplement: the chief model of the atrium mosaics was certainly the Early Byzantine codex of the Genesis. This went so far that even the mosaicists of the Moses cupola employed elements—facial types, figures, groups, architectural details—taken from the Cotton Genesis repertoire side by side with late Byzantine, Palaeologan features.

It is possible that the Genesis manuscript did not come to Venice accidentally, as part of the booty of the Fourth Crusade, but rather through Venetian commercial relations with Egypt. If so, it might have been sought out as an early Byzantine document brought from the place of Saint Mark's martyrdom. Either way, its use as a model should certainly be seen in the context of the politico-religious movement of the Venetian proto-Renaissance with its archaistic tendencies; as a parallel to the choice of an Early Byzantine model for the church of San Marco as a whole; to the use of Early Christian spoils or copies of early works for its architectural and sculptural decoration; and, generally, to the development, with the help of genuine and forged elements, of a "tradition" reaching back to the apostolic age. The "copying" of the Old Testament cycle of the Cotton recension in the mosaics of the atrium certainly represents the most consistently sustained effort in this direction.

There was, of course, no intention—nor was there the possibility—of copying the Early Byzantine manuscript exactly: there was space for only about one hundred scenes out of the 359 that the Cotton Genesis contained. Thus, a strict selection had to be made of what should be included in the narrative program, a selection on more than one level: first, the choice of what chapters should be illustrated; second, the choice of "significant" or otherwise important scenes; and, third, the pruning of these scenes of "insignificant" details. Perhaps the most important guiding principle on the first level was to select only larger chapters, not single episodes, chapters that were well known and popular: the Creation, the story of Adam and Eve, of Cain and Abel, of Noah and the Tower of Babel, the lives of Abraham, Joseph, and Moses. The most conspicuous gaps are the stories of Isaac and Jacob, gaps that are the more remarkable since these two chapters play such an important role in the Sicilian mosaic cycles. The Joseph cycle, on the other hand, is narrated in the broadest possible manner.

Within the narrative, certain elements were given special meaning. The inscription of the Sacrifice of Cain and Abel, apparently copied from the mosaic of the same theme in the Cappella di San Clemente, probably had a eucharistic meaning; the mosaic of the Hospitality of Abraham certainly did. The specific typological, christological interpretation in the San Marco cycle of the Life of Abraham is clearly expressed in the inscription that appears on the face of the supporting arch, in the main axis looking north that states explicitly that in Abraham Christ is signified. This christological signification of Abraham is the more conspicuous since the scene from the life of Abraham that is normally most heavily fraught with typological significance, the Sacrifice of Isaac, is missing. Actually, the phrasing of the inscription offers an explanation of the problem: the typological relationship of Abraham and Christ is presented as a very special one—here it is centered on and restricted to the rejection of the Hebrews in favor of the gentiles. This "anti-Hebraic" burden of the inscription gains in importance by the very fact that the parallel is labored, both sides of it being grossly exaggerated. Moreover, this is not the only tendentious inscription that points in this direction—the scrolls held by some of the prophets in the pendentives of this and the following cupolas contain parallel utterances: Isaiah 1:2, "I have nourished and brought up children and they have rebelled against me"; and 2 Sam. 12:10–11, "Thus says the Lord: The sword shall never depart from thine house. Behold, I will raise up evil against thee out of thine own house."

Most likely these utterances are to be understood as religious propaganda in the context of the hoped-for conversion of the Jews, which was a very widespread medieval theme but had gained a particular significance in the twelfth and thirteenth centuries. Here again we encounter the shadow of Joachim of Fiore, whose treatise *Adversus Judeos* had a great influence among his followers and did much to foster the belief in the final conversion of the Jews before the end of the world. Among the other episodes from the life of Abraham, Joachim pointed to the patriarch receiving the three angels as a demonstration to the Jews that one of the central doctrines of Christianity, the concept of the Trinity, was already contained in their sacred books and that the Hebrews were thus from the beginning predestined for conversion. This does not, of course, prove that Joachim had a hand in fashioning the program of the atrium mosaics of San Marco, where the Hospitality of Abraham occupies a place of honor. The difference between the date of Joachim's possible visit to Venice on the one side and that of the mosaics on the other is too great.

If the christological references in the Abraham cycle are very specialized and concern only the "Hebraic question," those of the Joseph story are very general indeed. A general christological symbolism of the Joseph story was dominant in Christian literature from the second century, often mixed with elements of moral significance. Both meanings seem to be adumbrated in our mosaics, although there is no suggestive inscription like the one connected with the Abraham cycle. But the representation of the evangelists in the pendentives of the last cupola of the Joseph cycle seems to point to a certain typological connection with the New Testament and the appearance of allegories of the virtues on the arches between the three cupolas could be connected with the moral symbolism of the Joseph story.

157

In San Marco, there may have existed a different motive for giving such prominence to the Joseph story, namely, the fact that Egypt, the "land of Mark," plays such an important part in the legend. In our mosaics, two complete bays are filled with the Egyptian story of Joseph, that is, considerably more than two-thirds of the space allotted to the Joseph narrative as a whole. Thus, the scene of Mark's ministry, the country of his patriarchate, and the place where his relics rested and from which they were recovered by the Venetians dominates the narrative. An additional motif pointing to Egypt, especially to the episcopal see of Mark in Alexandria, may be seen in the representation of the evangelist (together with the other three) with the episcopal pallium in the pendentives of the third cupola of the Joseph story. This dominant motif also appears in the last bay with the story of Moses, of which the Egyptian part occupies half of the available space. It may be going too far to parallel the exodus of the Hebrews from Egypt with the "salvaging" and exporting of the relics of the evangelist: the connection of Egypt and Mark in the general sense is more likely to have been in the mind of the program's author.

Certainly no typological symbolism can be found in the mosaics of the last bay of the atrium. Moses, it is true, is frequently understood as a *typus* of Christ, with some scenes of his life being paralleled with New Testament scenes; even more often he is equated with the apostles, especially Peter. However, there are no accompanying motives that would suggest any meaning beyond that of straightforward narrative, and possibly the connections with Mark's Egypt. The four prophets in the pendentives have nothing to do with the main theme of the bay but point to the enthroned Virgin above the Porta della Madonna.

Less clear is the meaning of the Queen of Sheba in the apex of the arch that precedes the dome. She is often equated with the "church of the Gentiles." It is possible that the "anti-Hebraic" theme is here suggested again, or that her representation is connected with the group of inscriptions and images introducing the theme of justice and judgment, as she was evoked in the Gospels, "the queen of the south shall rise up in judgment with the men of this generation and shall condemn them" (Matthew 12:42 and Luke 11:31).

Generally speaking, the typological, christological overtones in San Marco are rather faint. The chief meaning of the mosaics is narrative pure and simple; all other aspects are secondary, with the exception, perhaps, of the reference to Egypt as the country of the evangelist. The Old Testament cycle was certainly in the first place intended as a supplement and an introduction to the program of the interior, with the Moses cycle providing a fitting historical transition from the *ante legem* period to the *sub lege,* which is the first chapter of the grand historical sequence beginning in the east dome. That the primary meaning of the Old Testament cycle is, indeed, "history" is corroborated by the tenor and form of the bulk of the inscriptions.

Arrangement and Placing of the Old Testament Cycle

The arrangement of the mosaics in clearly defined chapters was certainly determined by the architectural articulation of the atrium in six domed bays and two broad barrel vaults, the latter on either side of the entrance bay. Each bay was treated as an entity, even in the case of the Joseph story, spread over three bays of the north wing, each bay containing a clearly defined chapter in the life of its hero: his youth up to his being taken to Egypt, his troubled life there, and his triumph. Unconnected with the main theme are the figures and medallions of the transversal and longitudinal arches, and only loosely connected are the representations in the pendentives, with the exception of those of the second cupola of the Joseph story, which are integrated into the narrative. The latter always begins in the east axis of the cupola and circles around clockwise; it is continued in the lunettes and apse-like niches, also in a clockwise direction. The two barrel vaults are treated as belonging together, the story of the Tower of Babel and the Dispersion being regarded as a sequel to the Noah story. The principle of continuity was the determining factor of the arrangement, in spite of the difficulties it may have entailed for the "composer" of the decoration. The next fixed point for the arrangement of the Old Testament program was certainly the placing of the Hospitality of Abraham in the east lunette of the next bay. This is not only a very conspicuous place, apt to enhance the importance of the subject, it is also the counterpart of the lunette above the Porta San Clemente, the Sacrifice of Cain and Abel, thus bringing out the eucharistic connotation of the scene. While the Sacrifice of Cain and Abel was regarded as the First Sacrifice, the meal that Abraham served to the angels became the prefiguration for the eucharist. One might think that the Sacrifice of Isaac, which is omitted from the program, would have been more important than the Birth of Isaac and Circumcision, which are represented. However, the first seems to have been necessary as the logical sequel of the annunciation of the birth (the Hospitality of Abraham)—the principles of logical sequence and of the order of reading being strictly adhered to in the entire Old Testament cycle. In addition, the place in which the Birth and Circumcision appear is divided by a window and so badly lighted as to make it entirely unsuited for an "important" representation. Did the Venetians, then, simply resolve to pass up the Sacrifice of Isaac? As a matter of fact, there does exist a seventeenth-century representation of this scene in the interior, in a lunette below the east vault of the south transept. It is just possible that there existed, somewhere in the interior, an earlier representation of the Sacrifice of Isaac, which was destroyed at that time and replaced. The earlier representation of the Sacrifice in the interior might have caused its exclusion from the atirum cycle. However, since we cannot with certainty point to the original place, this must remain questionable.

The next chapter, that of the Joseph story, is the most extensive: it fills three bays. The first part, filling in the corner, is more restricted than that of any other bay, for it occupies only the cupola itself. If the first chapter of the Joseph story is the shortest, the second is the longest. It contains so many episodes that the pendentives had to be integrated into the narrative, although there were, in addition to the cupola itself, a lunette and an apse-like semidome to fill. The third chapter and the Moses story again do without pendentives; they were the only two bays with an equal measure of surfaces to fill.

The variation in the extent of the mosaic surfaces in the various bays shows a remarkable skill and elasticity on the part of the director of the work. Most of the scheme must have been laid down before the actual mosaic work began, perhaps even before the north wing was completed architecturally, but such details as the elimination of the west lunette from the narrative of the first Joseph cupola, and contrariwise, the integration of the pendentives in the following bay, must have been worked out as the mosaicists went along. The same applies to the placing of the saints.

The Saints

The idea of placing medallions in the arches seems to have turned up comparatively late in the course of the decoration, for with few exceptions, there are none in the west wing. This increase parallels the general enrichment of the decor, the ever-growing part played by ornamental motifs, that is, the scrolls and tendrils in the transversal arches and pendentives in the later areas. But there must have been another incentive for augmenting the number of saints represented.

Not all figures or medallions that belong stylistically to a later period need be regarded as later additions or substitutions, but the authenticity of the figure of Saint Geminianus and the medallion of Saint Catherine are open to doubt, and it is almost certain that the four standing figures in the vault above the tomb in the fifth cupola bay were added in the fourteenth century. None of the figures of the original series seems to be missing, except perhaps those that may have been supplanted by Geminianus and Catherine.

Clement was a state saint and a patron of seafarers, a cloister, and a hospital. Peter was a state saint. Alipios does not seem to have any specific importance for Venice and may have been introduced as a companion piece for Simeon opposite, one or the other of the famous stylites. Phocas of Sinope was a patron of Black Sea and Adriatic mariners; seamen collected alms for the poor in his name. His counterpart opposite is Christopher, patron of seafarers, travelers, and pilgrims. Agnes, the Roman martyr, had a church in Venice from at least the eleventh century; the only specific reason that could be adduced for her inclusion is that Agnes was the name of the first wife of Doge Lorenzo Tiepolo. Catherine was the archmartyr of Alexandria. Her cult in Venice—if not introduced by the Fourth Crusade—was at least strengthened by it, and her representation is part of the Alexandrian theme. Silvester was especially popular in the thirteenth century. Venice possessed some of his relics, and his church in the city was the chapel of the Venetian patriarch of Grado. Cecilia shared the *titulus* of the ancient church in Venice with Cassianus, the bishop and martyr of Imola, who may have been included for political reasons. Venice possessed relics of Cosmas and Damian after 1154, and a church in their name existed at least from the early twelfth century. The group is completed by Gaudentius and Marinus, who may have been included because of a treaty Venice concluded in 1260 with Rimini, where they were venerated. They may have been a compliment to that town, whose alliance was of great value to Venice. A different set of motives seems to have determined the choice of saints represented in the arch between the fifth and last cupolas, Blaise and Nicholas, Dominic and Peter Martyr. They may have been introduced in connection with the reluctant introduction of the Inquisition in 1249. Blaise and Nicholas, two state saints, may be understood as neutralizing the Dominican inquisitors beneath the Queen of Sheba, "rising up in judgment"—a kind of pictorial commentary on the official attitude in Venice toward the Inquisition.

The last group of saints is the string of medallions surrounding the Crossing of the Red Sea, all from the seventeenth century. Of these, Paternianus of Fano had an old *titulus* in Venice and his cult may have gained added interest during the Adriatic wars of the thirteenth century. In addition, Lorenzo Tiepolo had been *podestà,* the highest magistrate, of Fano prior to his dogeship. Fantinus of Calabria belongs in the same category; his cult in Venice, where he had a church at least from the early twelfth century on, may have been introduced or revived because of the commercial ties Venice had with the Calabrian saltworks. Juliana most likely had a church in Venice, as did Augustine at least after the eleventh century; his was the parish church of the Tiepolo family. Magnus is among the protectors of Venice, his relics having been transferred there in 1206.

Lucia of Syracuse became very popular in Venice when her relics were transferred in solemn procession to her newly erected parish church in 1280. The terminus is not absolutely binding, however, because the cult of the saint was well established in Venice before that date. All the saints represented on this arch were also patrons of trades; it is, thus, not unlikely that they were chosen for this reason and that their representation was owing to (or even paid for by) the respective *arti*.

Generally speaking, the hagiographic program of the atrium incorporated saints whose veneration had gained some sort of actuality in thirteenth-century Venice. In this respect, the series is analogous to the "additional" saints of the interior, and stands in contrast to the "pantheon" of the great original program of the church which is, so to speak, abstract and timeless. In addition, the program seems to have been shaped by functional criteria: helpers near the west entrance, "political" figures in the east part. Criteria of functional importance and not of "greatness" or "holiness" seem to have dictated also the choice between full-figure representation and medallions.

There exists no intrinsic relationship between the main theme, the Old Testament, and the series of saints.

The Virgin with Saints John and Mark

The iconography of the mosaic in the apse-like niche at the east end of the atrium's north wing fits exactly the place in which it appears. The representation of the Virgin above a side entrance of the narthex is quite common in Byzantine programs; perhaps the most monumental example, in the shape of the *trimorphon,* is to be found above the door of the south vestibule in Hagia Sophia in Constantinople. But what makes the Venetian mosaic even more specifically adapted to its place is the choice of the two flanking figures. John connects the Porta della Madonna, which on the inside is named the Porta di San Giovanni, with the north transept, which was specifically dedicated to John, having an altar in his honor and scenes from his life in the dome. In the niche mosaic above the entrance to what was practically his sanctuary, he stands at the Virgin's right and thus takes precedence, even over Mark.

The scheme is so similar to that of the Deesis that it could almost be called a Deesis of the Virgin. As a matter of fact, the inscription around the niche leaves no doubt that this is exactly what it was meant to be. The inscription not only states that the image is one of intercession, it also specifies the content of the image: it is Christ who is called upon to allow the Virgin and the two evangelists to intercede for the beholder—which makes the message of the image one of double intercession. The iconographic type of the central figure is one of the most frequent representations of the Virgin, and the iconographic types of the other figures also conform to Middle Byzantine standards. It is quite in keeping with the central idea of the representation that they are not depicted turning toward the Virgin with hands lifted in prayer—they are not interceding with her, but add the weight of their merit as Gospel writers to the Virgin's intercession with Christ. It is perhaps characteristic that they hold their books in much the same manner as the Virgin holds the Christ Child.

The Genesis Mosaics and the
Cotton Genesis Miniatures

19

ELABORATING J. J. TIKKANEN'S FUNDAMENTAL OBSERVATION that there exists a very close relationship between the Genesis mosaics of the narthex of San Marco and the miniatures of the so-called Cotton Genesis in the British Library (Cod. Cotton Otho B VI), Kurt Weitzmann has been able to identify general principles governing the conversion of the manuscript illustrations into monumental decorations, as well as the specific modifications that occurred in Venice. The Cotton Genesis is a prolifically illustrated Greek manuscript from about the end of the fifth century, evidently produced in Alexandria or perhaps Antinoë in Egypt. Unfortunately, the manuscript was virtually destroyed by fire in 1731 and now exists only in shrunken fragments, which is one of the main reasons why a controversy has arisen over whether the Cotton Genesis itself served as the direct model for the mosaics or whether another manuscript—very similar to it in style and date but now lost—was the source. The reluctance to accept the Cotton Genesis as the direct model for the mosaics derives from the numerous differences that exist between the mosaics and the miniatures. The question is whether these differences require the assumption of a second source or whether they can be explained as alterations made by the mosaicists who apparently did not feel obliged to copy the model slavishly and to adhere to every detail.

The custom of using miniatures as models for monumental art seems to have arisen in classical art and continued throughout the Middle Ages. Yet, in the whole history of art, there is no parallel to the narthex mosaics of San Marco, where a manuscript model was used on such a large scale and apparently with the intention of making as faithful a copy as circumstances permitted. No doubt the different surface areas of the narthex walls needed adjustments and prevented the mosaicist from following the model in every detail. Yet it should be realized that the necessary changes are due not so much to the individuality of the Venetian mosaicists but are of a nature that would lead to very similar and often identical solutions wherever the transmission of miniatures into monumental art is involved. In other words, the alterations follow certain principles that are of a general validity and would be applicable totally or in part in all periods and cultures wherever the copying of miniatures by monumental artists is involved.

Selectivity. No matter how much wall space a monumental painter or mosaicist had at his disposal, it was never sufficient to accommodate full miniature cycles comparable to those of early Bible manuscripts. The Genesis cycle in San Marco comprises 110 scenes; the Cotton Genesis originally had 359 framed miniatures comprising about 500 individual scenes. The mosaicists selected only about one-fifth of the available episodes, concentrating on intact sequences.

Alteration of format. The majority of the mosaics are in frieze form, that is, a format of predetermined height and flexible width; in the Cotton Genesis, the width was determined by the writing column whereas the height was flexible. The result is that on occasion the imagery from the manuscript had to be abridged.

Condensations. The ever-present pressure to economize on free space led on occasion to extreme condensation. In the depiction of the Lord Speaking to Abraham, for instance, the mosaicist allowed just the width of the Abraham figure for this scene, while the segment of sky is placed above the preceding scene. In the Cotton Genesis, an entire miniature is devoted to the episode and, in it, the sky with the Hand of God is prominently displayed.

Omissions. Details, sometimes essential ones such as the serpent behind Eve in the Defense of Adam and Eve, are omitted to save space.

Additions. Because of the economizing tendencies of the mosaicists, additions were rarer than omissions, but they do occur where special conditions existed. In Abraham Sending Out Soldiers to Liberate Lot, a second and third row of soldiers were added to give the impression of a great army. Of a more decorative than iconographical nature are the rich baldachinlike structures in the third Joseph cupola.

Conflations. A further step in condensation is the conflation of two successive scenes in order to save space. In the scene of Noah Releasing the Dove, the raven is included which in the Cotton Genesis was a separate episode.

Compositional changes. A primary motivation for compositional changes that the San Marco mosaicists share with all artists working in monumental art is the desire to centralize a composition, to make each scene more independent and self-contained. Thus, in the Curse of Adam and Eve in San Marco, the Creator sits in the center of the throne, creating a static, symmetrical, and hieratic composition out of a more directional, narrative one.

Iconographic changes. The scene of the Curse of Adam and Eve was, in fact, inspired by a Last Judgment scene. It, like many others, was the result of a conscious effort to introduce christological elements in the Old Testament imagery.

Stylistic changes. The larger scale of the human figures in the mosaic gave the mosaicist the chance for greater elaboration of details in the drapery and elsewhere, and he was able to apply conventional workshop formulas. Furthermore, the mosaicist was interested in setting the figures with a sharp, clear outline against a hieratic golden background, which often replaces the atmospheric background found in quite a number of miniatures.

Process of transmission from one medium into another. It should not be assumed that the mosaicist took the original manuscript with him on the scaffold. He must have made intermediary drawings that were then used as the basis for the *sinopie*. This process explains to a large extent various differences and affects first of all color.

Overriding similarities, as well as some aspect of these principles, are apparent in nearly every one of the San Marco Genesis scenes for which the Cotton Genesis counterpart can still be discerned. For example, in the Spirit above the Waters the dove is included as the symbol of the Holy Spirit, and the three-ringed structure stands for the Trinity, Christian interpretations derived from the Cotton Genesis. As in the manuscript model, Christ was portrayed as the agent of creation in the second scene; the angellike figure is a personification of the day. In the Cotton Genesis the day personifications wore wreaths, which in the mosaic were changed to fillets. To keep Christ in the Creation of the Plants equal in size to the figures in the other episodes, the mosaicist omitted a row of shrubs, flowers, and additional trees portrayed along the bottom of the miniature (fig. 64). He also displayed a greater concern with physical reality, replacing the straight gold striation lines of the model with a plastic rendering of the folds. Most striking, the plants behind the figures and the blue sky are eliminated and replaced by the gold ground. The division of the Creation of the Birds and Marine Creatures into two scenes follows the manuscript model in showing the creation and the blessing. In the latter, the veiled *palla* replaces the sleeveless *peplos* worn by the personifications to indicate solemnity. The heraldically paired birds may suggest God's command to multiply and seem to have been added by the mosaicist. The emphasis on quadrupeds in the scene of the Creation of the Terrestrial Animals may be due to the mosaicist's desire for greater visibility. Because this scene was already missing from the manuscript in the thirteenth century, it may be based on the Naming of the Animals.

The Forming of Adam shows the Creator completing the shaping of the man from the dust of the earth, indicated by the dark gray color (fig. 65). This represents the first of the three stages articulated in Genesis 2:7 and so is out of place in this position. Again, the mosaicist—probably faced with a lacuna in his model—borrowed an appropriate image from later in the manuscript. The inconsistencies in the scene of the Blessing of the Seventh Day suggest that here, too, the mosaicist tampered with his model. First of all, the Creator's blessing arm is very awkward and would be much more appropriate for a Creator facing the personification. What is more, there is an inconsistency in the garments of the personification of the seventh day. In the model, the Creator probably stood at the left, turning toward a group of bowing personifications of whom only the one actually blessed reflects the original pose. Apparently it was the desire to create a more hieratic and more monumental image and, at the same time, to infuse a christological element by adopting for the Creator the type of a Christ in Majesty that caused the mosaicist to transform a dynamic composition into a static one.

In the Animation of Adam, the soul is personified by a classical *psyche,* presumably found in the Early Byzantine model. The Introduction of Adam into Paradise may be the result of a conflation of two separate actions, the introduction and the admonition not to eat from the Tree of Knowledge. The four rivers are denoted in classical fashion by male personifications holding urns. As in other scenes, the jewel-studded throne and footstool in the Naming of the Animals are changes of the model by the mosaicist. Putting Adam's left hand on the head of one of the lions, an action not called for by the text, is apparently a touch of thirteenth-century realism. Adam's presence in the Temptation of Eve may be understood either as an interpolation from the Admonition scene or as a borrowing of an adjacent scene in the Cotton Genesis showing the Admonition of Adam and Eve, in accord with an apocryphal account. The representation of the tree as a fig, rather than an apple, follows an eastern tradition. The

Judgment of Adam and Eve was totally recast in terms of Last Judgment iconography (fig. 66). Christian elements were introduced into the Expulsion, too; the golden cross alludes to the tradition that the cross of Christ's crucifixion was cut from the Tree of Knowledge (pl. 43). The gold birds outlined in red are phoenixes, which according to legend were allowed to remain in paradise. The cherubim in the pendentives relate to the cherubim stationed to guard Eden. Eve enthroned and holding spindle and distaff in the scene of Labor is a Mariological element that refers to the identification of Mary as the "new Eve." In comparing the cycle of the first cupola with the Cotton Genesis, it must be stressed that the mosaicist followed his model so closely that he omitted only two scenes and otherwise resorted to condensations and conflations to reduce the scope.

Cain is portrayed in the scene of the Sacrifice with upright hair, an Early Christian and medieval symbol of evil. Abel is shown carrying a sheep on his shoulders—an allusion to Christ the Good Shepherd that may have been in the Cotton Genesis. The *sinopia* discovered underneath the scene of Cain Talking to Abel shows Abel wearing a sleeved tunic, which must reflect the Cotton Genesis and which was altered by the mosaicist.

When the mosaicist decided on the Noah story for the decoration of the south and north vaults, he skipped about twenty miniatures of the Cotton Genesis mostly devoted to genealogical episodes. In the scene of Noah Bringing the Terrestrial Animals into the Ark, some species are represented in numbers greater than two and as many as seven, reflecting the difference between clean and unclean animals. The timberwork of the ark reflects thirteenth-century realism. Noah and His Family Leaving the Ark is twice the size of the others and actually conflates four scenes. It is full of contradictions: the family should be represented leaving rather than approaching the ark; the animals, instead of roaming around a rocky landscape with "snowcaps" should be walking out of the ark; one lion is lifted by Noah in a very unconvincing manner out of (what appeared to the artist) as a window rather than a door. We know that the leaf in the Cotton Genesis containing this scene was missing before the fire, and it seems likely that the mosaicist resorted to the earlier episode of Noah and His Family Entering the Ark to build this composition. The Animals Leaving probably was taken from a separate episode, and the rainbow surely was derived from the scene of the Covenant with Noah. The Sacrifice of Noah was also lost in the Cotton Genesis and this scene in San Marco also is a composite, using the altar from the Sacrifice of Cain and Abel. In the subsequent Noah scenes, the mosaicist followed the manuscript very closely.

The mosaicist wanted to make the tower of Babel "whose top may reach into heaven" impressive and so reserved the full height of one side of the vault (fig. 72). The Appearance of the Lord at Babel and the Confounding of Languages were depicted separately in the Cotton manuscript (pl. 47b). The man pointing to his mouth indicates the confusion of languages; Christ's mandorla, footstool, and the increased number of angels are the result of medievalization.

When the mosaicists laid out the second cupola with illustrations from the life of Abraham, choosing sixteen scenes and lining them up in one frieze, they started with chapter 12 of Genesis, skipping about fifteen miniatures from the rest of chapter 11 that contained mostly birth and death scenes and the beginning of Abraham's life, his marriage to Sarah, and his journey to Haran. The subsequent scenes closely adhere to the Cotton Genesis, which in this sequence is relatively well preserved. In the scene of the Hospitality, the eucharistic element is emphasized by converting the plate into a chalice; the two knives are the result of thirteenth-century realism (pl. 50). In the Birth of Isaac, the figures at the right are an addition, apparently inspired by a New Testament birth scene (pl. 49b).

Following the Abraham cycle, the artist omitted scenes from seventeen chapters of Genesis—containing 108 episodes—apparently in order to display the Joseph story more prominently. In the first Joseph cupola, the mosaicists followed the manuscript model with particular care, both with regard to the accuracy of individual scenes and to their dense sequence (pl. 51). Rather than omitting scenes, the mosaicist preferred to make use wherever possible of extreme condensation, not shrinking from relocation of compositional parts, for example, by combining the two dreams in one picture or placing proleptically the arrival of the Midianites at the banquet (pl. 52). In at least one instance, he did transform a narrative composition, refashioning Jacob after a Christ in Majesty in the episode of Joseph Telling His Father and Brethren His Dream.

The second Joseph cupola with its adjacent pendentives and lunettes also follows the Cotton Genesis closely, leaving out only four complete scenes (pl. 53). As in the previous cupolas, the mosaicists used the principles of condensation and conflation freely, but in addition, they took greater liberty in making changes of gestures. The greatest liberty they took was with the setting, where contemporary structures or architectural elements either replace simpler structures or add architecture where there was none in the model. Such unusual features as the crucifixion of the baker were already in the Cotton Genesis.

Compared to the earlier Joseph cupolas, the last one shows a slightly increased number of omissions, but not so many that they disrupt the flow of the narrative (pl. 56). The main difference is greater freedom with regard to the manuscript model. This does not so much affect the compositional layout—which is still close enough to confirm the relationship to the miniature model—as some details that do not interfere with the iconographical content. Most deviations result from the desire for greater naturalism as, for example, in the way corn is gathered and distributed. Such emotional expressions as the dejection of the brothers increase, but these should not be understood as individual achievements of the mosaicists, but as typical of the later thirteenth century in general. The architectural setting becomes ever more fanciful and permeated with Gothic elements. There are, however, scenes where the miniatures are richer in architectural details. The pyramids and beehive-shaped granaries were features of the Cotton manuscript (fig. 81).

There has been some speculation about whether the Joseph cycle continued in the north lunette, now destroyed. Although there is no way to be certain, the fact that the cycle breaks off at a rather insignificant episode suggests more was planned. If a fourth Joseph cupola was envisioned, the Cotton Genesis offered numerous further episodes for continuation.

The mosaics preserve to a remarkable extent the purely narrative character of the model, being unparalleled by any other monumental cycle that depends on miniatures. Frequent alterations of format do, on occasion, affect the iconography, as for instance in the Curse of Cain when a new type of figure had to be invented to fit better the curve of the lunette. Condensations also appear in the mosaics on a considerable scale, but the mosaicists remained remarkably faithful to the model and omitted few details. Additions also are rare, except where the artist strove toward greater realism. Because of the efforts to preserve as much as possible the fluency of the pictorial narration, conflations appear less often than might be expected. Every scene can be traced to the manuscript model and there is no reason to imagine a second source. The Cotton Genesis was, indeed, the direct model of the San Marco atrium mosaics.

The Mosaics of the Atrium: Composition, Iconography, and Style

20

THE COMBINATION OF THE CREATION and the story of Cain and Abel in one unit is not unique; neither are the accompanying cherubim. The placing of cherubim in the pendentives so as to create the compositional scheme of a "winged dome" has parallels in San Marco itself but was most common in Byzantium. The decoration is complete but sadly disfigured in detail. By and large, the material and technique have parallels in the interior mosaics of the first half of the thirteenth century, though there are some new shades.

The scenes in the Creation cupola are arranged in a manner quite different from that in the other cupolas, namely, in three concentric rings separated only by inscriptions (pl. 40). The origin of the scheme must be sought in late antique cosmological representations and their medieval derivatives. The scheme may thus be based on the close connection, in medieval thinking, between paradise, the world, and the dome of heaven. With this scheme San Marco also followed the widespread tendency in Italian and especially Roman painting to compress the story of the Creation into as compact a composition as possible. To read the sequence must have been rather difficult, even for a medieval beholder. The only indication of where to begin is the one radius that continues across the entire scheme, the only unbroken spoke of the wheel. In spite of the elimination of frames, the mosaicists preserved the "picture" character of the single scenes.

While it is possible within certain limits to determine the attitude of the mosaicists toward their model as far as the composition of the single units is concerned, it is much more difficult to assess the measure of their dependence with regard to style. On the one hand, too little is preserved of the details of the miniatures, but, on the other, too much damage has been done to the mosaics by unscrupulous and clumsy restorers. Certain features and qualities of the mosaics can, however, be ascribed with certainty to this dependence, among them the proportions of the squat, square-built figures with their large heads, so different from the prevailing mode in contemporary Venetian art, the crude realism of the nudes, with their "naive" sexual characterization, and to a large extent their attitudes and clumsy movements, often with both knees bent (fig. 66). While in almost all representations of the Creator, the general shape of the large, round head was certainly copied from the model, the particular forms are thirteenth-century Venetian. The outstanding feature in the shaping of the faces is the double curve that separates the chin from the rest of the face, swelling the lower part of the cheek to a kind of pouch. The faces of the "angels of the Days" show the same peculiarity but are on the whole less mannered and more "antique" (fig. 65). The interpretation of the Early Byzantine model by the thirteenth-century mosaicists also makes itself felt in some of the draperies. While those of the Days follow the model pretty closely, the folds of the Creator's mantle in most scenes are shaped in a way that, in spite of a general resemblance, is essentially different from the painterly freedom of the late antique miniatures. The drapery in the mosaics conforms to the current Middle Byzantine linear pattern with the characteristic hip design, the oblique fold separating the curving triangle of the thigh from the knee, and the fan-shaped bundle of folds descending from the gathering grasp of the veiled hand. This drapery pattern and the design of the faces are only two of many similarities between the mosaics of the Creation cupola and a group of works in the interior comprising the Agony in the Garden, the angels above the treasury entrance, and the prophets and saints in the aisles.

Nevertheless, there are palpable differences between the two groups. To make up for their lack of Gothic refinement, the mosaics in the cupola exhibit artistic qualities not to be found in those of the interior, especially an unparalleled painterly naturalism in the depiction of the animals. The source of this naturalism was certainly the late antique model, but there is a decorative wealth in the shapes and colors of the animals, even a kind of monumental grandeur in the way they are spread out in the surface without losing the "natural" character of their shapes and movements, which goes beyond anything that could have existed in the miniatures. It is in this bold and decorative colorism, where gold is used as a "normal" color, combined with the astonishing realism, that the true achievement of the atrium workshop must be seen. The same bold colorism shaped the color composition of the whole. It is in this transformation of the single forms and in the combination of the relatively minute parts into a composition which—in spite of its additive character—does not lack monumentality that the achievement of the designer and the mosaicists of the cupola must be seen.

The three lunettes of the Cain and Abel cycle differ compositionally between themselves. While the Begetting appears as a picture with its architectural framework (pl. 44b), the figures of the Sacrifice are isolated against the gold ground and placed so far apart from each other that they seem connected only by the force of their centripetal movement toward the altar in the middle. The composition of the Birth of Abel stands between the two: the two outer figures seem to have "slipped out" of the columnar frame but are still part of the pictorial unit. In the Begetting as well as in the Birth, the original frame of the miniature has been eliminated and its function given to the inner framework of the architectural setting. The south lunette contains no pictorial units at all. The four scene motifs are isolated against the expanse of the gold ground, which is articulated only by the compact lines of the inscriptions. Studying the three lunettes, one gets the impression that the designer was not yet sure of his methods and that he proceeded experimentally with rather limited success. It seems to have taken him some time to find the right key for the translation of the miniature model into wall mosaics. He wavered between the two possibilities of preserving the "picture" intact or of arranging the illustrative matter primarily with regard to the architectural framework to fill the shapes of the surfaces.

By and large the figures are less awkward in build and movement than

169

those of the cupola. They are somewhat closer in style to the prophets in the north aisle than to the figures of the Agony. Thus the Venetian elements seem to be considerably stronger in the mosaics of the lunettes than in those of the cupola, which represent a considerable step forward in the process of emancipation from the Early Christian model. A careful study of the border ornament and paleography suggests a date close to 1225.

The vaults south and north of the entrance bay offer surfaces better able to accommodate rectangular picture units than any other surface in the atrium. In the mosaics of these vaults several different attitudes can be noticed in the translating of the "pictures" of the model into the narrative units of the mosaic cycle. The four surfaces represent four chapters of the narrative: the Building and Entering of the Ark, the Flood, the Drunkenness of Noah and His Burial, and the Tower of Babel. Each is treated somewhat differently, with a growing tendency toward monumental composition and consequently toward emancipation from the model. With the two Babel scenes, the chief organizer of the decoration seems to have found his feet: from here onward there are still some experiments but no uncertainty, no awkwardness.

The palette is somewhat richer than in the first bay; some of the colors, especially the blues and greens, are more brilliant. The technique is, in principle, the same but more masterly and especially more differentiated. The brilliantly painted animals are certainly among the great masterpieces of medieval colorism. The modeling of the faces is bolder than in the Creation cupola and the time-honored drapery formulas are hardly to be found. They have become "deschematized," more adapted to the plastic shape and the movement of the body.

There are, of course, numerous ties with mosaics of the interior, fewer with the Agony than with the series of prophets. The Dispersion seems to be especially close to the latter, and there can be no doubt of the direct descent of the Jehovah figure from the Emmanuel inside (pl. 47b). This is not the first case of an earlier mosaic in San Marco itself serving as a model for a later figure, but it is the first time that this happened during the work on the mosaics of the Old Testament in the atrium, which as a body depended on an entirely different prototype. It is perhaps the most conspicuous of many indications of the gradual independence from the model, a process that affected more the stylistic than the iconographic aspects of the work.

As a whole, the palette of the Abraham scenes is somewhat more subdued than that of the Noah cycle. Strong colors are missing and the general impression is rather one of tinged white and gold. The technique is not as brilliant as that of the Noah story, either, although the principles are the same. In short, the whole looks somewhat tired. The east lunette, showing the Hospitality of Abraham, is an exception, first, because the lunette is well lighted and closer to the beholder; second, because the subject is more important; and finally, because the court costumes of the angels invite showier treatment.

The general aspect of the cupola represents the greatest possible contrast to that of the Creation: instead of being covered with numerous small pictures so that the golden ground is scarcely visible, the Abraham cupola contains only a comparatively small central medallion and a loosely arranged frieze that fills only about one-third of the large golden expanse (pl. 48). There is no continuous strip of terrain, only a very few linear contours of hills in the golden ground. The principal components of the frieze are figures, single and in groups, in a largely isocephalic arrangement. This cupola scheme seems so simple and unproblematic that it has rarely been analyzed. All the elements of the scheme appear already in the Saint John dome from the first half of the twelfth century, and it is not unlikely that it was first worked out there as a variant of the "normal" cupola scheme with single figures and was taken up again and developed to serve the detailed narrative of the Old Testament.

The beginning of the narrative in the east axis is marked, very discreetly, by a white vertical line in the golden ground. The scenes melt into each other so completely that without knowing the story, it would be difficult in some cases to decide to which scene a figure belonged. In the Hagar story and Circumcision episodes, the scenes have retained more of their picturelike coherence. There is also a tendency toward forming larger units, in part irrespective of iconographic logic.

In the east lunette, the main scene is moved a little toward the right of the central axis and the tree along with an additional line of the inscription reestablish the equilibrium. At the same time, the main accent rests on the meal scene surmounted by the tent, and especially on the central figure at the table, and above, the bust of Sarah appearing in the opening of the tent. Thus, the Trinitarian and eucharistic aspect of the scene is strongly accentuated (pl. 50).

The types, attitudes, and movements of the figures are identical to those of the Noah story, as are the drapery and modeling. There can be no doubt that the mosaics of the dome are the work of the same workshop as those of the Noah and Babel scenes and that they were made immediately after or at the same time as these. The prophet figures in the medallions are clearly derived from the prophets of the south aisle and hence must be dated a little later.

The palette and technique of the mosaics of the first Joseph cupola are the same as those of the Abraham dome (pl. 51). The types of figures are closely akin, though there is a certain change as regards the projections, attitudes, and movements. There are, for example, fewer profiles, and awkward back-views are lacking. The figures stand and move in a more organic manner, and their stance is more stable, approaching a kind of contrapposto. There is also a new rhythmic quality in the movements and a certain lyrical expression in the faces. While the general composition is the same, the single forms are a little larger, the episodes are more clearly separated, and the story is more "readable." The beginning of the story is again marked by a white line in the east axis. There is not the slightest attempt at representing solid objects, let alone objects in space. It is quite likely that these changes are part of a continuous process of emancipation from the model, of redesigning compositions and figures in accordance with tendencies of the period. They are the latest phase of a slow development toward more organic, even "classical" forms, with its corollary, the gradual elimination of Middle Byzantine elements.

The activity of the workshop that set the mosaics of the west wing of the atrium breaks off with the arch between the third and fourth cupolas. The interruption of the mosaic work in the atrium seems to have lasted a considerable time, for when the work was taken up again, with the second cupola of the Joseph story, it was done in a different spirit as regards the decorative arrangement and the interpretation of the model, with a different technique, and in a different style. If one leading master (with his workshop) can be held responsible for all mosaics of the west wing, those of the second cupola of the Joseph story must be ascribed to a different, younger master presiding over a different, newly recruited workshop (pl. 53).

Compared with the preceding cupolas, the palette has changed fundamentally. The colors are no longer restricted to light tones but are employed in comparatively large patches of local color in strong, even violent, hues. Most of the intense colors are liberally shot with gold: a new sumptuousness has taken the place of the restraint exercised in the earlier mosaics of the atrium. The technique has become more complicated, especially to produce painterly effects. The profound difference between this and the preceding bays can also be seen in the decorative arrangement. Here, the pendentives are filled with scenes and the arch between this and the following cupola is more richly decorated. Within the cupola itself, the central medallion is considerably larger and its filling pattern more vigorous than in the preceding cupolas. Since the figures are also larger, the free expanse of the gold ground is much smaller than before and is reduced to the role of background.

The narrative begins, as usual, in the east axis, with the scene of Joseph Being Sold to Potiphar, but, contrary to the usage in the preceding cupolas, the beginning is not marked in any way. The single scenes are presented in greatly varying forms. Some were given architectural settings, others not, as determined by purely artistic reasons of accent, balance, rhythm, or simply the available space. As a rule, architectural motifs were inserted wherever it was feasible. Thus, they play a very important part in the formal aspect of the whole. An experiment was adopted in the lunette of placing the figures on a strip of terrain so that they really seem to stand on firm ground. This is the third phase in a process that began in the Creation cupola with the copy of the Late Antique way of placing the figures on an elaborately described "realistic" ground. In the next phase, the ground was eliminated so that the figures not only stand against the empty golden ground but also seem to tread on air. At the same time, an ornamental strip of hillocks and plants was introduced to serve as lower frame of the golden surface in lunettes and vaults, although this had no connection with the figures. The solution that first appears in the lunette of the second Joseph cupola introduces the third phase, the beginning of a new, thirteenth-century development that is not just a return to the Late Antique illusionistic figure-terrain unity but the development of a new system, not optical but functional. Since according to the new "logic," figures had to stand on something, they were provided with some sort of base. It is the same logic that placed firm socles under the feet of Gothic statuary.

The architectural motifs follow the same trend of "logic": they become "practicable," and in some cases appear almost inhabitable. This is, of course, connected with an increase in scale as well as in three-dimensionality. The new feeling for the spatial relations between figures and architectural framework is as yet in an embryonic stage. The mode of projection is foreshortened frontal, which means that it is still the mode normally used in antiquity. Thus, the possibility of representing an interior closed on three sides and covered by a roof is still far distant, but the step toward a new interpretation of three-dimensional space has been made in these mosaics, a step that leads away from Middle Byzantine conventions toward new methods heralding Palaeologan art but in which the Western development also has its place.

Like other forms, the figures are large and bold, of a rather powerful, even heavy build, with sturdy muscular legs. They stand in a firmly planted stance with knees a little apart or move in powerful strides and lunges. The energetic move is shared by entire groups so that the action takes on a dynamic character. There are few classical attitudes; instead we find highly mannered postures and movements, among them an exaggerated posture with crossed feet, a kind of stylized dancing step derived not from Byzantine but from Western models. The expressions of the faces, too, are active, anxious, or defiant. The forms of the drapery have changed profoundly. Some Middle Byzantine formulas are still used, it is true, but even these have been transformed by the new plastic interpretation that has superseded the earlier linear, form-designing manner. In fact, the garments seem to detach themselves from the bodies, announcing a new conception of the draped figure, with a clear distinction between body and garment, in the place of the earlier unity. They show something of the freedom of Early Gothic drapery.

The realistic treatment of certain surfaces, on the other hand, and the painterly quality reflect an interest in optical effects irrespective of the nature of the objects on which they are to be observed; it is not descriptive but impressionistic.

Given the bad state of preservation of the cupola mosaics, it is difficult to decide whether all the mosaics of the bay are the work of one or of several masters. Deciding is made even more difficult by the fact that those parts of the decoration that are nearer to the beholder were executed with more finesse as regards both material and technique. In any case, one master must have designed and supervised the whole. His approach to the model was certainly freer in comparison with the preceding parts of the atrium's decor—perhaps still somewhat experimental but clearly tending toward a new and consistent style, which included a very vigorous colorism and a new interpretation of plastic forms and spatial relationships. It is an early variety of the volume style, the development of which dominated artistic trends in the second quarter of the thirteenth century in Byzantium as well as in the West. Our master must have been acquainted with both the Byzantine and the Western varieties. Nonetheless, the style probably grew out of the Venetian tradition.

Although there was an interval between the work on this cupola and that on the preceding one—due perhaps to the fact that the north wing of the atrium was still being built—it was not a complete gap. The style recalls that of the *preghiera* and *apparitio* panel inside, not so much as regards motifs or vocabulary as the sharing of some general principles. There is in both works, for instance, a tendency to break away from the Byzantinizing tradition, although this is achieved in different ways. The common tendency that strikes the beholder most forcibly is that toward a strong colorism, the preference for saturated, even harsh colors. Both also share an inclination toward three-dimensional represen- tation. In addition, the figures have acquired more body, greater solidity. Bold projections aim at implying movement in space, and architectural forms are represented in a similar mixture of flat and three-dimensional projections. Finally, another quality common to both groups of mosaics is that of painterly technique aiming at a realistic rendering of details. Thus, both groups belong to the critical period of breaking away from the tradition of the precious linear style of the first half of the thirteenth century; both are on the way toward the volume style of the second half. The cupola is more organically developed, however, and thus should be dated later than the panels.

In the third and last cupola devoted to the story of Joseph, the state of preservation is much better than that of the preceding one (pl. 56). The palette is more differentiated, and the colors generally are less glaring and more fully blended together. The technique is more sophisticated: dark contours have largely disappeared, and the tesserae are more varied in size and shape.

The beginning of the narrative, like others in the east axis, is not marked in any way. The scenes are fused into an almost perfect continuum, much denser than in the preceding cupola. Nevertheless, most scenes are shaped as self-contained units, the pictorial units being more complicated, more picture-like than those of the earlier cupolas. The architectural settings all have roofs or attic-shaped superstructures that cause them to appear three-dimensional. In details, the architecture combines Western or Westernized motifs with Byzantine, a characteristic of this group of mosaics.

Generally speaking, almost all figures stand or move on firm ground, which is usually represented as a green strip of terrain consisting of a row of hillocks and plants in a pattern that, compared with the lunette of the second Joseph cupola, has lost something of its ornamental character and become more freely shaped. Thus, it marks a further step in a regular "progress" toward three-dimensional picture space, even if this space is as yet only a shallow stage. This progress is continued in the lunette under the third cupola, where the strip of terrain begins to lose its quasi-ornamental regularity. In addition, the upper scene of the lunette is also provided with a strip of green terrain, though its relation to the golden ground still seems to have caused some difficulties for the mosaicists, which led to the artificial joining of this strip with the architectural motifs of the lower scenes, especially on the left. It is only slowly, step by step, that the new logic of spatial representation is fully realized. There is as yet hardly any attempt to create spatial receptacles enclosing the figures. So far the plastic style of the cupola mosaics affects only the solid bodies: it does not create space. The tendency toward three-dimensional treatment also extends to individual objects, and the figures also have more body than in the preceding cupola. In this as in other respects, the mosaics of the lunette are even more modern. The figures are also more classically proportioned, in spite of their almost herculean build. Their movements are more subtly differentiated and motivated psychologically than in the older mosaics. Entire groups are swayed by one intense emotion and individuals are represented in all the expressive attitudes and gestures contained in the Byzantine repertoire.

The modeling of the draperies is softer, less rectilinear and abstract than in the preceding cupola. The graphic element is reduced; soft folds design the relief of the bodies in parallel curves, observing the logic of falling, hanging, sagging, and stretching, as in classical or classicizing reliefs. There is a marked increase in technical skill of suggesting three-dimensional values and in psychological refinement as regards the representation of both single figures and events. One feels that the leading master was at the height of his powers and that the workshop had definitely reached the high point of the thirteenth-century classical style.

LIFE OF MOSES AND DEESIS OF THE VIRGIN

Although a number of elements were remade in the seventeenth century and later, the entire program of the last bay as it appears today is most likely authentic (pl. 60).

The palette is practically the same as in the preceding cupola except, perhaps, that the colors are a little softer and more broken by white lights. The mosaics seem to be the work of more than one hand, but making attributions to the various mosaicists is difficult if not impossible in view of the disfiguring restorations.

The general aspect of the cupola and semidome differs fundamentally from that of the preceding ones: instead of an approximately isocephalic frieze of figures silhouetted against the golden ground or framed by architectural motifs also of equal height, we have here an irregular up and down of forms, primarily landscape and architectural scenery. The figures seem rather secondary, being of various sizes and distributed in different layers. They are not only framed but contained in the scenery. In fact, so completely integrated are they in their environment that some of them are rather difficult to make out at first glance. The eye cannot simply progress from one figure or group to the next, because the complicated narrative sequence has to be unraveled by examining the picture units analytically. One experiences an entirely new compositional principle at work here, the negation of the principle of geometric regularity that dominated the compositional schemes of all the other cupolas and domes of San Marco. The firm, schematic design has been replaced by a free, picturesque arrangement, in which landscape, architecture, figure, and inscription play almost equally important parts.

The San Marco cycle is richer than that in the Middle Byzantine Octateuchs but does not contain one of the most important events, the Giving of the Law on Mt. Sinai. Why were the miracles in the desert preferred to the receiving of the Law? This question is perhaps connected with another: Why was the entire narrative between the Burning Bush and Crossing the Red Sea left out (the story of the plagues and the preparations for the Exodus) that takes up a great deal of space in most pictorial cycles? The likeliest explanation is that the cycle was conceived not as a narrative of the history of the Chosen People but as a "biographical cycle." The scenes were chosen not for their typological and theological message but for their importance in depicting the life of the protagonist, as in all chapters of the Old Testament cycle in the atrium. That the choice of scenes to be represented was intentional and was not merely dependent on the existence or absence of illustrations in a cycle that served as a model can be concluded from the fact that all cycles that might be considered as prototypes contain a large number of illustrations of plagues. Nevertheless, it is certain that the model followed by the designer of our mosaics was a Byzantine illuminated manuscript.

The scene of the Ordeal of Moses is an apocryphal episode that is neither contained in the Bible nor illustrated in any of the known Octateuchs. It is certain that the ultimate source of the scene must be sought in Jewish commentaries on the Bible. Although no representation of the episode has come to light so far in Byzantine art, the way in which the scene is rendered in the cupola mosaic certainly presupposes a Byzantine model, more specifically an Early Palaeologan miniature: the architectural background, grouping of figures, costumes, and armor all clearly support this assumption.

Quite apart from the question of the principles of selection, for which the designer of the mosaics may have been largely responsible, it can be stated that the iconographic tradition to which the model belonged had hardly anything to do with the tradition followed by the illuminators of the Byzantine Octateuchs. None of the Middle Byzantine cycles is as detailed as the one from which the designer of the San Marco mosaics selected material to shape into a continuous narrative of the Life of Moses. Nonetheless, it seems likeliest that the manuscript model was an Early Palaeologan manuscript, dating to the third quarter of the thirteenth century.

In analyzing the style of these mosaics, what will have to be taken into account is whether all parts of the cycle were derived from the supposed model, or whether some parts must be regarded as having been copied from other sources, or, finally, whether these parts were more or less freely invented and shaped by the Venetian designer. It is certain that about half of the cupola, beginning with the Basket with Infant Moses Put into the River, was in the Palaeologan model. To this group should be added the Watering of Jethro's Flock and, at least in part, the Miracles of the Desert. In the other scenes, the figures are not integrated into the landscape but stand and act solely in the foreground, with the landscape and architecture added only as backdrops. This conservative treatment, as well as such outmoded architectural forms as the two houses of the Jethro scenes, is close to the repertory of San Marco itself. How can this heterogeneity be explained? Most likely either the model contained the scenes in a form that made them unsuitable as models, or the manuscript itself retained some traditional, even antiquated, pictorial elements inherited from a still earlier version and not modernized. Equally conservative, that is, taken from the old repertory of the atrium workshop, are the half figures of the prophets in the pendentives and all of the ornamental decor, which is in great part identical with that of the preceding cupola.

The most spectacular Palaeologan elements appear, of course, in those scenes of the Life of Moses that depend directly on the Palaeologan manuscript that served as their model. The dominating elements in these are the landscape backgrounds in the form of steep rock towers, which consist of sloping platforms split vertically (fig. 86). The origin of these crystalline rock structures can be traced back to late antiquity. The form was revived in the renaissance of the tenth century, and from that time, it was never completely forgotten. In our mosaics, the landscape forms were certainly copied from the early Palaeologan model. It was, in fact, in manuscripts that these forms were first revived, certainly at an earlier date than in monumental painting. San Marco may actually be one of the earliest examples of the use of these forms in mosaic.

More characteristically Palaeologan than even the rocky landscape motifs of the Moses cupola is the architectural shape of the palace that serves as a stage and background for the scenes of Moses' childhood, which also goes back to the manuscript model. This architectural representation is the earliest attempt in San Marco to enfold space in the form of a large niche. The building is, more or less, a rational structure, exhibiting none of the fantastic inconsistencies and willful distortions of spatial relations that appear in High Palaeologan structures. The type lived on in Venetian painting of the fourteenth century.

The figures are not yet completely integrated into the scenery, whether architectural or landscape, but are either placed in shallow niches or appear from behind flat coulisses. In some scenes, however, a first step has been made toward creating a closer relation between the figures and elements of the stage, namely, by a kind of interweaving. Generally speaking, there is as yet no conception of unified, homogeneous space. Every scene has its own space and every action takes place between its specific coulisses, which provide a kind of sounding board for the dramatic events.

The attitudes and movements of most of the figures that were taken over from the Palaeologan model serve to enhance the dramatic element as regards not so much the speed of the action but its intensity. The style of the narrative is not dynamic but expressive. This means that the attitudes and movements of the figures seem especially conditioned for the actions they perform or the emotions they express. Some of the figures are represented in unusual views and projections. In the cupola there are no fewer than five figures seen from the back, all of them drawn in a manner characteristic of Palaeologan art, combining two or more discordant projections of various parts of the body. The facial types of the figures are not much different from those in the preceding dome, but they are a little smoother, one might even say prettier. All the figures, even those involved in dramatic scenes, show a certain equanimity, a lack of participation that contrasts oddly with the dramatic movements and postures portrayed. The conservative forces of the workshop were still strong enough to prevent a complete surrender to the new trends in Byzantine art. This is also true of much of the drapery design: conservative forms can be found even in some of the figures copied from the "modern" parts of the Palaeologan model. However, side by side with the traditional schemes of drapery design and techniques there are figures in which the form-designing drapery has given way to an entirely different "modern" type of surface relief of the draped figure, that is, to a glittering pattern of highlights in playful forms without any linear structure. Here we must reckon with a direct influence from Palaeologan painting that went beyond the copying of iconographical patterns and figural types. In San Marco, however, the highlights still follow the relief of the drapery and the faces in the form-designing curves, to bring out the structure and not merely to convey effects of light. Thus, the form-designing technique of the mosaics of the Moses cupola does not show any influence from the Palaeologan panel-painting technique.

There is just enough left in the nineteenth-century reworking to permit us to recognize the mosaic above the Porta della Madonna as a work closely connected with the workshop of the Moses cupola. Some peculiarities of modeling make it almost certain that the mosaic was, together with the lunette (Saint John) on the inside of the doorway, the latest product of the workshop. Taken as a whole, the mosaic decoration of the last bay of the atrium is an experimental work, conservative in some parts, bold and immature in others. It is a work of transition in a time of revolutionary change.

Faced with a lack of unity of style, or at least of stylistic material, a question again arises that has already been asked with regard to the Agony in the Garden mosaic in the south aisle. How did the lack of homogeneity, of stylistic uniformity, affect the beholders and even the artists themselves? And again it must be said that differences of style do not seem to have disturbed either of them at all. The main interest of the public was surely the subject matter and the decorative—not stylistic—unity. If a new stylistic language enlivened the subject or made the narrative more compelling, it was surely welcome. It should also be kept in mind that this plurality or, in the case of San Marco, duality of styles has nothing to do with eclecticism and that the more recent style was not chosen willfully but obtruded itself with the model. It may indeed have been welcomed as something new and interesting and was thus admitted for parts of the work while for others the older style was still valid. To the present-day beholder, the side-by-side existence of the two styles shows how sudden the inroads of the new forms were. It also proves that the new style, which made such a sudden appearance, was not native to Venice but imported, for there was not even sufficient time for the new leaven to transform the older vocabulary.

The mosaics that decorate the ciborium in Parenzo, dated 1277, are a byproduct of the San Marco workshop, created by at least two of its mosaicists, one of whom was an assistant of the master of the second Joseph cupola, while the other was closely connected with the work in the Moses cupola. The date of

177

the ciborium thus provides a most important basis for dating the later phases of mosaic work in the cupola. The second Joseph cupola, though certainly a good deal earlier, cannot have been so far removed in date that one of its mosaicists could not still have been working in 1277, which means that its date can hardly be much earlier than about 1260. The Moses cupola, on the other hand, must have originated very close in date to the Parenzo mosaics, that is, between 1275 and 1285.

In spite of the imperfections that this situation brought about, there is a freshness about these mosaics, a youthful promise of things to come. Yet, this promise was not fulfilled. The new effort came at the very end of the great campaign of the thirteenth century. With this last bay the mosaic decoration of the atrium was completed. We do not know where else the masters continued working, if they continued at all. It was certainly not in San Marco itself.

CHAPTER TWENTY

Mosaics in the Vault of the Cappella Zen

THE PRESENT SEPULCHRAL CHAPEL of Cardinal Battista Zen was installed in the original southwest entrance hall between 1503 and 1515. This "antevestibule" was originally open toward the south and served as one of the main entrances to the church, a kind of sea gate. In the early fourteenth century, the lower part of this inner porch was remodeled by the addition, or possibly enlargement, of nine niches framed with columns and filled partly with mosaics (full figures of Christ Emmanuel and four prophets) and partly with statuettes of four prophets taken from another context.

Although it is unlikely that the vault was left unadorned throughout the twelfth and thirteenth centuries, there is no possibility of ascertaining what manner of decoration existed there prior to these mosaics. As now preserved, the iconographic schemes and compositions can be trusted although the specifically stylistic qualities have to be regarded with great caution. The palette is in several respects similar to that of the second cupola of the Joseph cycle, but the contrasts of light and dark shades are more strongly marked, the dark shades are duller, and some of the new material is rather crude and glaring in color.

In each of the two halves of the barrel vault are six scenes of the Life of Mark arranged in two tiers (pl. 64 and fig. 88). The cycle begins in the upper northeast corner of the vault and ends in the lower northwest corner and consists of the following scenes:

Mark Writing the Gospel
Mark Presenting Gospel to Peter
Mark Baptizing in Aquileia
Mark's Dream-Vision in the Venetian Lagoon
Peter Consecrating Hermagoras
Mark Healing a Demoniac
Mark Ordered by a Dream-Vision to Go to Alexandria
Mark's Voyage to Alexandria
Mark Healing Anianus
Mark Strangled at the Altar
Mark Dragged and Killed
Burial of Mark

The Life of Mark, which is continued on the facade with the history of the Translation of the Relics from Alexandria to Venice, was not placed outside because the *translatio* was part of the state legend. The church's claim to be the

Fig. 88. Cappella Zen, vault, west half

CHAPTER TWENTY-ONE

shrine of the evangelist's relics, his resting place, had to be demonstrated first, on the "title page"—the story of his life was an amplification, a commentary. Even in this commentary, the motif of the relics and the divine right of Venice to their possession occupied an important place. This is, in fact, the *raison d'être* for retelling the story of the saint's life, a story that was already represented twice in the church, each time in connection with the narrative of the translation. In the elaboration of the state legend the cycle of the vestibule also presented the *praedestinatio,* the divine message to the saint that his body would eventually find its resting place in the lagoon, that is, in the exact location of San Marco, a thirteenth-century offshoot of the legend. It was not, however, the only addition to the narrative as it had been represented in the vault of the Cappella di San Pietro. The vestibule cycle begins with two scenes missing from the San Pietro sequence, a theme that is alluded to in a most monumental form in the figures of Peter and Mark in the main apse, namely, Mark Writing the Gospel and Mark Presenting the Gospel to Peter.

Another scene not contained in the San Pietro cycle is Mark Healing a Demoniac. The inscription locates the scene in Egypt. It serves as a connecting link between Rome and Egypt, together with the dream-vision in the Pentapolis, in which Mark receives the divine command to go to Alexandria. The last of the new scenes in the Cappella Zen cycle is Mark Dragged and Killed. To make room for the additions, a number of scenes that figure in the San Pietro chapel sequence were eliminated. The result was that the series no longer underscored the claims of the Grado and Venice to ecclesiastic primacy over Aquileia but established and advertised the city-state's divine right to the possession of its patron's relics. Thus, Mark appears not so much as the founder of the patriarchate but as the author of the Gospel, as a popular miracle worker and martyr. It is a more Venetian emphasis, with Venice presented as the heir of Alexandria, for here we encounter the same preponderance of the "Egyptian" motif as in the north wing of the atrium.

The iconography of the single scenes is to a certain extent dependent on the two earlier cycles, the Pala d'oro and the San Pietro vault. Other images were based on representations of the Life of Christ.

As far as the precarious state of preservation permits any definite judgment, the mosaics of the vault are the work of one master with perhaps one or two assistants. The principles that govern the compositions of the single scenes are the same throughout the entire cycle: all units are self-supporting, compact, and well-balanced "pictures," and most are tripartite; together they constitute a "minuscule" pictorial text without any claim to monumentality. In general, the twelve scenes are conceived as integral pictures, clearly separated from each other, in most cases cut off by the vertical trimming of the background. The rectangular delimitation of the pictures even if they are unframed suggests that the cycle was conceived as a series of clearly distinct pictures, in the manner of book illuminations. This does not mean that the mosaics were copied directly from an illuminated manuscript or panel painting. It is much more likely that the preparatory drawings or paintings that were to serve as the mosaicists' model were expressly created for this purpose by a Venetian master who took his cue from miniatures or panels or was even an illuminator or a panel painter himself. Everything in the style and iconography of the mosaics is thoroughly Venetian; in some details the artist who prepared the pictorial model even reverted to much earlier mosaics in San Marco itself.

In the arrangement of the whole there are no mirror effects as there are in

181

almost all the vaults of the interior. The designer treated the two sides of the barrel vault as if they were parts of one stretch of vertical wall. The only principle governing the whole is the uniform direction of the movement. This lack of overall compositional pattern appears as a falling off of artistic quality, and in other respects, too, the work is not of the highest quality.

Judging from the best-preserved faces, it seems very likely that the mosaicist who shaped them was trained in the workshop of the second cupola of the Joseph cycle. At the same time there are differences, especially in the expressions: the heavy types, with the defiant, truculent expressions have been replaced by mild, nondescript faces devoid of expression. In this respect, the faces recall rather those of the Moses scenes. The movements and attitudes of the figures are as unspecific as the faces: they are very much subdued, quite unlike those of the later chapters of the Old Testament cycle. The most striking feature of the garments is the zigzagging and undulating seams which recalls the mosaics of the second Joseph cupola. This play of lines adds to the impression of flatness, an impression that is created chiefly by the movements and attitudes of the figures. They are all conceived parallel to the picture plane and do not at all imply spatial depth. Nor does the modeling create the effect of strong plastic volume, and the apparent relief is extremely shallow. This flatness stands in odd contrast to the three-dimensional schemes of some of the architectural motifs and their grouping, which are, in fact, the most "modern" features in the entire decoration of the vestibule. Side by side with completely flat architectural forms, we find outbuildings jutting out in front, miniature terraces with railings, cupolas, roofs with excrescences, and even a tower set in a miniature courtyard. These forms suggest that the designer knew something about the more recent development in the field of architectural representation.

The mosaicist must have been a master of the third rank, trained in the workshop of the second Joseph cupola. Moreover, he must have been an old man when he was given the task of decorating the vestibule, most probably in the 1270s.

Facade Mosaics

NOTHING CAN BE SAID of the program of decoration of the original eleventh-century facade of San Marco, which has been overlaid by the rich architectural, sculptural, and mosaic decoration of the thirteenth and following centuries. Fate has not been much kinder to this second set of mosaics, however: of the nine large compositions and several single figures only one mosaic is left, that above the Porta Sant'Alipio (fig. 89); all the others were completely remade after new cartoons in the seventeenth, eighteenth, and nineteenth centuries. The program of these later mosaics, however, follows the original one.

Fig. 89. Facade (Porta Sant'Alipio): Mark's Relics Transferred into Church *(Alinari)*

Fig. 90. Gentile Bellini: *Procession in Piazza San Marco,* Venice, Accademia *(Anderson)*

Upper Story: Christological Cycle
    Descent from the Cross
    Harrowing of Hell
    Resurrection
    Ascension

Niche above the Central Porch
    Last Judgment

Lower Story: Translation of Mark's Relics from Alexandria to Venice
    Body of Mark Is Taken from Its Tomb
    Body Is Covered with Pork
    Muslim Guards Are Repelled by the Pork
    Relics Are Placed in the Ship
    Arrival of the Ship in Venice
    Relics Are Taken from the Ship
    Doge and People of Venice Venerate Relics
    Body of Mark Is Taken into the Church

Figure of saints, Peter, Liborius, Nicholas, Paul, Mark, Vitus, Christopher, and Gerardus, as well as the Virgin were done in the seventeenth century.

The program of the thirteenth-century mosaics can be ideally reconstructed with the help of literary and pictorial sources—from a record of the inscriptions and from Gentile Bellini's procession panel painted in 1496 (fig. 90).

Judging from a comparison with the preserved scene of the *translatio* of Mark's relics into the church, the Bellini painting seems faithful enough even in certain details. There are discrepancies, however, among them certain alterations in the proportions of various parts of the architecture, deviations in the grouping of figures, articulations of the groupings, and other elements. Iconographically, and to an even higher degree, stylistically, the "reproductions" must therefore be treated with the utmost caution. What can be taken for granted are the subject matter and the broad lines of the composition.

The christological cycle is not a simple repetition or enlargement of the cycle in the interior, but a series of images especially selected for the facade and culminating in the *Adventus Domini* (Second Coming of Christ) mosaic above the central door. The eschatological tenor was made clearer through the original inscriptions. The reason the cycle began with the Deposition, rather than with the Crucifixion, may have been because the Deposition was already missing in the interior. What is more, it stressed the death of Christ and his victory over death by his resurrection. The Anastasis was, of course, de rigueur in a Resurrection cycle. More problematic is the inclusion of the Resurrection in the form of Christ stepping out of a sarcophagus, the specifically Western Resurrection image, which in a way duplicates the theme represented by the Byzantine image of the Anastasis. Both the inscription and the image itself, however, contain the motif of the resuscitation of the just in anticipation of the Last Judgment. Moreover, the inclusion of both Byzantine and Western Resurrection images in one cycle is not infrequent in works that originated near the boundary between the two worlds. The Ascension, finally, is explicitly connected with the Resurrection by its inscription. It is also connected with the culmination of the entire christological program, the Second Coming through the allusion to the *Adventus* contained in the basic source, Acts 1:11. Thus, the christological program is a well-thought-out whole.

The christological cycle was continued and reached its completion in the great mosaic above the central porch; the nineteenth-century work was preceded in the thirteenth century by the mosaic recorded in Bellini's painting. It pictured the *Adventus Domini,* in preparation for the Last Judgment and is thus the crowning center of the great program of the central doorway. In fact, it represents the main theme that gives to the other sculptural parts their specific meaning. The original mosaic thus had the same function as the Judgment or *maiestas* reliefs in the tympana of Romanesque and Early Gothic facades. Equally characteristic is the absence of specific elements of the Judgment, motifs that must have been part of the representation of the Last Judgment in the interior of the church. The grand compositional pattern of the mosaic, with its strict symmetry and clear disposition of the figures and groups silhouetted against the golden ground fits its function as the crowning motif of the central porch, even as the chief accent of the entire facade.

What can be derived of it from the Bellini rendering indicates that the scene of the Removal of Mark's Body from Its Tomb depended on the rendering in the Cappella di San Clemente. The depiction of Venetians placing the relics in a basket, however, was not in the earlier cycle and is an embellishment. The Venetians carrying the basket away again corresponds roughly to the mosaic of the interior, as does, to a certain extent, the deception of the Muslim guards. The loading of the relics into the boat, recorded in the inscription, is not pictured in the Bellini painting and the transfer of the basket is difficult to make out. The disputation bears some relationship to the interior cycle but is not the

185

same. The ship ready to set sail recalls the narrative in the Cappella di San Clemente. Mark saving the vessel from shipwreck and the arrival of the ship are hidden from view. The mosaic of the solemn reception of the relics must have been one of the most interesting representations of the dignitaries of the Venetian church and state; the left half must have been some adaptation of the reception mosaic in the vault of San Clemente.

The Solemn Deposition of the Relics is represented in the last and only extant mosaic of the original cycle. Although it has been restored, the representation may be regarded as authentic, and the central figural parts even as original. The mosaic represents the moment in which the open casket with the splendidly attired body of the saint is carried through the central door of the west facade into the church—not as at the time of the actual *translatio* in 828/29 but at the time when the mosaic was made, the "present" of the later thirteenth century. This substitution characterizes the twofold historicity of the representation, which depicts the reception of the relics in the guise of a ceremonial gathering of the Venetian society of the thirteenth century. It is, therefore, quite legitimate to inquire into the nature of this gathering.

What first strikes the beholder is that most of the participants in the ceremonial gathering are coming out of the four doorways instead of going in or waiting in front of the building. Thus, the situation depicted is *after* a ceremony. The fact that the body of the saint is carried into the church does not seem to arouse much interest: it is as if this central motif were merely an inset in the representation, which is either unspecific or has a different meaning, at least a sort of double entendre. The latter indeed seems to be the case: it even seems possible to determine the nature of the ceremony that provided the background for the *collocatio*. The roll in the doge's hand is without doubt the *promissio,* the document enumerating his duties, upon which the newly elected doge had to take an oath. Thus, it is more than likely that the situation represented is that immediately after the presentation and the investiture of the newly elected doge in San Marco, with the participants of the ceremony just leaving the church and the people waiting outside. Several features even make it possible to identify the newly elected doge as Lorenzo Tiepolo (1268–75). The chief figure in the left half of the picture is the dogaressa, Marchesina de Brienne, and the youth immediately to the left of the casket of the saint must be one of the two sons. Of the two clerics who carry the casket, the second on the right is distinguished by his crimson cope and his pallium and must, therefore, be the patriarch. The absolute prevalence of the lay element in this scene only confirms that the mosaic portrays a secular occasion, the last act of the election ceremony of the doge: it must also be realized that in the second half of the thirteenth century the *collocatio* was regarded more as a state and social ceremony than as a specifically ecclesiastic or religious event.

All in all, the mosaic represents one of the most splendid secular gatherings depicted in the ecclesiastic art of the time. The splendor of the scene is heightened by the magnificent backdrop, the representation of the facade itself of which the mosaic is a decorative detail, perhaps the finishing touch. The church is represented roughly as it appeared in the second half of the thirteenth century. The mosaic depicts the church with the cupolas heightened to their present form, with the decoration completed by columns, marble revetment, reliefs, and mosaics. The central lunette, of course, still has its original articulation, which disappeared only in the fifteenth century. Below this lunette the bronze horses are already in place. Despite a number of divergences, the

186

representation must be regarded as one of the most accurate "portraits" of a contemporary building in the third quarter of the thirteenth century.

The mosaic of the *collocatio* is the only part of the thirteenth-century mosaic decoration of the facade that offers stylistic details that can be compared with other mosaics of the church. The types and the treatment of the heads go somewhat beyond those in the second cupola of the Joseph story. The design and modeling of the drapery are also fairly close to the mosaics of that cupola, and the coloristic treatment, with crimson, light and medium blue, and several shades of green as the dominating colors, is almost exactly the same. A certain softness in the faces suggests that the mosaic originated a little later than the cupola but certainly earlier than the third cupola of the Joseph cycle.

A date in the late 1260s for the completion of the facade mosaics, suggested by the chronicle of Martin da Canal, is corroborated by the fact that the important work of beautifying the piazza was undertaken at that time—the paving in 1266/67 and the restoring of the palace of the procuratori in 1269. In the meantime, work was still going on in the atrium with the Life of Moses, which can be regarded as the last part of the great mosaic decoration.

Development of Mosaic Art in San Marco

23 ──

THE DEVELOPMENT of specifically Venetian monumental painting may well have begun as early as the first half of the ninth century, but it is only with San Nicolò al Lido, built in 1043, that substantial evidence is preserved describing mosaic pictures. As regards extant monuments, the two mosaic apses of Torcello Cathedral are certainly the most important Venetian monuments antedating the earliest mosaics in San Marco—belonging to two different periods, mid-eleventh century and the second half of the twelfth. The clear affinities of the south apse with sixth-century monuments in Ravenna suggest a revival of Early Christian and Early Byzantine traditions at this time. The political motor of this revival may have been the assertion of Venetian power in the Mediterranean. Some reminiscence may even have survived in the program of San Marco—for instance, the placing of the Sacrifice of Cain and Abel and the representation of the Lamb in the presbytery, the compositional scheme of the Reception of Mark's Relics in the vaults of the Cappella di San Clemente, which goes back to the Justinian dedicatory image in San Vitale—and perhaps also in the iconography and even the narrative style of the Marcian cycle in both side chapels.

Different from these bits of testimony of a revival of Ravennate ideas and forms are those reminiscences of pre- or at least Early Romanesque north Italian painting that have survived in the style of the local workshop. Some characteristics of this style seem to derive from an almost timeless popular art—a subcurrent that was almost always present in Venice, at times militating against the Byzantine current, at other times combining and fusing with it.

The analysis of the various cycles shows that the mosaic decoration of San Marco consists of a number of stylistically different groups of work, some smaller, some larger. By and large, the work seems to have progressed from east to west and from top downward, with the exception, of course, of those irregularities that were caused by the fire of 1106 and, perhaps, a second catastrophe of uncertain date. It begins, not in the main apse, but in the niches around and above the central door; in style the mosaics here relate to the apostles in the main apse of Torcello. Thus, it does not seem that the masters were newly called from Byzantium but that they had stayed on in Venice. This would explain the somewhat antiquated, somewhat tired style of the mosaics of the San Marco porch, even though it is a fairly pure Byzantine style (pl. 1 and fig. 4).

When the main apse was ready for decoration, around 1084, a different, more modern workshop was employed. Compared with true Byzantine works, however, these mosaics also did not represent one of the most modern currents of Constantinopolitan painting (pl. 3). Damaged by the great fire of 1106, the apse mosaics were subjected to extensive repairs by a master who was acquainted with contemporary Byzantine monumental painting with which he shared a new feeling for statuesque monumentality, a tendency toward the great pose and gesture and toward the humanizing and softening of the expression.

What remains of the post-fire campaign in the east dome has certain generic similarities with the neoclassical style of Byzantium but is more mannered, the pattern of the draperies being less rhythmical, more broken, and harder. The mosaicists were highly trained and refined artists and used a technique derived from the best Greek prototypes, but one showing local and perhaps also individual idiosyncrasies. Whether these mosaicists were Greek or not, they must have had a certain amount of Greek training, evident in the treatment of details and in the mastery and almost classical air about the figures. On the other hand, the mosaicists took quite a number of motifs and features from the San Marco apse, translating them into a more linear vocabulary with a tendency toward preciousness and nervous complication. Thus, we must reckon with the fact that the style of these figures was developed in Venice itself by mosaicists who developed a specialized manner of their own on the basis of the early Comnenian style of Constantinople.

In the mosaics made after the completion of the apse and east dome, there is hardly any trace of renewed Byzantine influence or any attempt on the part of the local craftsmen—for it was they who began work again at mosaics—to find out what was going on in Byzantium and to orient themselves accordingly. On the contrary, they seem to have been bound to local Venetian traditions of iconography and composition and, as far as they had any connections with Byzantine mosaic art at all, it was with models and, in part, with techniques of the eleventh century. What we find in the choir chapels of San Pietro and San Clemente is a change from a colonial to a local art.

The story of the evangelist, of the founding of the patriarchate of Aquileia, and of the *translatio* of the patron saint's relics from Alexandria to Rialto is told in a dry, sparse chronicle style (fig. 12). Technically speaking, they are rather primitive though fairly competent works. On the other hand, the technique lacks the refinement of genuine Byzantine mosaics. It seems that as they went along, the mosaicists reestablished, step by step, a certain amount of contact with at least some currents of Byzantine art. By the time the work in the choir chapels was completed, the workshop seems to have split or sent off several branches that produced an enormous amount of work, filling practically the entire church with not very attractive, almost mass-produced mosaics.

Neither the branch that grew into the north transept nor that of the south rose above the level of moderately competent craftsmanship. Both depended on Byzantine miniatures as models for their simple iconographical compositions, and both made do with a very few figure types derived in part from the apse mosaics. Compositional schemes and figures are stereotyped to a degree hardly ever found in Byzantine art: one even has the feeling that the designer consciously aimed at stereotyped regularity. The technique, too, has been regularized, to conform with almost geometrical patterns. Nothing in Byzantine art is quite so schematic or formulaic as this technique. The same principle of schematic, even geometric regularity also dominates the overall composition of the north cupola with its concentric rings of ornaments, inscriptions, and

189

figures, as well as every single scene built on the same principle (pl. 8). The final effect is one of firmness and stability—something more akin to Romanesque schematism than to Byzantine monumental decoration.

In the south dome the same principle of geometric regularity did not succeed because of the poverty of the program (pl. 11). The four comparatively small single figures of saints were hardly sufficient to organize the vast golden surface. While the mosaics of the two domes were being set, a number of more or less independent groups of workmen, all connected with the local school, were busy on the vaults and walls of the transept. Though monumentalized, the Miracle scenes of the north transept were copied, more or less faithfully, from Byzantine miniatures of the late eleventh or early twelfth century (pl. 12a). The latest part of the decoration of the north transept, the cycle of the Life of the Virgin, also copied from a Byzantine manuscript, and remade by a north Italian workshop, shows no adaptation at all (pl. 12b). A much better-led and better-equipped branch of the local workshop set the mosaics on the south vault of the central dome, with four christological scenes, undoubtedly based on an eleventh-century Byzantine Gospels. The compositions are extremely sober, mere strings of silhouettes held together by a tenuous rhythm. If, in the north dome, it was the radial and concentric articulation of a dome that dominated the composition, here it is the smooth and even surface of a broad vault that provides the principles of organization. The single scenes consist of rectangular, paratactic sequences of similar motifs without any pictorial centering.

The next surviving unit of the great campaign is the west dome with the representation of the Pentecost (pl. 13). Although this was completed some time later, it still shows numerous ties with the north dome and the south vault. The grand geometrical organization of the dome as a whole is common to both cupolas, down to the arrangement of the inscriptions and their paleographic forms. The designer, however, had to turn again to Byzantium. Indeed, the apostles testify to a renewed and profound study of Byzantine monumental prototypes, the first direct contact of this kind after the completion of the first phase of mosaics in the east dome. These prototypes must have been fairly modern, exhibiting a style that must have been leading up to the dynamic style. Some characteristics of the figures can only be explained by newly established direct communication with Byzantine mosaics or mosaicists. What is especially striking about the forms found here is the emergence of a perfectly integrated rhythm of the linear pattern, a rhythm that reached its climax in works of the middle and second half of the twelfth century (pl. 14).

The mosaics of the west dome are the latest work of the local school; as a matter of fact, they already go beyond its normal possibilities by following "modern" Greek models and incorporating contemporary Byzantine techniques. The school must have had a fairly long life: in spite of the indubitable connections between its earliest products in the Cappella di San Pietro and its latest works in the Pentecost dome, it is a far cry from the art of the choir chapels to that of the west dome. The difference in time may not have been great. More important, certainly, was the different relation to the living Byzantine art of the period. From this point on, this connection was never to be lost although the interpretation of Byzantine models and methods varied and became, by and large, increasingly free.

During the last third of the twelfth century extensive repair work was done in San Marco. The parts most affected lay along the main axis: the east dome, central dome, west vault, and south vault of the west arm. A complete renewal was necessary in the central dome and the west vault, which are de novo creations of the late twelfth century, albeit perpetuating the main themes of the original programs. However, the designers in the late twelfth century were not content with reproducing faithfully the destroyed or heavily damaged mosaics, but introduced such new features as the allegories of the virtues in the central dome and the four rivers of paradise in its pendentives, both clearly Western elements that cannot have been part of the original, predominantly Byzantine program. Among other new and distinctly Western additions are the tablets in the pre-Passion scenes with their inscriptions dramatizing the narrative.

The actual repairs seem to have begun in the east dome, where ten and a half figures were newly designed and set. The master must have known some Byzantine works of the earlier phases of the dynamic style, but the most important roots of his art must be looked for not in Byzantium, but in Venice itself, namely, in the apostles of the west dome. Some of the stylistic principles and even technical details of the two domes—the latest work of the pre-catastrophe period and the earliest of the repair period—are fairly close. Thus, the style of the east dome seems to have been a Venetian growth, a development of the style of the west dome in the direction of the dynamic style of Byzantine painting without, however, fully realizing this dynamic ingredient (pl. 15).

The style of the east dome was certainly the basis of the further development in San Marco. This development is characterized by an increase in expressive mannerism on the one side and by a growing awareness of what happened in Byzantium proper on the other. Byzantine styles of the last quarter of the century seem to have found their way to Venice very quickly and to have been assimilated as rapidly. Taken as a whole, the development from a neutral and static style to a dynamic and expressive mannerism can be regarded as an almost automatic process.

Work on the east dome may have gone on for some time. It is also likely that after its completion, the mosaicists did not immediately move to the central dome, which in style is appreciably different. With the mosaics of this dome and the adjacent vault with its scenes from the Passion and Resurrection of Christ, Venetian mosaic art reached its maturity and soon its peak as well (pl. 17). The mosaics of this group, which were made under the supervision of a major artist, are surely among the great monuments of medieval painting, powerful and refined at the same time. In a very brief period, fifteen or twenty years, the workshop went through the whole gamut of possibilities evolved from later Comnenian art, from the storm style to a kind of rarified fin de siècle style, a sort of Byzantine art nouveau, and finally to the new monumental style of the turn of the century. Although echoes of all these styles and currents can be found in the mosaics of the central workshop, none of them was adopted in its purely Byzantine form, nor were the extreme forms of these styles accepted, and certainly not the extreme baroque of the storm style. Most of the figures in the dome are standing, quietly stepping out, or turning—their extremely slender bodies with spindly limbs confined within straight perpendicular contours. The draperies are not flowing freely but appear almost glued to the bodies (pl. 19a). The colors are subdued, the expression of the faces not expansive, let alone aggressive, but nervous, anxious, appealing; some even have a kind of lyrical quality. If these qualities are hardly to be found in the works of the storm variety of the dynamic style, they are certainly present and even preponderant in the "art nouveau" style.

The mosaics of the west vault show the gradual differentiation and

191

disintegration of the workshop of the central dome (pl. 22a). No fewer than five different hands can be distinguished in the scenes of the Passion and the Resurrection, to say nothing of a number of assistants employed by these masters. One of them seems to have been the chief master of the dome who probably was also responsible for the design of the whole vault. There are in some figures a certain hardening of the details in the drapery folds, a more linear treatment, and the almost complete disappearance of an integrated shading of the figure as a whole, which could be explained by assuming a somewhat later date, probably less than a decade. In others, these differences are much more strongly accentuated. There is nothing left, in these stiff and almost motionless forms, of the sinuous movement of the central dome.

The abstract-decorative style was not the last impulse to come out of Byzantium before the fall of Constantinople in 1204. There is very good reason to suppose that at about the turn of the century there originated in the capital an entirely new current that aimed at a return to the great classical art of the tenth and eleventh centuries, a monumental, neoclassical style. It was characterized by a new simplicity and grandeur, by a feeling for the totality of bodily volume, a melodious flow of line, and a new humanism. In San Marco its first traces appear in some faces of the Passion mosaics.

Both styles, the complicated late Comnenian and the new monumental style, lived on into the thirteenth century when they appeared side by side in the grand panel of the Agony in the Garden (figs. 48–49). The symbiosis of several styles in one mosaic, already present in the west vault, is perhaps a characteristic of the time around 1200. The almost glaring discrepancies, not only in design but also in color and technique, do not seem to have disturbed either the artistic supervisor of the decoration or the beholders.

In San Marco there must have existed an iconographic program that ordered the arrangement of the several parts and cycles of the decoration, though the completion of this program was not achieved within a short time but stretched out over a long period, progressing in fits and starts and interrupted by stalemates and catastrophes. It was inevitable that this should have led to a rather motley accretion of much smaller units. There must have been times when only one or two masters, with some assistants, were at work in different parts of the church on the immense task of encrusting the large surfaces with mosaics and other periods when four or five masters worked side by side in one dome or vault.

How and where did the mosaicists who worked in San Marco receive their technical and artistic training and where did they get the models? The answers are different for different tasks and periods. With all due caution, it can be assumed that the earliest mosaics—porch, apse, and east dome (phase I)—are the work of Greeks who had already lived for some time in Venice and used Greek model books that were already somewhat out of fashion and were modified, in various degrees, according to the Venetian taste. A great change occurred in the early twelfth century, when Greek influence weakened and a large Venetian workshop took over that used neither Greek material nor Greek pattern books, at least not in the early stages of its activity. In the later stages Byzantine illuminated manuscripts served the Venetian craftsmen as models for whole compositions and single figures. Only in the latest stages of their work, in the west dome, did direct Byzantine influence appear again in San Marco, and with it the use of specific Byzantine model books for monumental painting. In the last quarter of the twelfth century, Veneto-Byzantine masters of high rank took over, who knew Byzantine mosaics firsthand, probably because they traveled as journeymen, perhaps even as far as Constantinople, and took cognizance of the most modern trends of Byzantine painting. The model books they used were most likely of their own composition.

The Western factor is more difficult to define. With the exception of the early works of the local school and some features in the later mosaics, it consists not so much in compositional and figural motifs but in the interpretation of the Byzantine patterns and formulas, from the technique to the decorative principles. Perhaps the most interesting aspect of the Western factor is the geometric character of the compositions, especially that of the north and west domes—that is, in the mature and late works of the local school, where a severe and at the same time organic synthesis of figural, epigraphic, and sparse ornamental forms had been reached, a synthesis that would be sought in vain in Byzantium. Even the technique, with its circular patterns, obeys this overriding principle of geometric regularity.

As they stood completed according to the plans laid down in the early twelfth century, the mosaics of San Marco must have constituted the most richly differentiated monument of Italo-Byzantine mosaic art of the time— perhaps even of medieval painting in general. Sicily and Rome, the other two important contemporary centers of mosaic art, had nothing to show that could compare, as a single monument, with San Marco. True, Sicily has a greater number of mosaic ensembles than Venetia, and Monreale has certainly a grandeur that is perhaps more impressive at first glance than San Marco, but none of the Sicilian monuments, taken singly, has anything like the wealth and differentiation of San Marco.

THIRTEENTH CENTURY

The next phase in San Marco can be traced only from about 1215, with the earliest part of the Agony in the Garden panel. In spite of probable interruption in the work, the style of these earliest extant mosaics of the new century is still quite clearly connected with that of the last phase of the Late Comnenian style as it is represented by the work of the Ascension master and his school. The somewhat later date of the sleeping apostles of the Agony panel is confirmed by their greater bulk, the handsome, less expressive types, and the more organic, regular, and even mellifluous draperies. The new style is still preponderantly linear, but the linear drapery envelops a body that is beginning to take on volume, even if this is still largely the volume of a relief.

With the work of the second master of the Agony, which can be dated with a high degree of probability to the years from 1216 to 1218, a new style turns up in San Marco, if only as a brief interlude. This style is characterized by the grand design of the five figures, which corresponds to the sober, monumental, and statuesque forms that appear in the work of Greek masters of about 1208/9, e.g. in Studenica. The severe figures of our master have shed all reminiscences of Comnenian art, with the exception of the spiral pattern on the hip of John, who lies at the feet of Christ. The presence of this antiquated detail suggests that the grand schemes of the figures were in fact a recent import from Byzantium. The new conception of the monumental figure, however, is combined with a broken, splintery treatment of the drapery. On the one hand, this treatment points forward to later Byzantine works, and, on the other, it bears a certain

193

resemblance to the so-called zigzag style that dominated much of German painting of this time. Taken as a whole, the style of the second Agony master is anomalous with regard to the Venetian development. It even seems that the style was not at all well understood by the master who introduced it in San Marco. At any rate, it disappeared when he left Venice—for Rome, as the evidence indicates. Nevertheless, the grand statuesque design of the figures of the second master was not without some influence on the style of his followers, for it set a standard of scale for the rest of the figures in the panel, and the drapery design of the standing Christ became the model for the drapery patterns of the other standing figures of Christ.

The master (or masters) who succeeded the second Agony mosaicist reverted more or less to the traditional style of the first master, without, however, completely escaping a renewed influence from contemporary Byzantine painting. In the meantime, the severe phase of the monumental style had been succeeded by a more pliable variant, a statuesque style richer in form-designing or other kinds of modeling details and with a somewhat fuller volume in the figures—reminiscent of contemporary Byzantine developments. The new Byzantine influence was felt rather superficially, however, and was not the decisive stylistic factor. Apart from the older Venetian tradition which again came to the fore, quite new tendencies also made their appearance—tendencies that deflected the development in San Marco from a course strictly parallel to that of Byzantine monumental painting, comprising such decidedly Western elements as a new kind of Gothic elegance visible in the shaping of the supple bodies, especially the hands and feet. This early Gothic style is echoed, faintly at first, in the figures of the third Agony master. His work constitutes the first of several successive phases of a "precious" style. A second phase is represented by the figures of prophets in the north aisle in which we find a rich lineament in seams and contours that also creates a highly differentiated relief, a shimmering, metallic surface. In a third phase, which includes the figures opposite on the south wall and some of the saints in the west part of the church, this relief is flattened out, and disappears almost completely in the stiff and rectilinear figures of the prophet-kings or else is reduced to slightly curved planes from which the drapery seems to have been carved out. There also appear richly patterned backgrounds that are clearly derived from Gothic stained glass, enamel, or metal work. In the last phase of the precious style, which includes the saints in the central part of the church, the decorative effects become a little coarser and the technique more summary. There are no convincing parallels, let alone prototypes, for these phases of the Venetian development that constitute the "precious" style. The style is a Venetian growth in which Gothic elements appear grafted onto the Veneto-Byzantine art of the first master of the Agony. The intrusion of these Gothic influences was perhaps the most important stylistic factor in the first half and the middle of the thirteenth century.

Parallel to the crystallization of the precious style and its development toward a flat decorative style was a process triggered by the impact of Late Antique illusionism, which reached Venice in the model of the Old Testament mosaics of the atrium. Translating the Cotton miniatures into mosaic must have been very difficult for workmen trained to follow models especially created for monumental work. The "relief style" of the third master of the Agony had to be modified in order to render some of the illusionistic qualities of the new small-scale models. To a certain extent all this may have retarded and even deflected the development—and may explain the lack of sureness—in the initial parts of the work of the atrium. It was only step by step that the designer and the mosaicists learned to cope with the new task.

The new element of illusionism, which was, after all, a kind of naturalism, was mastered more easily in the representation of animals than of human figures. In the latter field, the weight of the Venetian tradition was great enough, soon after the completion of the first cupola, to cause a return to the style of the third master of the Agony and of the prophets of the north aisle. There is a further development of the style with a tendency toward classical beauty, harmony, and even elegance in the first Joseph cupola. This seems to have been specifically Venetian, not directly influenced by any foreign factor. What appears Western in this style is derived from the mosaics of the interior, the later prophets and saints.

With this saturated, harmonious phase, the development breaks off suddenly and is followed by an almost complete gap of about twenty to thirty years (c. 1230 to c. 1255–60). This gap can be filled only to a certain extent. A few figures of saints in the interior may have originated in the 1240s and early 1250s. The mosaics that can be dated (if only hypothetically) to the early fifties are marginal works that do not exhibit a consistent style. In fact, even the two most important mosaics of this date, the *preghiera* (pl. 33) and the *apparitio* (fig. 52), seem only loosely connected with the main development, and they may, in fact, be the work of outsiders. In any case, the style, or rather the two different styles of the two mosaics, owe hardly anything to Byzantine art, nor can they be attributed to any other outside source. The only Byzantine element is the new highlight technique in the faces of the figures of the *preghiera*. The physiognomic realism of these faces is to be seen as a Venetian development, perhaps in the realm of secular painting. The same is true of the unsuccessful attempts at representing three-dimensional space in the depicted interiors.

In the Deesis above the main door of the west wall—apparently the latest part of the decoration of the interior—Byzantine influence reasserted itself (fig. 62). Not only is the Byzantine highlight technique further developed than in the *preghiera,* the volume style that dominated the development of painting in the Byzantine area from the middle of the thirteenth century also makes its appearance. The bodies begin to fill out and their draperies are modeled in a new, painterly manner.

A different, more mature version of this transitional style can be seen in the second cupola of the Joseph story, which recommenced the new activity of mosaic decoration in the atrium in the late fifties or early sixties. The master of the new workshop approached his model in a new spirit: he was open to some of the leading tendencies of his time as they appeared in Italy with their new plastic vigor and their sharply delineated pattern of the drapery (pl. 54). The design and modeling of the draperies have also profited from contemporary Byzantine art. The master seems, however, to have been at least as much interested in French forms and tendencies. This is especially evident in the architectural and ornamental details but to some extent in the drapery patterns and the figure style as well, where we find the first traces of these proto-Renaissance tendencies that dominate the style of the next cupola. At the same time the painterly practices that first turned up in the *preghiera* seem to have been developed further, including the new and bold colorism that first appeared in the Deesis. Although some characteristic qualities of the style of the second Joseph cupola thus seem to have been taken over from the *preghiera* master, neither these nor any other mosaics in San Marco can really fill the gap between the first

195

and the second cupolas of the Joseph cycle. We can only assume that, if there was a continuous development between the two styles, it must have taken place outside San Marco itself.

The mosaics of the Cappella Zen and of the facade—offshoots of the workshop of the second Joseph cupola—do not seem to have contributed a great deal to the further development of the new style. The end of the workshop's activity can be dated to the 1270s with the last mosaic of the facade.

Up to and, to a certain degree, also including the mosaics of the fifties and sixties, Byzantine linear formulas more or less dominated the design and modeling of the draperies. From then onward they began to be superseded and were finally completely ousted, first by classical lineaments and fold schemes and finally, in the last three decades of the century, by the new glittering light technique and the bulging plasticity of Palaeologan art. The mosaics of the seventies—those of the third cupola of the Joseph cycle—are the chief works of what can be termed the classical phase of thirteenth-century Venetian art. It is in these works that the proto-Renaissance found its most perfect realization in the field of mosaic. All those elements that appeared virtually separate in the mosaics of the preceding cupola seem here to have entered into a perfect synthesis. Neither Western nor Byzantine elements predominate, but are completely amalgamated. The "classical" quality of these mosaics did not have its roots in the Cotton Genesis model, but was an independent growth. In fact, the mosaics of the third Joseph cupola are more "classical" in a sculptural way, that is, in type, design, movement, and modeling of the figures, and in part even in the costumes and "beautiful" faces, as well as in the motifs of the architectural backgrounds with their shell-shaped niches. These motifs and forms owe more to the Venetian proto-Renaissance than to the manuscript model.

Of course, the very fact that an Early Christian model was used for the mosaic decoration of the atrium was in itself due to the proto-Renaissance tendencies that began to develop soon after the capture of Constantinople. Some effects of these tendencies in the early thirteenth century are evident in the choice of the material and motifs of the San Marco decoration, in the archaistic return to Early Byzantine techniques as they appear, for instance, in the mosaics of San Vitale in neighboring Ravenna, and in the increased use of medallions. In its pure form, however, the classical style appears only in the third quarter of the century in the third Joseph cupola, in those mosaics that are indeed more classical than the works of the parallel phase of Byzantine painting. In San Marco, the feeling for organic, classical form outweighs the tendency toward the emphasis on volume; in Byzantium it is the other way around. Nevertheless, the two phases in Venice and Byzantium are in a way evolutionary parallels.

With the Moses cupola, the last of the atrium, the development of style takes a sudden turn: the "classical" style has been suddenly ousted by the influx of Palaeologan art. The cupola is filled not with a frieze of more or less crowded figures and architectural elements, but with large picturelike compositional units of landscape, architecture, and figures in complicated arrangements (pl. 63). To a large extent Palaeologan forms also dominate the landscapes and the architectures themselves, as well as the types, movements, and modeling of the voluminous figures. However, not all the cycle was conceived and executed in the new style, for some parts look as if they had been transferred unchanged from the preceding cupola. In the greater part of the cupola and the north apse, the new technique of glittering lights playing over the entire surface of the figure has supplanted the earlier drapery designs, but in other parts, Byzantinizing and classical drapery patterns are still in use. This existence, side by side, of earlier traditional elements and modern, Palaeologan ones is proof that the new forms came from outside, introduced from Byzantium together with the iconographic model for the greater part of the Moses cycle. This prototype was most likely an Early Palaeologan manuscript, probably of the early 1270s. The date of the mosaic itself could be about a decade later.

The sequence of movements and stylistic episodes that has been summarized in the preceding pages does not constitute an organic, continuous development. Rather, it was a complicated process, shaped in part by foreign influences that at times deflected the evolution from its "normal" course. In addition, there existed in most periods several strands of development that diverged from each other because several masters worked side by side. And there are, finally, gaps in the sequence as it appears today, partly because of losses in the decoration of the church itself, partly because work on the mosaic decoration seems to have been interrupted altogether in certain periods or continued only at a slackened rate.

During the thirteenth century, mosaic was certainly the leading branch of the figural arts in Venice. As far as can be determined, it was not influenced by either Venetian wall painting, panel painting, or miniature. The relationship between mosaic and sculpture seems to have been somewhat different: it is certain that sculpture was in some respect under the influence of mosaic, but sculpture may also have had some effect on the development of mosaic style. Sculpture seems to have strengthened certain tendencies, as, for instance, the readiness to receive and amalgamate French stylistic elements on the one hand, and on the other, the influence of the proto-Renaissance movement, which developed more strongly and perhaps at an earlier date in sculpture than in painting.

Byzantine influence reached Venice in several waves of various intensity during the thirteenth century: two or three waves in the first quarter, one rather faint wave after the middle, and another in the late seventies or early eighties. Each of these waves may have carried several different impulses. Where did they come from? This question is, of course, connected with the problem of the survival in and continued radiation of monumental art from Constantinople during the Latin occupation between 1204 and 1261.

We can probably regard those Byzantine influences that reached Venice when the great Agony in the Garden mosaic was made as coming from Constantinople itself. This would explain the generic similarity between the figures of the oldest part of the Agony and some of the earlier series of prophets on the north aisle, on the one hand, and certain Serbian frescoes on the other. However, while the latter were most likely the work of Constantinopolitan painters themselves, the Venetian mosaics were probably made by Venetians after drawings by masters from the Byzantine capital and were certainly influenced by their style or rather styles as these appear in the three successive parts of the Agony panel. The second of these parts, with the broken surface treatment of the draperies, may well have been influenced by an early manifestation of the Byzantine style that otherwise came to the fore only in the last third of the century.

It has been shown that this two- or three-fold wave of Byzantine influence gradually subsided in the third decade of the century. A new impact made itself felt only after the middle of the century. The most important testimony of the new wave is the Deesis above the west door, if the few Byzantine elements

197

appearing in this and other works of the time can be taken as evidence of a "wave." In any case, this latter influence can hardly be connected with Constantinople: the model, with its technical and stylistic innovations, must have come from some other source. Oddities of the Venetian mosaics seem to point to a locality where provincial, antiquated, and modern elements were all mingled. As a matter of fact, most of the Byzantine paintings of the middle of the thirteenth century show this synthetic style, with its harsh colorism, its almost brutal types, and hard modeling of the shadows in faces and draperies. It is hardly possible to localize the sources of the Byzantine influence that helped shape the Venetian mosaic style of the 1250s and 1260s. In addition to individual works, probably icons, that may have reached Venice at that time, we must also reckon with a kind of general infiltration of new forms and techniques from provincial regions. Salonica, where Greek domination was reestablished, may have played an important part among these sources, perhaps by way of Serbia.

It was only in the seventies that relationships between Constantinople and Venice were resumed. It can hardly be doubted that the new wave of Byzantine influence that reached Venice in the seventies and eighties came directly from Constantinople. This influence first made itself felt in the infiltration of the volume style, visible in some of the figures of the third Joseph cupola and lunette, and soon afterwards in the sudden appearance of a Palaeologan model as the main source of the Moses cycle. In addition, the designer of the cupola and lunette mosaics must have been conversant with the new principles of cupola composition, and the mosaicists must have been able to learn something about early Palaeologan modeling techniques. It may be questioned whether these ultramodern trends had established themselves in Constantinople so soon after the reconquest of the city. This would certainly have been impossible if Byzantine artists had to start from scratch in the newly regained city: they must have brought with them an almost fully developed style, which, in the hothouse atmosphere of a period of restoration and renovation of many metropolitan churches, would have evolved at a rapid pace. The place where the preparatory fashioning of the Palaeologan style took place was either Salonica or Nicaea or both. It is certain that the Palaeologan style whose influence so drastically changed the traditional style of the leading San Marco workshop was fully developed in resurrected Byzantium at least as early as the eighth decade of the century.

Neither the first monumental style of the recovered capital nor the volume style reached Venice or was fully accepted and appreciated there. It attained the peak of its development in the 1260s, when Venice was more or less cut off from Byzantium. The extreme variety of the style, with its bloated forms, would in any case have hardly found favor in Venice at a time when the proto-Renaissance movement was at its height. Another fact that should be stressed when considering the effect of contemporary Byzantine influences on the San Marco mosaics is that the antique elements that are so strong in the third cupola of the Joseph cycle were in no way the result of this influence: this was a Venetian development. If Byzantine models played a part in the development of this growth, they were Early Byzantine and not medieval works, because Byzantine thirteenth-century art had nothing to do with the upsurge of classicism that was part of the Venetian proto-Renaissance.

The transmission of the various waves of Byzantine influence that reached Venice between 1204 and 1280 must have been effected by a variety of means. Apart from the Early Byzantine Cotton Genesis, there must have been one or two Byzantine painters, who may have contributed to the modernizing of the

198

Late Comnenian style of the leading workshop by preparing model drawings. In the period about the middle of the century, this role was played by chance encounters with contemporary Byzantine works, probably icons. A slight infiltration of new forms and methods in the sixties and seventies was followed by the adoption of an almost contemporary, early Palaeologan manuscript as the model for the Moses cycle. This must also have led to an ever growing familiarity with the new Byzantine style. Perhaps the most important role played by Byzantine influences in the development of the Venetian mosaic style in the thirteenth century was not a positive one. The influence of the Cotton Genesis miniatures may have interrupted for a time the growth of a specifically Venetian style, as a continuation of the style of the Ascension workshop. The influence of the monumental style was not strong enough and the chance encounters with contemporary modeling and highlight techniques did not provide a sufficiently broad basis for the development of a truly painterly style. Finally, the influence of Palaeologan miniature painting—in the model for the Moses cycle—cut short the organic evolution of the Venetian proto-Renaissance as it manifested itself in the third Joseph cupola, without, however, leading to the adoption of the fully grown Palaeologan style.

The tracing and evaluation of Western influences in the thirteenth-century mosaics is made especially difficult by the fact that certain elements and tendencies in Venetian art that might be regarded as due to Western influence were actually indigenous to Venice. Venetian art was never for any length of time purely Byzantine: the Western component always asserted itself soon after the arrival of any new wave of Byzantine influence. The difficulty of separating indigenous from imported elements is increased by the evolutionary parallelism of Eastern and Western art, which became even more strongly marked in the thirteenth century than it was in the twelfth. With regard to the development of style, this parallelism may in certain cases give rise to doubts about whether the chief tendencies active in one or the other phase of the art of Venice—which lies between the two worlds—belonged by Byzantine or to Western art.

In the Agony panel, traces of specifically Gothic influence can be discerned in the first section. The influence becomes even more obvious in the third section, reaching a peak in the panels of the aisles (Christ, Virgin, prophets). In the latter, the precious style of French Gothic has entered into a perfect synthesis with the Veneto-Byzantine style of the early thirteenth century. French influence is not confined here to details of figures but shapes the entire form of the panels. It transforms the traditional color scheme and the patterned grounds, as well as the functional role of the frames in a way that approximates Western images, so that they serve, not only as boundaries, but also as integral parts of the pictorial units.

The gradual change in the rendering of the relief of the bodies from the rich drapery patterns modeled by form-designing curved lines in the figures of the north aisle, to the almost flat surface, bounded and cut across by straight lines in the figures of the south aisle, follows exactly the development of Early Gothic figure design and modeling. This brief return to a flat decorative style as it appears in Venice and in the West in the later second and the third decade of the thirteenth century has no exact counterpart in the otherwise parallel development of Byzantine painting. On the other hand, it would be in vain to look for specific models for the prophets and saints in French or German painting. Here it seems to be only the effect of a general influence exerted by what proved to be a rather brief phase in Western painting.

199

Whether Western influence was also responsible for those specialized forms that parallel the German zigzag style is an exceedingly difficult problem, especially if one realizes that the broken surface variant occurs in Venice earlier than in the North, while the linear zigzag, although an age-old Byzantine element, was fully developed—and exaggerated—in the North at least one whole decade before its comparatively tame manifestation in the San Marco prophets. It is very likely that this was a most complicated give-and-take process in which not only two but three partners were involved: Byzantium, Venice, and the North.

The influence of Western Gothic appears again briefly in the second cupola of the Joseph story. It must be assumed, however, that it was also present in the quarter-century between the later prophets and saints of the interior and the cupola, the mosaics of which mark the resumption of work in the atrium. In this case, the Western influence can be clearly defined as French. With the third Joseph cupola, the Gothic influence comes to an end, ousted first by the classical proto-Renaissance and after that by the new wave of Byzantine influence in the Moses cupola.

The transmission of Western, that is, preponderantly French, influence seems to have been effected by artists trained in France, working in Venice. It must also be noted that Venice belonged in some general way to the French sphere of influence: French was widely spoken and understood there. Further, while the crusades may have intensified the French element in Venetian culture, it is unlikely that crusader art, whether French or not, specifically contributed anything to the development of the Venetian mosaic style. There seem to be no sufficiently strong arguments in favor of influence from Tuscany or northern Italy.

Considering the importance of the foreign contributions to the style of the San Marco mosaics, it might appear as if the art of the thirteenth century in Venice were little more than a mixture of Byzantine and Western elements, without any substance of its own. Nothing, however, could be more erroneous. Quite apart from the fact that the two main ingredients were not completely foreign, belonging as they did to the very essence of Venice, their meeting in Venetian art did not result in a mixture but in a genuine synthesis from which sprang something essentially new. In addition, at least from the twelfth century, there existed something authentically Venetian. First among the Venetian characteristics is, of course, a subtle colorism; another, a sense of rhythmic composition developed from the frieze—a trait that led to the preference for broad, oblong formats with a horizontal spreading-out of the content, as against the strictly confined "picture" compositions of most other Italian painting. Connected with this is the leisurely unrolling of the narrative as against dramatic concentration. Yet another Venetian trait is the penchant for the decorative, for splendor and sumptuousness, the striving for harmonious "beauty," for the classical as against the characteristic and expressive.

One of the most important characteristics of twelfth- and thirteenth-century mosaic-making in San Marco was the multiplicity of styles, the possibility of several artists working side by side with an amount of personal freedom hardly to be found in other medieval ensembles. A well-known document of 1258 indicates that several mosaicists with their apprentices worked side by side, independent of each other, in San Marco. This apparently "anarchic" situation had a very positive effect: it made possible the rise of personal freedom, the development and assertion of artistic personality even under conditions of close cooperation.

About the artists who worked in Venice in general and in San Marco in particular, there is little contemporary documentary evidence. Writing in the late eighteenth century, Zanetti mentioned a few names of painters, but they are only names and not otherwise well documented. The sole interesting fact about them is that they either are Greek or are referred to as Greeks; they may have been immigrants from Constantinople. The one thirteenth-century Venetian mosaicist whose name has come down to us is Apollonius, a Greek. Vasari tells us that Andrea Tafi met him in Venice and took him to Florence to assist him in the mosaic work of the Baptistery. An interesting point in Vasari's narrative is that Apollonius instructed Tafi in the production of raw materials for making mosaics, enamel, and stucco. The evidence suggests that during those times when they were needed in San Marco, the mosaicists were virtually serfs of the Procuratoria and were not allowed to leave town. The granting of permission for mosaicists to take up work in other places was more or less a matter of state policy. This policy certainly contributed to Venice's virtual monopoly in mosaic during part of the thirteenth century, but it may have prevented or minimized the spread of the Venetian mosaic style and technique; the instances of which we know are very few indeed.

The only documented cases of "export" of the Venetian mosaic style or emigration of Venetian mosaic workers in the thirteenth century concern Rome and Florence. The mosaic of the apse of San Paolo fuori le mura was, in large part, the work of Venetian mosaicists. The few original pieces of it that remain are so close to parts of the Agony panel in San Marco that they must be regarded as works of Venetian hands or executed under close Venetian supervision. It seems, however, that the foreign milieu, and perhaps the pressures of a large work to be completed in a short time, were detrimental to the quality of the work. The activity of the Venetian mosaicists does not seem to have exerted any further influence in Rome.

Venetian work in Florence is less well documented. The parts of the Florence Baptistery dome assigned by Vasari to Venetian and Venetian-trained mosaicists are among the most purely Tuscan portions of the entire work.

The influence of the San Marco mosaics elsewhere in Italy is confined to wall-painting. North of the Alps, the impact of Venice can be detected but did not go very deep, and although Venetian or Venetian-trained artists also worked in the Greek East, they seem not to have had a determining effect on the formation of the Palaeologan style.

More important was the impact of the formal qualities of the mosaics on later Venetian painting. Venetian painters never completely lost sight of their great national church. Something of the mosaics' iconography lived on, not merely the themes but also their compositional schemes, for instance in the work of Paolo da Venezia and his school. More important was the impact of the formal qualities of the mosaics on later Venetian painting—which would not have developed as it did without the influence of San Marco. The actual inclusion of mosaic apses in Venetian paintings of the later fifteenth and early sixteenth centuries provided a coloristic and spatial framework that, since these apses almost always seem hollowed out of a wall parallel to the picture plane, was sufficiently flat to suit the preference of Venetian Renaissance painting for

201

shallow spatial compositions. These golden apses also very often set the key for the entire harmony of color. It was this golden twilight that made it possible for the figures to be integrated in those niches and the shallow stages in front of them not as plastic but as coloristic entities.

The literal reproduction of golden apses in the paintings disappeared in the course of the sixteenth century to be replaced by more sophisticated renderings of the golden light of the mosaics. The intangible, immaterial character of the warm backgrounds of Venetian portraits and iconlike representations of saints was a kind of analogue to the golden ground of the mosaics and a product of the painters' dealings with them. Other characteristics of the Venetian sixteenth century may have been strengthened by the influence the mosaics exercised on leading artists, including the dominant ornamental character, the tendency toward flatness, a certain kind of rhythm, and the absence of a decisive effect of the frame on the composition as a whole. Down to the eighteenth century, the walls and vaults of Venetian churches were often covered by a vast array of paintings with hardly any plastic articulations dividing the surfaces and with one picture running into another—all of them looking together as if they were part of a large, unbroken surface similar to the continuous crust of the mosaics. Within the several entities, the shapes are connected with each other by linear means, with a noticeable trend to continue the contour of one shape in that of another; groups and masses of figures are pointedly opposed to each other in the two halves of frequently oblong compositions, as in most of the San Marco mosaics. Most scenes are enacted parallel to the picture plane, with the figures given as colored silhouettes against a luminous background. There are strong contrasts of light and dark but little variegation of color: Venetian paintings are never motley, but rather fit into the atmosphere of their ambience. Venetian artists also often employed the technique of highlights on parallel ridges of drapery, frequently connected with each other by light "bridges" across dark "valleys" of folds, and continuous modeling was often replaced by a bold juxtaposition of light and dark or of contrasting colors without transition. It is certainly difficult to distinguish those qualities that can be firmly connected with the mosaics of San Marco in particular from those that were inherent in Venetian painting as a heritage of its Byzantine past in general. But there can be no doubt that such specific influences did exist and that the mosaics of San Marco thus had a certain share in preparing the ground for that kind of painterly painting one might call specifically European. The "afterlife" of San Marco was, thus, after all, a very real life.

CHAPTER TWENTY-THREE

Index

Christ, scenes (cont.)
    Temptation, 43, 101
    Transfiguration, 89
    Washing of the Feet, 43, 44
Church fathers, 28, 39, 42, 95
Colorism, 169, 173
Compunction, 66
Constantinople
    Apostoleion, 5, 72, 86–88, 92, 98
    booty from, 13, 14
    Hagia Sophia, 96, 161
    relations with Venice, 5–6
    taking of, 6, 13, 14
Contarini, Domenico, doge, 3
Cotton Genesis miniatures, 155, 156,
    162–67, 194, 198, 199
Creation cycle, 130, 131, 132, 164–65,
    168–70
Cupolas, principles of decorating, 41,
    46, 88, 198
    see also Ascension dome; Joseph
    cupolas; San Marco

D
Dal Pozzo, Leopoldo, 9
Dandola, Andrea, 13
Deesis, 11, 123, 124–26, 161, 195, 197
Doge. See names of individual doges
Doges, representations of 110, 111

E
Earthquakes, 14, 86, 127
Eli, 142
Evangelists, general, 15, 17, 56, 67, 146
Evangelists, individual. See John; Luke;
    Mark; Matthew
Evangelist symbol, Luke/ox, 61, 89, 93

F
Falier, Ordelafo, doge, 3
Falier, Vitale, doge, 3, 110
Fire, 14
    of 1106, 5, 86
    of 1419, 25
    of 1439, 7
Florence, 201
Fortitude, 66
Frederick II, emperor, 154

G
Genesis. See Adam and Eve; Cotton
    Genesis miniatures; Creation cycle;
    Old Testament cycle
Golden ground, 98,
    in choir chapels, 36
    in south vault, 45
Grado martyrs, 46

H
Hades, 72, 73, 74
Haggai master, 59, 61
Hetoimasia, 55
Honorius III, pope, 6, 105

Hope, 143
Hosios Lukas, 17

I
Inscriptions
    Capella de San Pietro, 92–93, 97
    Capella Zen apse, 23
    Greek, 28, 97
    horizontal vs. vertical, 21
    inscribed scrolls, 70–71, 76, 97
    Judgment of Solomon, 154
    Latin, 28, 97
    Leonine Hexameter, 97
    main apse, 23
    main porch, 19
    Old Testament cycle, 157
    south vault, 43
    Virgin, in atrium, 161
Isaac, 138, 159, 166
Isaiah master, 59–60

J
Jacobus Veneticus Grecus, 98
Jesse Tree, 8, 48
Joachim of Fiore, 9, 98, 157
John, 17, 39–41, 94–95, 126, 146, 151,
    161
    Agony in the Garden, 101
    Ascension dome, 64
    Crucifixion scene, 71, 72
    Destruction of the Temple of Diana,
        39, 41
    Last Supper, 43, 44
    life of, 38–41
    martyrdom of, 79, 80
    Pentecost dome, 57
    Poison Test, 39
    Raising of Drusiana, 39, 40
    Raising of Stacteus, 39
    Resuscitation of the Poisoned Men, 39
John II Comnenus, emperor, 5
Joseph cupolas
    first, 138, 142, 143, 144, 157–59, 166,
        171, 195
    second, 142, 145, 166, 171–73, 195,
        200
    third, 146–50, 166, 174, 196, 198, 199
Joseph story, 157–59, 166
Judgment of Daniel, 99, 106, 155
Judgment of Solomon, 142, 154–55
Justice and judgment theme, 154–55

K
Kiev, Saint Sophia, 47

L
Lamb of God, 188
Landscape, trees and plants,
    representations of, 78, 176
Last Judgment, 8, 91, 99, 106, 165, 184,
    185
Literary sources for Life of Mark, 30
    see also Models; Sources
Liturgy and rites, 95–96
Luke, 17, 18, 55, 57, 64, 146

M
Magister Petrus, 20
Malachi master, 59, 61
Malchus, 69, 70
Mariological cycle. See Virgin Mary
Mark, 15, 17, 19–23, 57, 64, 94, 123,
    146, 151, 161
    Ascension dome, 64
    Baptizing Athaulf, 30
    Baptizing in Aquileia, 179
    Baptizing in the Pentapolis, 30
    Body Being Removed from the
        Tomb, 31, 34
    Burial of, 30, 79
    Consecrated as Bishop of Aquileia, 30
    in Deesis, 123, 125–26
    Dragged and Killed, 179
    Dream-Vision in the Venetian
        Lagoon, 179
    Healing a Demoniac, 179, 181
    Healing a Leper/Athaulf, 30
    Healing Anianus, 30, 179
    Hermagoras Baptizing, 30, 32
    Hermagoras Consecrated by Peter, 30,
        179
    life of, 30–31, 36, 179
    main porch figure, sixteenth-century,
        15
    Martyrdom of, 30, 33
    Mission to Alexandria, 31, 36, 179
    Pentecost dome, 57
    Preaching in the Pentapolis, 30, 31
    Presenting the Gospel to Peter, 179,
        181
    Reception of the relics, 33, 34–35,
        188
    Relics Being Carried Away, 31, 34
    Relics Being Transferred into Church,
        183
    Sailing to Alexandria, 30, 31, 36, 179
    Saint Peter Consecrating, 30
    Ship Arriving in Venice, 33
    Ship with Relics Being Examined by
        Muslims, 31, 34
    Strangled at the Altar, 179
    Vessel Being Saved from Shipwreck,
        33, 34
    Vessel Departing from Alexandria, 31,
        34
    Writing the Gospel, 179, 181
Mark's relics, 13, 31–36, 108–14, 184,
    185–86
    apparitio, 100, 108–14, 195
    legend of, 1, 2–3, 28, 31, 36, 94, 109,
        181
    Translatio, 30–31, 33, 36, 179, 184–86
Martin de Canal, 6, 187
Martyrdom cycles, 82, 90, 94
Master of the Anastasis, 78
Master of the Thomas scene, 76, 77,
    78
Matthew, 17, 28, 84, 85, 94, 146
    Ascension dome, 64
    Baptizing King Egippus of Ethiopia,
        79, 80, 82

martyrdom of, 80, 82
Pentecost dome, 57
Medallions, 159
Miracle cycle, 48–50, 89
Models, 14, 192
  for Agony in the Garden, 100, 103,
    104
  Apostoleion mosaics, 87
  for Betrayal of Judas, 70
  for Miracle cycle, 50
  for Moses cycle, 175–76
  for Reception of Mark's Relics scene,
    34–35
  see also Cotton Genesis miniatures;
    Literary sources; Sources
Monaco, Pietro, 9
Monreale, cathedral, 13
Mosaicists, 7–10, 192–93, 201–2
  Byzantine, 13, 18
  following preparatory drawings, 129–
    30
  Greek, 189, 192
  Venetian, 6, 7
  see also Agony masters; Ascension
    master; Isaiah master; Malachi
    master; Master of the Anastasis;
    Master of the Thomas scene
Moses cupola, 151–54, 158, 159, 174–
  78, 196–97, 199, 200

N
Narrative cycles, 89–90
Nations, in Pentecost dome, 56
Noah, 132, 133, 134, 135, 163, 165, 170

O
Old Testament cycle, 91, 127, 155–59,
  168–74, 194–95
  gaps in scenes chosen for, 156–57,
    159, 175
  placement of, 156, 158–59
  reasons for choosing, 155–56
  selection of scenes for, 156–58, 162–
    64, 175
  significance of Abraham in, 157
  significance of Joseph in, 157–58
  see also Adam and Eve; Cain and
    Abel; Joseph cupolas; Judgment of
    Solomon; Susanna, story of; Tower
    of Babel

P
Painting, importance of, 201–202
Palma, Jacopo (il Giovane), 8, 106
Paolo da Venezia, 201
Paradise. See Last Judgment; Rivers of
  Paradise
Parenzo, cathedral, 6
Partecipacius, Justinian, doge, 3
Passion scenes, 69–73, 76, 77, 89, 91,
  191
Pentecost, 11, 54–57, 87, 88, 93, 94
Philip of Courtenay, 110
Piazzetta, Giambattista, 9
Pietro, 7, 8

Pilate, 70
Preghiera. See Apparitio Sancti Marci
Program, 86–98
  authors of, 96–98
  Byzantine elements, 88–91
  choir chapels, 90
  compared to Apostoleion's program,
    87–88, 92
  domes, 88
  episodic execution of, 86
  grouping of saints in, 95
  inscriptions and, 92–93
  liturgy and rites and, 95–96
  original, and changes in, 10–11; of
    tribune cupolas, 114
  pendentives, 88
  political theme, 94–95
  possession of relics and, 94
  Romanesque elements, 93–94
  side chapels, 90, 91
  Western elements, 91–92
Prophets, general, 58, 116, 170
Prophets, individual
  Daniel, 25, 27, 43, 138
  David, 43, 58–61, 72, 116–17, 151
  Elijah, 28
  Ezekiel, 116, 138
  Habakkuk, 25, 26, 27, 142, 154
  Haggai, 58–61
  Hosea, 58, 59, 61, 116, 118
  Isaiah, 58, 59, 60, 64, 116, 117, 138
  Jeremiah, 25, 26, 43, 116, 117, 138
  Joel, 116, 117
  Jonah, 58, 59, 61
  Malachi, 58, 59, 61, 151
  Micah, 116, 117
  Moses, 29, 43; see also Moses cupola
  Nathan, 142
  Obadiah, 25, 26, 27
  Samuel, 142, 154
  Solomon, 58, 59, 61, 72, 116, 142,
    151, 154–55
  Zephaniah, 58, 59, 61
  Zechariah, 43, 58, 59, 61, 151

Q
Queen of Sheba, 146, 158, 160

R
Radi, Lorenzo, of Murano, 10
Ravenna, 92, 189
  San Vitale, 35, 188, 196
Relics, 3, 121
  choice of saints included in atrium
    and, 160
  program and, 94–95
  see also Mark's relics
Resurrection scenes, 73–75
Restorations, 9–10, 13, 190–91
  after twelfth-century catastrophe, 25,
    36
  fifteenth and early sixteenth centuries,
    7, 8
Ricci, Sebastiano, 9

Rivers of Paradise, 67, 92, 191
Rome, San Paolo fuori le mura, 105,
  201

S
Saccardo, Pietro, 10
Saints, general, 95, 155, 159–61
Saints, individual
  Agnes, 143, 160
  Alipios, 138, 160
  Ambrose, 28, 39, 42
  Anthony Abbot, 121
  Anthony of Padua, 146
  Apollinaris, 146
  Augustine, 28, 151, 160
  Bacchus, 29, 94
  Basilissa, 121
  Bassus, 121
  Benedict, 121, 122
  Blaise, 46, 95, 146, 160
  Bonifacius, 121, 122
  Cassianus, 146, 160
  Catherine, 121, 143, 160
  Cecilia, 146, 160
  Christopher, 142, 160
  Clement, 28, 29, 36, 46, 94, 95, 160
  Constantius of Ancona, 94
  Cosmas, 146, 160
  Damian, 146, 160
  Dominic, 146, 160
  Dorothea, 46, 47, 95
  Epiphanius, 94
  Erasma, 46, 95
  Euphemia, 46, 95
  Fatinus, 151, 160
  Francis of Assisi, 121, 122, 146
  Gaudentius, 146, 160
  Geminianus, 143, 160
  George, 47
  Gerardus Sagredo, 121
  Gregory of Nazianzus, 28
  Helias of Grado, 29, 94, 96
  Hermagoras, 20–23, 30, 31, 32, 53,
    94, 95, 179
  Hermogenes, 121
  Hilarion, 121, 123
  Homobonus, 121, 122, 123
  John. See John
  John Chrysostom, 28
  Julian, 53, 95, 121
  Juliana, 151, 160
  Leonard, 46, 91, 94, 95, 99, 107–108
  Lucia, 151, 160
  Luke. See Luke
  Macarius, 121
  Magnus, 151, 160
  Marinus, 146, 160
  Mark. See Mark
  Mary Magdalen, 121
  Matthew. See Matthew
  Nicholas, 20–23, 46, 94, 95, 146, 160
  Pantaleon, 28, 94
  Paternianus, 151, 160
  Paul Martyr, 121, 123, 146, 160
  Paul the Hermit, 121

Pl. 1a. Main porch: Philip and Simon

Pl. 1b. Main porch: Mark

Pl. 2. Main apse, view looking east

Pl. 3a. Main apse: Peter

Pl. 3b. Main apse: Mark

Pl. 4. East dome, view from below

Pl. 5a. East dome: Jeremiah and Isaiah

Pl. 5b. Cappella di San Pietro: Consecration of Hermagoras

Pl. 6a. Cappella di San Pietro: Martyrdom of Mark

Pl. 6b. Cappella di San Pietro: Interrogation of Peter by Herod

TELLVS ADEST NAVTE DIC VELVM PONITE CAVTE

S MARCV

ESTVARIE

ES CLERVS PELS DVX MTE SERENVS LAVDIB AO CHORIS EXCIPIVNT DVLCE CANORIS

Pl. 7. Cappella di San Clemente: Ship Saved by Mark

Pl. 8. North dome, view from below

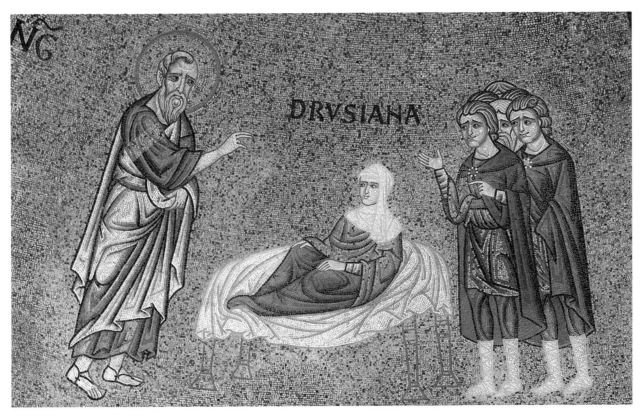

Pl. 9a. North dome: Raising of Drusiana

Pl. 9b. South vault, view looking north

Pl. 10a. South vault: Third Temptation of Christ,
Christ, half-figure

Pl. 10b. South vault: Third Temptation of Christ,
angels, half-figures

Pl. 11. South dome, view from below

Pl. 12a. North transept: Healing of the Paralytic

Pl. 12b. North transept: Annunciation at the Well and
the Handing-over of the Purple to Mary

Pl. 13. West dome, view from below

Pl. 14a. West dome: Matthew

Pl. 14b. West dome: Bartholomew, head

Pl. 15. East dome: Haggai, Zechariah, and Malachi

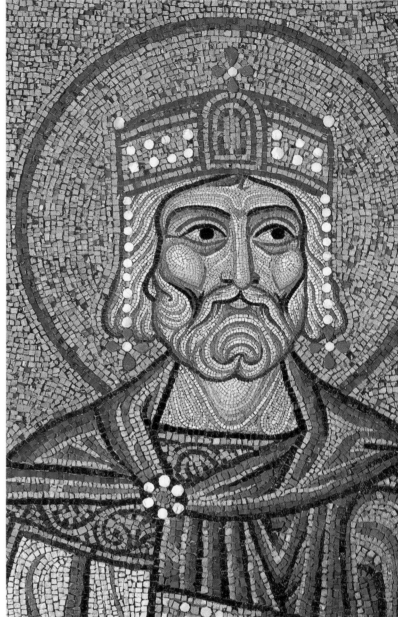

Pl. 16a. East dome: Isaiah

Pl. 16b. East dome: David, head

Pl. 17. Central dome, view from below

Pl. 18. Central dome: Christ

Pl. 19a. Central dome: Paul

Pl. 19b. Central dome: John, half-figure

Pl. 20a. Central dome: Karitas (Charity)

Pl. 20b. Central dome: Misericordia (Mercy), head

Pl. 21. Central dome: River Tigris

Pl. 22a. West vault: view looking east

Pl. 22b. West vault: Betrayal and Mocking of Christ

Pl. 23a. West vault: Betrayal, Peter and Malchus, half-figures

Pl. 23b. West vault: Mocking, Christ, head

Pl. 24a. West vault: Crucifixion, right section

Pl. 24b. West vault: Crucifixion, Virgin, head

Pl. 25. West vault: Anastasis

Pl. 26a. West vault: Anastasis, John, David, and Solomon, heads

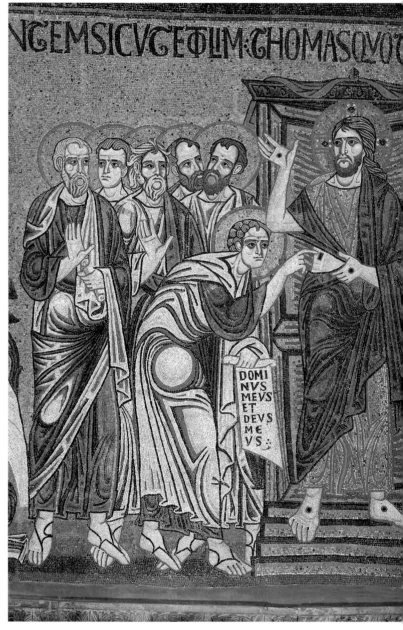

Pl. 26b. West vault: Incredulity of Thomas, left half

Pl. 27. South aisle vault, east half

Pl. 28a. South aisle: Bartholomew Preaching

Pl. 28b. South aisle: Matthew Baptizing King Egippus

Pl. 29a. West arm, south wall: Agony in the Garden, kneeling Christ at left

Pl. 29b. West arm, south wall: Agony in the Garden, central part

Pl. 30. West arm, south wall: Agony in the Garden, sleeping apostles at left

Pl. 31. West arm, south wall: Agony in the Garden, Peter, Andrew, John

Pl. 32. West arm, south wall: Agony in the Garden, standing Christ at right, head

Pl. 33. South transept: *Apparitio Sancti Marci*, Prayers for the Discovery of the Body

Pl. 34a. South transept: Prayers for the Discovery of the
Body, group of bowing men at left, left section, busts

Pl. 34b. South transept: Discovery of the Body,
female figures at left, upper parts

Pl. 35. South transept: Discovery of the Body, doge, councillors, heads

Pl. 36. West arm, north wall: Christ Emmanuel

Pl. 37a. West arm, south wall: Virgin

Pl. 37b. West arm, south wall: Ezekiel

Pl. 38a. West arm, north wall: Jeremiah, head   Pl. 38b. Northwest pier of west dome: Gerardus, head

Pl. 39a. Northwest pier of central dome: Julian

Pl. 39b. Southwest pier of west dome: Hilarion

Pl. 40. Atrium, Creation cupola, view from below

Pl. 41. Atrium, Creation cupola: Separation of Light from Darkness, God

Pl. 42. Atrium, Creation cupola: Creation of the Birds and Marine Creatures

Pl. 43. Atrium, Creation cupola: Expulsion

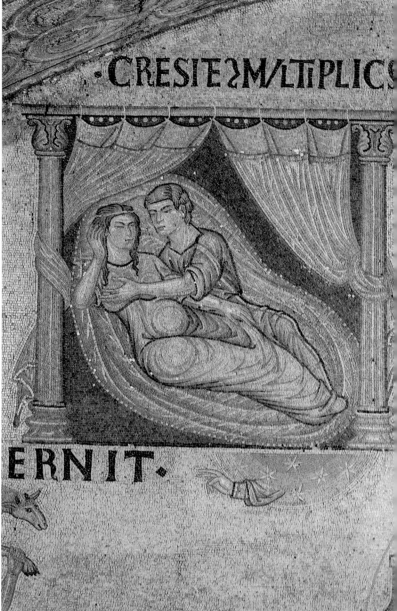

Pl. 44a. Atrium, Creation cupola, northeast pendentive: cherubim

Pl. 44b. Atrium, Creation cupola, east lunette: Begetting of Cain

Pl. 45. Atrium, entrance bay, south vault: Noah Bringing Fowl into the Ark

Pl. 46. Atrium, entrance bay, north vault: Ham Seeing Noah Naked

Pl. 47a. Atrium, entrance bay, north vault:
Burial of Noah, Noah, bust

Pl. 47b. Atrium, entrance bay, north vault:
Appearance of the Lord at Babel and the Confounding
of the Languages, God, angels

Pl. 48. Atrium, Abraham cupola, view from below

Pl. 49a. Atrium, Abraham cupola: Departure to Canaan

Pl. 49b. Atrium, Abraham cupola, west lunette: Birth of Isaac

Pl. 50. Atrium, Abraham cupola, east lunette: Hospitality of Abraham, central section

Pl. 51. Atrium, first Joseph cupola, view from below

Pl. 52. Atrium, first Joseph cupola: Joseph Thrown into the Pit and Brethren Feasting

Pl. 53. Atrium, second Joseph cupola, view from below

Pl. 54a. Atrium, second Joseph cupola: Potiphar's Wife Displays the Garment
to the People of Her House

Pl. 54b. Atrium, second Joseph cupola: Pharaoh Throwing the Butler
and the Baker into Prison

Pl. 55. Atrium, second Joseph cupola: Butler Serving Pharaoh

Pl. 56. Atrium, third Joseph cupola, view from below

Pl. 57. Atrium, third Joseph cupola: Joseph Gathering Corn, worker at right, bust

Pl. 58. Atrium, third Joseph cupola: Joseph Selling Corn, Joseph and guards, busts

Pl. 59. Atrium, third Joseph cupola: John the Evangelist

Pl. 60. Atrium, Moses cupola, view from below

Pl. 61a. Atrium, Moses cupola: Ordeal of Moses

Pl. 61b. Atrium, Moses cupola: Moses Driving away the Shepherds, Moses, head

Pl. 62. Atrium, Moses cupola: Moses and the Daughters of Jethro at the Well

Pl. 63. Atrium, Moses cupola, north apse: Desert Miracles of Moses

Pl. 64. Cappella Zen, vault, east half: Legend of Mark